BRING THE **KINGDOM** TO YOUR CITY

BRING THE KINGDOM TO YOUR CITY

Lessons from EPHESUS

Alan Vincent
with Eileen Vincent

Copyright © 2023 by Eileen Vincent

All rights reserved under International Copyright Law. This book may not be copied or reprinted for commercial gain or profit. The use of short quotations or occasional page copying for personal, or group study is permitted and encouraged. Permission will be granted upon request.

Unless otherwise identified, Scripture quotations are taken from the New King James Version. Copyright © 1982 by Thomas Nelson, Inc. Used by permission. All rights reserved.

Scripture quotations marked ESV are taken from The Holy Bible, English Standard Version. Copyright © 2001 by Crossway Bibles, a publishing ministry of Good News Publishers.

Scripture quotations marked NRSV are taken from the New Revised Standard Version Bible, copyright © 1989 by the Division of Christian Education of the National Council of the Churches of Christ in the United States of America. Used by permission. All rights reserved.

Scripture quotations NIV are taken from the Holy Bible, New International Version®, NIV® copyright © 1973, 1978, 1984, 2011 by Biblica, Inc.® Used by permission. All rights reserved worldwide.

Emphasis within Scripture quotations is the author's own.

Outpouring Ministries

Paperback ISBN: 979-83-9656-8242

Hardcoved ISBN: 979-83-9656-9010

Bring the Kingdom to your city
Lessons from Ephesus

by Alan Vincent with Eileen Vincent

CONTENTS

My Appreciation 7

Introduction 9

Section 1 – Moving into Kingdom Christianity

01 – Jesus Draws the Line 13

02 – Repossessing the Gates 25

03 – Bringing the Kingdom 37

04 – Miracles Required 47

05 – Faith, Anointing, and Sonship 57

Section 2 – The Assault on Ephesus

06 – Five Stages of Preparation 69

07 – Paul's First Encounter with Ephesus 91

08 – A Living Church in a Demonized City 105

09 – Paul's Letters to Timothy 119

Section 3 – Ephesians Chapter 1

10 – The Greeting 133

11 – Our Divine Identity 147

12 – The Spirit of Revelation 161

Section 4 – Ephesians Chapter 2

13 – The Power of the Cross 177

14 – Seated Together with Christ 195

15 – Two Become One 205

Section 5 – Ephesians Chapter 3

16 – Biblical Mysteries 217

17 – Mysteries Being Revealed in this Season 231

18 – Revelation of the Father 241

19 – Fathering and Warring Maturity 257

Section 6 – Ephesians Chapter 4
20 – Crucifying the Flesh and Walking in the Spirit 269

21 – Walk in His Purpose 279

22 – Walk in Unity 287

23 – The Mind of Christ 309

Section 7 – Ephesians Chapters 5 and 6
24 – Walk in Love, Purity, Light, and Wisdom 323

25 – Walk in Submission 331

26 – A Warring Church 349

Section 8 – Lessons from the Writings of John
27 – Jesus' Letter to the Church in Ephesus 359

28 – The Gospel of John 367

29 – The Letters of John 377

Afterword 391

Other Books and Resources by Alan and Eileen Vincent ... 395

MY APPRECIATION

I am hugely indebted to a number of people who have made this book possible.

First, thank you Steve Telzero for your amazing undertaking transcribing the whole five day School of the Word.

Then my appreciation to Amy Calkins who turned the transcript into a book using her expert editing skills.

Duncan Vincent designed the cover. Duncan, it is excellent.

Thank you David Hickson for designing the book so that it is a pleasure to hold.

Thank you to each of you and all those who encouraged me.

BRING THE **KINGDOM** TO YOUR CITY

INTRODUCTION

Over a period of about twenty years, Alan Vincent taught Schools of the Word. These were the delight of his life. Hundreds of students from many nations came to drink deeply from the wells of his revelatory, prophetic teaching gift. While explaining a scripture, he would often say, "I need a whole week to teach this." The Schools of the Word were his opportunity to do just that!

You are holding a book in your hands that is an edited transcription of the School of the Word, "Ephesus, The Pattern for City Taking and Regional Transformation". I owe a huge debt of gratitude to Steve Telzerow, a missionary in Slovenia, who painstakingly undertook the task of transcribing every word from recordings of this school. This transcription is of the school taught in San Antonio, Texas, U.S.A. in 2001. You may feel that you are in the room as Alan is teaching, because at times there is interaction with the students.

We live in days when the nations are in upheaval; the church is under attack with horrendous persecution in many places. But at the same time, believers worldwide are waking up. It is as if the ten virgins are being roused from their slumber. The bridegroom is coming!

It's time for the harvest of souls to be reaped worldwide. The apostle Paul's strategy for expanding the Kingdom of God into virgin territory is outlined in these chapters. There is urgency to raise citizens of the Kingdom of God who understand what it means to live under the rule of our glorious God and Savior Jesus Christ, who walk in obedience to His Spirit and word and learn to live His sacrificial life. This book is truly a manual for the church today. We must gain the ability to live during conflict in a manner that glorifies God. As we stand against the enemy in our authority, filled with the Holy Spirit, following the blueprint shown to us in the history of Ephesus, we shall possess our cities and nations.

In a comprehensive manner, Alan covers practical and doctrinal understanding for the growing church. He exposes how deeply the world system has invaded the church, how unbelief cripples faith, how acceptable traditional religious ways hinder the advance of the Kingdom of God and lull believers into satisfied small expectation when all the magnificence of the life of Christ is available to all believers. This is not a comfortable book for those who are happy with the status quo. It will shift your thinking, drive you to search the scriptures, confront you with the need to live the crucified life. There is no space here for mere head knowledge; truth must be lived and so the life of Christ manifested.

Preachers and teachers will be delighted as the scriptures they have read dozens of times, and even preached, suddenly are flooded with fresh light. They are taken on a tour as if in a mine to discover hidden seams of gold to delight the heart of the diligent seeker. Many have found these teachings to be a wealth of sermon outlines that will continue to expand as they are applied to the congregation.

In speaking, Alan was not tied to notes, but would often tell stories of his own walk with God; his manner of delivery allowed him to illustrate a spiritual point with a testimony, and his transparency was greatly appreciated. He worked hard to explain spiritual truths. Some of his carefully thought-out illustrations to emphasize a point will never be forgotten.

In these pages, you will meet the whole gamut of styles used by Alan to present truth. He would say, "The Lord has told me to feed sheep not giraffes." So, you will find the careful teacher, the preacher, the storyteller, and the prophet who is after transformed hearts rather than informed heads. Alan's desire would be that all who read this book would not only gain knowledge, but also be enlightened and motivated by faith to fulfill their high calling in Christ Jesus.

I pray you are blessed and equipped as you read this book and that you are empowered to carry forth its strategies within your own sphere.

Eileen Vincent

SECTION 1
Moving into Kingdom Christianity

1

JESUS DRAWS THE LINE

The purpose of this book is for you to receive tools in order to take cities. This needs to be practical. I feel that God has shown me the biblical model of how the city of Ephesus was overtaken by the Kingdom of God. We must learn these lessons in order that our communities can be powerfully impacted by the power of God. Right now, around the world, communities are being transformed by God's power.

The first thing I want us to see is the preparation that led to the assault upon the city of Ephesus. The first thing we must get clear in our mind is *the difference between John the Baptist Christianity and the actual coming of the Kingdom*. There is a large difference between talking about the Kingdom and seeing the Kingdom come. It puzzled me for years that when Peter first came to Jesus, in their first encounter, the Lord left him with a simple prophetic word that his name would be changed. Approximately eight months went by until Jesus came and preached the gospel of the Kingdom of God. Then Jesus called the people to repentance and to believe in this gospel.

Section 1 – Moving into Kingdom Christianity

This took place after John the Baptist was put in prison. John the Baptist's ministry was a God-ordained ministry, fulfilling prophetic scripture and preparing the way of the Lord. Gabriel the archangel came to announce his birth, and Jesus testified about John. But with all these wonderful things, a point came when all the preparation had to end in order for the Kingdom to come. This truth bursting in my heart gave me revelation about what must happen in our society if we want to see the breakthrough.

We will see that when Paul finally came to Ephesus, along with Priscilla and Aquila, they were already kingdomized people. They had been with Paul long enough to become fully kingdomized. Yet, they discovered a small group in Ephesus who had not yet transitioned from John the Baptist Christianity to real Kingdom living. Until this condition was corrected or changed, there would be no practical possibility of an effective assault upon the city of Ephesus. We need to see why this change was necessary and what the distinctions are between John the Baptist Christianity and Kingdom Christianity. We need to look at ourselves and the churches we lead to see on which side of the line we live and move. Jesus drew a definite line in the sand, making John the Baptist and all that came before him a past tense experience. Then He said, "Now the Kingdom has come!"

The Kingdom Suffers Violence

In Matthew 11:11–15, we find the testimony of Jesus regarding John the Baptist. Jesus begins with the phrase, "Verily, Verily," or "I tell you the truth…" We could modernize this phrase for effect in order to understand the force of what Jesus was saying. He could have said, "Listen guys, I really mean this…" He says,

> Assuredly, I say to you, among those born of women there has not risen one greater than John the Baptist; but he who is least in the kingdom of heaven is greater than he (Matthew 11:11).

Chapter 1 – Jesus Draws the Line

This is an amazing statement. There is no one born of women greater than John the Baptist. Yet notice that the least in the Kingdom of heaven is greater than John. Jesus continues,

> And from the days of John the Baptist until now, the kingdom of heaven suffers violence, and the violent take it by force (Matthew 11:12).

Two forces are being described here. First of all, every time there is the slightest manifestation of the Kingdom, there is a violent reaction against it by demonic powers. This is the first principle we must learn: *If you begin thinking Kingdom, teaching Kingdom, and propagating the Kingdom, please know that you will receive a strong demonic attack against you for daring to advance the Kingdom.*

This is automatic. You can be a happy, clappy charismatic church, and while the devil does not like it, he will not resist or bother you, because you are no danger to him. If a church begins to have Kingdom intent for living, teaching, and advancing God's Kingdom, the devil takes notice and will stoutly resist any attempt to do so. When a group of churches comes together with Kingdom intent, all the knees in hell start knocking. They will do all they can to not allow such a movement to continue.

On our side, we must have an aggressive, forceful intent of advancing the Kingdom against all opposition. The devil will not sit around and allow us to establish the Kingdom without a fight. We will have to fight every inch of the way in establishing and advancing the Kingdom. If we learn the lessons of this kind of Kingdom warfare, then we can win every time.

Finally, nothing can stop the Kingdom! But we must recognize that even talking about the Kingdom begins to stir the nest in the spirit realm. If you have no stomach for war, then do not get into the Kingdom.

The Kingdom of God involves violence and forceful advancement. It requires forceful men and women to do the job.

Focusing on the Kingdom

Then Jesus says in Matthew 11:13, "For all the Prophets and the Law prophesied until John." All the prophets and the Law (the Old Testament) gave a constant testimony about the Kingdom of God up to and including John the Baptist. Many spoke about the Kingdom. Many saw the Kingdom. Many had incredible visions of the Kingdom, including Daniel, Isaiah, and Zechariah. This was the burden of their hearts. Finally, John the Baptist was sent by God to prepare the way of the Lord.

One of the things I had to learn was that John the Baptist had a two-fold purpose in what he was preparing the way for. First, John was preparing the way for Jesus, the King of the Kingdom. This was a personal preparation. But what I missed for years was the preparation John accomplished for the Kingdom itself. Jesus was very aware of this dimension, and we will look at scriptures later where Jesus clearly indicates, "Don't only look at Me, but see also what I am establishing! It is not *just* a person, but also thing, a dimension of life called the Kingdom."

I believe we have missed this for years and years. We have totally focused on the person of the Lord Jesus Christ while missing what He came to establish. Someone might ask, "How can it be wrong to focus on the person of Jesus?" The answer is that if we do not include the revelation of the Kingdom, about which He was so concerned, then we are not hearing Him correctly.

In the book of Acts, we are told that the apostle Paul went everywhere preaching Jesus *and* the Kingdom (see Acts 19:8; 28:31). Obviously, the two are closely connected, but they are *two dimensions of one great truth*. I believe we have been very deficient in our preaching of the Kingdom, even when we may have effectively preached Jesus.

Preaching Jesus without the Kingdom does not produce city transformation. The prophets prophesied about the Kingdom, but none of them, including John the Baptist, could bring the Kingdom in. John had the closest look at the Kingdom. It was right before his eyes. He had a relationship with the King of the Kingdom. He could see and actually touch it. John gave the best proclamation of the Kingdom that had yet been heard. Nevertheless, John could not bring people into the functional reality of the Kingdom. This was something only Jesus could do. That is why there is a line drawn between John the Baptist and Jesus.

Ruined Cities Restored

The next thing I want you to see is that the prophets spoke about ruined cities being restored. I could turn to many scriptures about this, but I want us to look only at a few. Jesus quoted Isaiah 61 when He began His ministry. He was anointed with the Holy Spirit after having been in the wilderness winning that incredible battle. He came back from that wilderness with the power of God upon Him. He came to His own home town, took the scroll of the book of Isaiah, sat down, opened the book, and read these famous verses:

> The Spirit of the Lord God is upon Me, because the Lord has anointed Me to preach good tidings to the poor; He has sent Me to heal the brokenhearted, to proclaim liberty to the captives, and the opening of the prison to those who are bound; to proclaim the acceptable year of the Lord… (Isaiah 61:1–2).

I want you to notice where the thrust of the gospel lies. If you could summarize this passage, you could say that the gospel is for the "needy" people of our society. This includes the brokenhearted, the bound, the prisoners, the poor, and so on. This was the gospel He came to preach. Many of us in middle class suburbia must ask, "We give a gift to downtown missions organizations, but how many of us are involved in that sector of society as we should be?"

Section 1 – Moving into Kingdom Christianity

When you get into that sector of society, you will find that everyone you meet is bound by demons. If you don't know how to deal with demons, you are no good in that sector of society. That is why many churches and many people have avoided that sector of society. We want nice, clean, respectable families to come to church, get saved without any fuss, begin giving a good tithe, and help the church grow. I am not saying this is wrong, but this cannot be all we should be doing.

Then Isaiah went on to speak about the day of vengeance of our God. However, Jesus did not quote this part in Luke 4. At the time Jesus began His ministry, that day of vengeance had not yet come. I have said publicly on several occasions that God gave me a word two years ago that the day of vengeance is coming. God said, "The time is coming for Me to show My anger." I can still remember as I was praying when the hair on my head stood up as God said, "This is the time for this scripture to be fulfilled. It is the day of the vengeance of our God." I saw in scripture that *the anger was not against lost sinners, but the anger was against the work and activity of Satan* and what he is doing to lost and needy people.

God said further, "Alan, the church has never seen Me angry." I began to tremble.

I asked, "What does that mean?"

He said, "In order for My anger to be manifested in society, I must have a people I can use. I must work through people. I need My sword."

I said, "Lord, here I am. Whatever You want me to do, whatever You want me to be, I am here. I want to be with You in this ministry."

The fury spoken about here is against the works of the evil one. Those who live in Texas and other parts of the country are well aware of the blatant, wicked arrogance of the occult, witchcraft, and New Age, which are assaulting all the pillars of our society.

It is the arrogance that is so blatant. There is no shame anymore. They will demand the right to come into our schools and at an early age pervert our children to believe that the homosexual lifestyle is a good lifestyle. God is angry about this. He must find an outlet for this anger, and the outlet must be prepared to establish the Kingdom properly.

If we look forward in Isaiah 61 to verse 4, we find part of the promise of what is going to happen in the day of God's anger. It is not destructive except for the devil and his kingdom. That is where the destruction takes place. But there is also something constructive happening during this time. We read in verse 3 how the intercessors' mourning has been turned to joy, their despair has been turned into a garment of praise. Then in verse 4 it says,

> And they shall rebuild the old ruins, they shall raise up the former desolations, and they shall repair the ruined cities, the desolations of many generations (Isaiah 61:4).

This is one of many promises the Lord makes regarding our times. I believe the Lord cannot come until there is a restoration of all things. I am not expecting Jesus to come tonight. There are certain scriptures that must be fulfilled. All of these great promises must be fulfilled. I believe that something incredible, amazing, and totally divine must happen in our cities before Jesus can come again. He will not come to demonized cities. He will come for cities where the power of the Kingdom has come and transformed those places.

In Isaiah 58:12 we find another important prophetic scripture that must be fulfilled before the end of the age. One of the results of the right kind of prayer and fasting is that those from among us will rebuild the old waste places. We will raise the foundations of many generations. We will be called the repairer of the breach, the restorer of streets to dwell in:

> Those from among you shall build the old waste places; you shall raise up the foundations of many generations; and you shall be called the Repairer of the Breach, the Restorer of Streets to Dwell In.

If you walk through some of our downtown areas in our cities, you will see things that need restoration. I have walked through the streets of Washington D.C., away from the tourist areas, and it is a mess. It broke my heart. There are certain areas of San Antonio that look very nice in the tourist section, but there are certain areas you do not travel through. That is true of every town and city we know about. Imagine that these places are transformed so that they become wonderful places where life and salvation are pouring through those streets. The power of God and the power of the Kingdom can accomplish this! This is what it is all about.

However, something phenomenal must happen in the spiritual realm before these things can be felt and seen.

> Thus says the Lord God: "On the day I cleanse you from all your iniquities, *I will also enable you to dwell in the cities, and the ruins shall be rebuilt.* The desolate land shall be tilled instead of lying desolate in the sight of all who pass by. So they will say, 'This land that was desolate has become like the garden of Eden; and *the wasted, desolate, and ruined cities are now fortified and inhabited*'" (Ezekiel 36:33–35).

Imagine walking through the downtown area of Boston and saying, "This city has become like Eden." There is no drug problem and no violence. Is this too hard for the Lord? I don't think it is. My God is big enough for these things. This is what the prophets were speaking about.

Now let's look at Amos 9:14. This verse follows a prophetic word in Amos 9:11 about the raising up of David's tabernacle.

Many of us understand that this is happening again. Places of prayer, worship, and intercession are rising up everywhere. These 24/7 permanent places of prayer are a sign of these scriptures coming to fulfillment. Then verse 14 says,

> I will bring back the captives of My people Israel; *they shall build the waste cities and inhabit them*; they shall plant vineyards and drink wine from them; they shall also make gardens and eat fruit from them.

We know in several scriptures it says that God will start with Jerusalem, but He will complete His work in every city.

From Describing to Demonstrating

Returning to Matthew 11, we see that Jesus drew a line saying that up until John the Baptist and including him, the Kingdom had been prophesied. But now violent men must be raised up in order to establish and advance the Kingdom. The inauguration of Jesus' life and ministry set off a violent reaction in the heavenlies. But these violent men will have the power to advance the Kingdom with force. Jesus was the beginning of a new breed of men and women in the spirit who will advance the Kingdom with violent intent. I will explain what this violence means later, so we all understand what Jesus meant.

We read that after John was put in prison Jesus declared the Kingdom of God. In Matthew 11:2, John was disillusioned and discouraged, having been overcome by Herodias. He asked Jesus the question, "Are you the Coming One, or do we look for another?" (Matt. 11:3). Jesus replied:

Go and tell John the things which you hear and see: The blind see and the lame walk; the lepers are cleansed and the deaf hear; the dead are raised up and the poor have the gospel preached to them. And blessed is he who is not offended because of Me (Matthew 11:4–6).

Section 1 – Moving into Kingdom Christianity

Jesus essentially says, "Here is the beginning of the manifestation of the Kingdom." For example, when you go through the gospels, you see in Luke 9 that when Jesus began His ministry, He sent out the twelve to heal the sick, cast out demons, and raise the dead. He said, "I give you power over small local demons that cause colds, but do not tackle the big boys!" Is that what is says? No, it says He "gave them power and authority over all demons, and to cure diseases" (Luke 9:1).

All of this was fulfilled in the book of Acts. There was not one church in the book of Acts that was not established on the manifestation of signs, wonders, and miracles. Paul said in Romans 15:18–19,

For I will not dare to speak of any of those things which Christ has not accomplished through me, in word and deed, to make the Gentiles obedient–in mighty signs and wonders, by the power of the Spirit of God, so that from Jerusalem and round about to Illyricum I have fully preached the gospel of Christ.

The preaching of the Kingdom in the scriptural, New Testament sense was inconceivable without the cutting edge of the Kingdom with mighty signs and wonders. You do not argue the gospel with Muslims, but you raise the dead and heal the sick. That is the end of any arguing. Secular humanism and cynical arrogant intellectualism need the raw power of God to wipe out the arrogance of many Americans and Europeans so that they might humble themselves before the feet of Jesus.

Years ago in Southern India, God gave me a powerful ministry into the Catholic Church. Today, there are thousands of born-again, Spirit-filled Christians moving in and out of the Catholic Church. I was invited to conduct a retreat for the Redemptionist Priests of the Catholic Church. They were the evangelists and revivalists of the Catholic Church. I was to conduct this meeting at the Jesuit headquarters.

Chapter 1 – Jesus Draws the Line

I was in this bizarre situation driving in a vehicle toward this retreat center. I had three days with these priests.

The Jesuits hosted the meeting and the chief priest, for whatever reason, was there to attend the meetings. I did my first session, and it was hard. When I started to speak from scripture, these men laughed at me condescendingly. They were educated, intellectual, and had brilliant minds, but they had no biblical foundation. They did not even see the need to have one.

This group of men was a challenge. I was offended and hurt. They openly ridiculed me and laughed at me.. I went into my room and said, "Lord, I want to go home. I don't want to stay here!" While I was praying, the Lord showed me a white stomach on a dark green background. In the corner of the stomach was a red blob that was pulsating. I knew God was showing me a stomach ulcer in its exact location.

When I went back to the next section, I drew what I had seen on a chalkboard. I said, "This is someone's stomach, and in this area you have a painful throbbing ulcer. God showed this to me. If you will come forward I will pray for you, and you will be healed." The man came forward and was powerfully healed.

Another older priest whose back was bent nearly 90 degrees from arthritis came forward and said, "Maybe you can help me."

I said, "I can't, but Jesus can."

The man came forward, and when I touched him it sounded like a series of rifle shoots went off, "Bang, Bang, Bang!" He straightened right up and began to run around the room.

All the priests sat there like lambs the following day. Every one of them was filled with the Holy Spirit. The chief Jesuit came to me and asked to have a private interview with me. I obliged.

I went into this man's study. He confessed to me of being a child molester. He was driven by uncontrollable lust. He said, "I know, despite my great public appearance and stature that I am hanging over the side of hell. Can you do anything to help me?" I prayed for that man and foul demons came out of him. He was totally transformed, gloriously saved, and filled with the Holy Spirit. He later left the Catholic Church and went out as a evangelist.

The cutting edge of the Kingdom includes the signs, wonders, and miracles that follow the preaching of Jesus and His Kingdom! Jesus sent out the twelve and the seventy saying, "You will preach the kingdom of God. Therefore, you must heal the sick, raise the dead, and cast out demons." These workers came back to Jesus saying, "Lord, even the demons are subject to us in Your name!" (Luke 10:17). He said, "Don't get excited about that. Just thank God that your names are written down in heaven" (see Luke 10:18–20).

Your salvation is more important than any instrument you might become for God to use. I believe God is looking for such people. There will be a grassroots movement across the body of Christ demonstrating the power of God. No one will be marked out as something special. If we are marked out in some special way, then we better stay humble. If you can't, then you need a good wife or a few good elders to say, "Look brother, we know God is using you to raise the dead, but you are becoming a little bigheaded about it. We want to pray for you that you won't be spoiled by the power that is flowing through you." This is the Kingdom. We must see it and advance it. This must become the norm and not the exception.

2
REPOSSESSING THE GATES

In the days of Jesus, John the Baptist went down in defeat. Jesus said, "Don't be offended. This is the Kingdom. Everything the prophets promised, including John the Baptist, is now fulfilled in me. I am the beginning of the manifestation of the Kingdom." John's experience of going into depression (even wondering whether Jesus was the one or if he should look for someone else) is typical of many men I knew who were once warriors with me, but are now completely out of the fight.

What happened to John the Baptist was identical to what happened to Elijah. Elijah challenged the social evil and moral compromise of his day. He had tremendous courage, but he did not end up in victory. Personally, I believe he did not enjoy the eventual victory because disillusionment overshadowed him. He went into the wilderness wishing he could die. God had to come and find his servant and minister to him a measure of restoration. He was a wounded general, someone who never went back into the fight. Sometimes, when men or women have experienced a certain level of demonic assault upon their lives, even though God loves them and can give a measure of restoration, they do not get back into the fight again.

Section 1 – Moving into Kingdom Christianity

If you look at the history of the healing ministry in America during the 1940s, many of those ministers ended up as a wounded general, including Branham, A.A. Allen, and many others. They went out in a power and anointing that began to forcefully advance the Kingdom. Even though they were not using those terms, that is what was happening, because that is the nature of the Kingdom. They went head-on with demonic spirits, and they had power to cast them out. Immediately, that will catch the attention of larger principalities and powers that rule this present world under Satan. There are demonic powers that have responsibility for certain parts of the world. When you start to establish the Kingdom, you draw their attention. If you cast out demons of sickness and disease and start advancing the Kingdom, with people becoming strong believers, it is not long before you become known in hell. Those demonic powers will come against you.

I believe, in the case of Elijah, that the demonic principality that came against him, which has become a known principality, was the same one that Paul confronted in his ministry. That principality found residency within the Queen Jezebel. I don't think the spirit is called Jezebel. This spirit does not only occupy women, but also men. There are certain characteristics about this spirit that we will look at because we will deal with this spirit if we want to advance the Kingdom in our cities and regions. This spirit has a tremendous fury against any true spiritual authority. It absolutely hates the Kingdom or anyone who dares to establish the Kingdom, because such people immediately challenge its power to have a kingdom of its own. It does not mind religious activity. In fact, it uses religious activity as one of its chief weapons.

This spirit will entangle itself in Christ-less religion, in political life, in the media, in the financial world, and even in the military realm. This spirit will even manipulate military power to keep and defend its power. When all of this is challenged, it comes against the challenger with great fury and anger. In the case of Elijah, the attack was purely spiritual, although Ahab hated him and tried to kill him. In that dimension, you could say there was a political attack against his ministry. But Elijah was enveloped in a deep depression with a strong sense of loneliness, "I alone am left." He ran into the wilderness with the desire to quit and die. He was not successful in overcoming this spirit, but the spirit was effective in bringing his ministry to an end.

A Better Way

I am spending so much time on this because God wants to make something clear to us. When the attack on Ephesus took place, God wanted the apostle Paul to succeed in establishing the Kingdom. He did not want Paul to end up like Elijah or John the Baptist. We will see the steps that God used to prepare Paul for this effort. We must be prepared for the very same conflict. We must pass through the same preparation, because God does not want us to end up as a wounded general. God does not want you to end up as another Elijah or John the Baptist. God does not want more casualties in this spiritual war.

What happened to John the Baptist was almost identical to what happened to Elijah. There are tremendous similarities in that they both challenged the demonic powers, the social wrongs, the moral degeneration, the spiritual backsliding, and the political evils of their day. Elijah ended up discouraged, disillusioned, and defeated. John ended up the same way. The demonic powers ruling the land were too powerful for their level of anointing. The demonic powers had strong gates that were working through Jezebel and Herodias.

Do you understand what spiritual gates represent? These are the power centers from which demonic powers exercise rule, control, and government over a city. In the Old Testament, these were physical gates. In those gates the elders sat and regulated anything that came in or went out of the city. At those same gates the elders exercised legislation and judgment.

Section 1 – Moving into Kingdom Christianity

When you move into the prophets, however, these gates gradually turned into spiritual entities which are now in the heavenlies and not on earth. They have the same function, however. They have the power to legislate over the lives of the people, and they have the power to control what comes in and what goes out of the city.

The gates you find in a modern city take two forms. They will be people that demonic powers influence or possess and use for their purpose of control and manipulation. These people will be located in positions of power in politics, economics, media, and education. The media and education realms are the places where minds are trained to think the devil's way. We have seriously lost the battle over the last decades about authority and voice in the realm of media and education. When a principle of a college or university is blatantly ridiculed and believed to be unfit for any place in the education system because he confesses to be a creationist, it is obvious who controls and influences that system. Can you see how much ground we have lost?

Jezebel and Herodias represented a tremendous gate. They were people that spirit could use to exercise its rule and power over an entire region. So certain people are the first manifestation of gates in our time.

The second manifestation of gates concerns locations where something has taken place, especially in places where there has been shedding of blood. Other places include the making of covenants, especially when blood is used. Certain places become strongholds because of what went on there historically. Until what happened there is undone in a proper spiritual way, the demons associated with that place continue to hold power and sway.

For example, on two occasions in the last decade Austria has dedicated the nation to the Virgin Mary. Several million people participated in this ceremony to consecrate the nation to the Virgin Mary.

This is a powerful covenant. It makes it difficult to break through the wall of Catholic prejudice, making room for the Kingdom to be established. That is why we have a battle in Austria to see any kind of breakthrough.

The only breakthrough we have seen in all the years I have worked in Austria is when God anointed an old baker with a mighty healing ministry with the power to cast out demons. He began to move in that ministry, and he caught the attention of the media. They did several television programs with this man as genuine miracles were taking place. A new church planted in a town called Villach, which struggled with eighty to one hundred people for quite some time, suddenly grew to hundreds, a phenomenal size for Austria. Once again, you advance the Kingdom with the power of signs, wonders, and miracles. I don't know any other way to do it.

I shared a conference with a man in England back in the 1960s. This man was an unobtrusive nobody that God was using. At that time, Indonesia was entirely Muslim. There was no measurable number of Christians in Indonesia. There were a few groups of Christians here and there, but all statistics regarded the nation as 100 percent Muslim. God told this man to go out into the streets of his town to heal the sick and cast out demons in the name of Jesus. He was not to do anything else except give them the healing power of God and the power to deliver for free. He just began doing this, and within a few weeks he saw over two thousand miracles. The whole region where he lived was in an uproar. Eventually, an evangelistic team came and began preaching the gospel. They spoke about the Jesus this man had first proclaimed through the power of signs, wonders, and miracles. God told this man not to try and get the people saved, but just tell them that it is by the power of Jesus' name that these miracles happened.

Section 1 – Moving into Kingdom Christianity

Praying in Secular Leaders

Even though Elijah was a wounded general, unable to get back in the fight, God gave him a final commission at the end of his ministry:

> Then the Lord said to him: "Go, return on your way to the Wilderness of Damascus; and when you arrive, anoint Hazael as king over Syria. Also, you shall anoint Jehu the son of Nimshi as king over Israel. And Elisha the son of Shaphat of Abel Meholah you shall anoint as prophet in your place" (1 Kings 19:15–16).

He gave Elijah a three-fold job to accomplish, but Elijah only carried out one of these jobs. Elijah did anoint Elisha, but he did not go and anoint the other two mentioned here by God. He never went to Hazael or Jehu. I can only conclude that he was so discouraged and depressed that he did not see the point and ended his ministry by disobeying the Lord.

I believe that Hazael represented the secular leader. God essentially said to Elijah, "This is My man. You must anoint him, because he will do My will." I believe that part of the preparation ministry of the Kingdom is recognizing secular rulers and appointing them with our prayers.

In the United States, we have a tremendous battle to see the right person come to the Presidency. In saying that, I am not suggesting that God is a Republican. If the Democratic candidate has a heart for God, we would all vote as a Democrat. We are after a person who will do God's will and have God's heart. I am praying for both sides of the political divide, that men and women of God can start to work together to see the Kingdom come.

The battle for the 2000 election was a furious battle. I felt such a weight come upon me on the eve of the election that I could not stay upon my feet. I had to get on my knees, and I was more or less in travail for the outcome. I am not much of an intercessor, because that is not my calling, but I felt that God was looking for everyone

Chapter 2 – Repossessing the Gates

He could find to get into this battle, because the outcome was so important. Toward the afternoon, before the results were known, I was released from that agony.

Several weeks before the election I saw a vision of a newspaper headline that said, "Bush Wins by a Whisker!" I prayed to that end over the next few weeks that what I saw prophetically would come to pass physically. For prophesies to come to pass, we must wage war to bring about their fulfillment. Just because God speaks things does not mean that is the end of it. Instead, it is only the beginning.

I believe we are called to the Hazael anointing, which is the appointing of secular rulers to places of government and influence. These people will facilitate the purposes of God in their arena of influence. It struck me, while studying the details of the rebuilding of Jerusalem and the fallen temple during the days of Nehemiah, Ezra, Haggai, and others, that their ability to fulfill the prophetic word depended upon who was on the throne in the capital city of the Persian-Median Empire. This is summarized in Ezra 6:14,

> So the elders of the Jews built, and they prospered through the prophesying of Haggai the prophet and Zechariah the son of Iddo. And they built and finished it according to the commandment of the God of Israel, and according to the *command of Cyrus, Darius, and Artaxerxes king of Persia.*

Having a favorable and influential king upon the throne was as important as the prophesying of the prophet. They both worked together to fulfill the command of God.

You may remember that Daniel's prayers were very powerful in causing Cyrus to come to the throne and subsequently allow the Jews to begin rebuilding Jerusalem and the temple. In four years after they began to restore the temple, two things happened almost simultaneously.

First, Cyrus died, but so did Daniel the intercessor. God lost his king and his intercessor in a very short period of time. As a result, all progress stopped for fourteen years. The son of Cyrus was a renegade son. He couldn't even wait for his father to die before taking the throne.

This son of Cyrus did something totally illegal, which was reversing the law of the Persians and the Medians. He passed an order that the temple must not be built. Contrary to the law, he overruled the previous favor of the king, and because there was no intercessor, nothing could be done to stop it.

The prophetic word of God was on hold until two new prophets came, Haggai and Zechariah. They prophesied and stirred the people to action. However, equally important was the fact that Darius came to the throne. When these two things were in place, the secular king and the prophetic ministry, they completed in four years what could not be done in fourteen years. These lessons are written in the Bible for our instruction.

We have a very serious responsibility to pray secular leaders into places of rule and authority. I believe America has been very negligent in obeying the command of scripture in 1 Timothy 2, as well as 1 Timothy 1:18, where Paul says to Timothy to wage a mighty war according to the prophecies he had received. In other words, the prophetic word is the equipment for war. It is not an automatic thing that falls out of the sky upon your head.

Although God has prophesied revival for the United States, we must still bring it to pass. This is almost a contradiction, which we will not understand on this side of heaven. It is my responsibility to see that God's irresistible and eternal word in prophecy is fulfilled. Please do not ask me to explain it, because I cannot. I am God's agent to make His word come to pass. Secular authority that is favorable toward God and His Kingdom will make a big difference.

From Assyria to Babylon

Israel represented compromised religion in the days of Elijah. They practiced syncretism, which is also common in our day. The Assyrians came in and mixed the religions together. They reestablished the worship of ancient gods in the land. The ten tribes of Israel ended up with a slightly Jewish form of syncretism. They worshipped the gods of the land. They worshipped other gods. Everyone was practicing religion in their own way. They thought this was fantastic. Surely, between them all, they would touch all the gods with favor.

The second thing the Assyrians did was to bring a complete destruction of the morality of the nation. Assyria's invasion of the land destroyed religious purity and moral purity. At the same time, it seriously undermined the institution of the family. The United States of America has been seriously attacked by the same spirit of Assyria. In the history of the civilization of the world, the attack upon morality and the simplicity of faith always precedes being taken over militarily. A great recent example of this is Germany. Remember that the Moravians came out of Germany. Remember that in Germany the one hundred-year prayer meeting happened. It is amazing to think that all of Europe, including men like John Wesley, was impacted by the movements coming out of Germany. We could move further back in that nation's heritage and remember Martin Luther.

But at the turn of the century, something went wrong with the way the Germans thought. There was an attack upon what we have come to know as thesis-antithesis thinking. This means that there are absolutes, non-negotiable truth which is eternal in nature. Anything but that truth is error. God thinks this way. This is the black-and-white nature of God. You will read many scriptures that say, "This is truth and that which is not this truth is error." God does not mess around and walk in grayness or confusion. He says, "There is one name under heaven by which we might be saved, Jesus.

Therefore, there is no other name, so don't waste your time on anything else." God is a total thesis-antithesis thinker.

Uniquely, Judaism and Christianity were trained by God to think this way. These civilizations were unique in having this kind of mindset and thinking. If you have lived in a culture, as I have, where they have never been impacted by this kind of thinking, you will find it does not exist. This includes Hindu culture in India or Confucianism in China and many of the primitive religions of Africa. This way of thinking is almost non-existent. There are no absolutes. Everything is changeable and variable.

At the turn of last century, Germans began to teach synthetic thinking. This thinking demands we go to every sincerely held point of view and find good in it. The final truth is an undefined mixture of all the different opinions about truth. If any view is sincerely held, that makes it truth and acceptable.

However, if truth is an opinion then everything is negotiable, and there are no absolutes. What was morally right last year is not necessarily right today. This destroyed the German nation. Unfortunately, this thinking spread to every learning institution in the Western world. If you are a black-and-white thinker and talk in absolutes, then you are considered intellectually naïve. You need to be reeducated to think in a more intelligent way.

This is what happened to the majority of the nation of Israel in the days of Jehu. The Israelites were seriously Assyrianized, and they were about to become seriously Babylonianized. Babylon represented the final military takeover. I believe America has been thoroughly Assyrianized, and if we do not wake up and change things, it won't be long before we are Babylonianized. Some kind of despotic government can take over this land of freedom, not because we did not love freedom, but because we stopped thinking like God.

The highest ranking demons of the world have longed to take this nation over for decades. We have a massive war on our hands right now. None of us have a choice in the matter. We must organize ourselves and our churches to be praying Hazael anointed prayers. We also need to be praying Jehu anointed prayers.

Praying in Religious Leaders

Jehu represents the leaders of religious systems that are not the pure evangelical gospel of the Lord Jesus Christ. It does not matter whether you like their religion or not. These people have tremendous influence and power in our nations.

Religion is the happy hunting ground for the Jezebel spirit. This is where most of the thrust and power of deception concerning morality come from. The LGBTQ movement has tremendous support and momentum in some of these movements. Some are even ordaining such individuals to lead their churches and teach their children. If a man like John Wesley would once again sit in the driver's seat of the movement he founded, think what that would do to Methodism.

We need to start praying prayers that bring godly change in all areas of authority. All we have said here is part of the John the Baptist ministry, or the Elijah ministry if you like. This ministry prepares the ground for our cities to be taken.

We received a shock in the recent elections in the United States. I asked God, "Why did Bush only win by a whisker?"

He said, "He won by a whisker because My church has been apathetic and half-hearted about praying these prayers. I have given them a fright." During the fiasco of the previous years, many Christians became desperate in prayer.

3

BRINGING THE KINGDOM

In the New Testament, Jesus came to fulfill the ministry of John the Baptist. This is what we must see and understand. We do not simply want the preparation. Instead, we want to usher in the fullness of God's Kingdom. It is one thing to announce that the Kingdom is coming, but it is another thing to actually bring in the Kingdom. Jesus came to finish the job with a new anointing and power to establish the Kingdom. This anointing and power is what we need. Jesus predicted the full manifestation of the forerunner ministry before His second coming.

Jesus came down from the Mount of Transfiguration, where Moses and Elijah had appeared to Him, and then:

> And the disciples asked Him, saying, "Why then do the scribes say that Elijah must come first?" Jesus answered and said to them, "Indeed, Elijah is coming first and will restore all things. But I say to you that Elijah has come already, and they did not know him but did to him whatever they wished. Likewise the Son of Man is also about to suffer at their hands." Then the disciples understood that He spoke to them of John the Baptist (Matthew 17:10–13).

John the Baptist was a fulfillment in preparing the way for the King of the Kingdom. But there will be a new preparation at the end of the age for the second coming of the Great King of the Kingdom. It will be the final glorious manifestation of the Kingdom. However, we must see the Kingdom come now on earth as much as is possible before He comes to consummate it.

I am not clear on how far this restoration will occur before Jesus comes. However, one thing I am convinced about: He will come to consummate a victorious church that has a few battle scars, a few cuts and bruises. She will still be standing on the devil's neck when He comes. This was the dominate view of the church until one hundred years ago. If you read the Puritan hope, you'll see that the church expected to be victorious and triumphant. It expected to herald in the coming of Christ by its victory, although battle-scarred and bruised. It is a triumphant church that will welcome in the final consummation of His coming.

The idea that the church becomes a worn-out, beaten, run-out-of-town, old hag before His coming is ridiculous, blasphemous, and complete heresy. The bride of Christ is without blemish, spot, or wrinkle. She is beautiful! It cannot be true that Jesus comes in a rescue helicopter to get us out of the mess before the devil takes complete control. This is unbiblical, and it has led the church astray. It has conditioned the church to expect the devil's takeover. I say this unashamedly: I see that doctrine as a serious heresy that hit the church of Jesus Christ about one hundred and fifty years ago.

I am not waiting for the rapture bus or rapture train to get me out of a destroyed world and defeated church. I am here to change the world and bring the Kingdom in by the power of His Spirit!

Chapter 3 – Bringing the Kingdom

The Kingdom Anointing

What I want you to see now is that Jesus draws a line. Up until this point, we have seen the John the Baptist anointing. The purpose of John's anointing was to prepare the way and not to be an end in itself. With Jesus the Kingdom has come, and with Him comes a Kingdom anointing. There are several things I want to mention about this anointing. *When you see a John the Baptist type anointing there are certain characteristics that mark it out.*

The first characteristic of the John the Baptist anointing is that it is very individualistic. The person with this anointing is a loner. He is on his own. Elijah said, "I am the only one left. There is no one but me." John the Baptist was a man on his own. He had no team and no relationships. He was there to do a great thing for God. He was incredibly powerful and effective in some ways, but it was the individualism and loneliness that made him vulnerable.

God has lifted up powerful individual ministries until this present time. However, we have come to the time when that phase is ending. Those individual ministries are not there to bring the Kingdom in. They are there only to prepare the way for the Kingdom to come. The purpose of great healing and evangelistic ministries is to bring forth a healing, evangelistic church. We should not be spectators and sit in passive admiration while someone does the ministry for us. The purpose of the Ephesians 4:11 ministries (apostle, prophet, evangelist, pastor, and teacher) is to bring the church to the work of the ministry.

If I am a successful apostolic ministry, then I cause the church to become apostolic. We together become the sent ones to forcefully advance the Kingdom. If I am an Ephesians 4 prophet, then I cause the church to become prophetic, to see prophetically, and to pray prophetically, which causes the word and purpose of God to manifest in our land. This is a corporate activity.

Section 1 – Moving into Kingdom Christianity

If I am an Ephesians 4 evangelist, then I cause the church to become evangelistic, training them to reconcile people with God, heal the sick, and cast out demons. I am not there to preach evangelistic crusades while everyone watches me in admiration. The power of signs, wonders, and miracles is for an impartation of faith to the church so it becomes normal for all church members to have this as their daily equipment. When they go out into the world and meet someone in the supermarket who is dying of cancer, they say, "Let me lay hands on you." Instantly, God does a miracle and that person can easily be led to Christ! This is the church moving in the power of the Kingdom.

One of the first things you see about the Kingdom as distinct from John the Baptist's ministry is that it is a corporate ministry and not an individual ministry. This is the first major distinction. The Kingdom by definition must be in plurality. The moment Jesus was anointed, one of His first acts was to get another twelve involved. Then He moved to get another seventy involved. Jesus knew the Kingdom is a corporate matter, not an individual matter. Jesus seemed to even violate time by getting these men to move in the power of the Kingdom so quickly.

I asked Jesus this question, "How did You get these men moving in the power of the Kingdom before You ever went to the cross?"

Jesus said to me, "Alan, I was so desperate to get the Kingdom moving. However, I could not do it on My own in a really significant way. So I used my Calvary Credit Card. I went to the Father and said, 'Father, when the time comes I will pay the full price at Calvary. But could I have Kingdom power by credit please before paying the price later? I cannot wait for the world to feel and experience the power of the Kingdom. I cannot do it by Myself, but I must do it by impartation to these men You have given to Me.'"

Chapter 3 – Bringing the Kingdom

From the very beginning, the coming of the Kingdom had to be a corporate experience. The individual, isolated ministry, as wonderful as it has been and continues to be, has come to a passing phase. Jesus did not go out and preach the Kingdom until John the Baptist had been put in prison. This happened because one era was ending so that another era could begin. He closed one before He could open the other.

When will the Kingdom come to your city? The Kingdom will come when individual ministries see the Kingdom as more important than their individual success. The Kingdom of God will come when we see the power of our corporeity as far more powerful than what even the most anointed of us could do in our individuality.

Jesus made this incredible statement about John the Baptist and the Kingdom. He said, "Although there has never been anyone greater than John the Baptist born of women, however, the least in the Kingdom of God is greater than John the Baptist" (see Matt. 11:11). If we look at the city of San Antonio, we can find several megachurches. Some of them are well known. They are on television continually and have a very effective ministry. But I want you to see something. Over the city of San Antonio there are great demonic principalities that sit in defiance and anger against any manifestation of the Kingdom of God. These principalities must be moved out of the way. The same is true for your city.

God gave me an illustration to help me understand this truth. Saddam Hussein was a very evil man. Let's pretend he represents an evil principality. Imagine now that James Bond goes to deal with him. There is no one more masculine or more fantastic and more equipped as an individual than James Bond. Mr. Bond arrives in the capital of Iraq to deal with this evil. He flies through the roof in some spectacular way and is ready for a one-on-one confrontation.

Now I believe Saddam Hussein has the intelligence, evil cunning, and equipment to deal with James Bond effectively. I doubt that James Bond would come out the winner, although he is very brave and very skillful. In this case, it would be a suicide mission.

Imagine now that we have a new ambassador for the United States of America. He is quite small and in no way does he have the stature of James Bond. Imagine he comes to Saddam Hussein and says, "I have a word for you from the nation I represent and the President I represent..." He proceeds to deliver a message saying that if he does not stop his illegal and horrifying activity then all the power and might of the United States will come against him within ten days. Which of these two scenarios do you think would make Saddam Hussein tremble more? This little man is not impressive as an individual, but what he represents makes him so powerful. It is what he is part of and joined to that makes him so powerful and worthy to be reckoned with.

In San Antonio, we have over one thousand churches on our database. Most of them have fifty or less people attending. In the south side of San Antonio, God is doing something amazing. Imagine that two hundred churches come together with an average membership of one hundred members. Corporately they represent twenty thousand believers, which is by far the largest church in San Antonio. Anyone of those pastors that lead a church of one hundred now has all the power of that corporeity behind him. Imagine what that would do for the Kingdom in a given city.

What if there were one thousand churches with one hundred people. That would amount to one hundred thousand believers. When one pastor goes to a demon in that corporate strength, although he only pastors one hundred, he has tremendous power and authority because of what he is part of. Can you see the beginnings of what the power of the Kingdom is all about?

Something Greater Has Come

In Matthew 12:6, Jesus says, "I tell you, *something* greater than the temple is here" (ESV). Jesus is trying to get these men to see that they should not only look at Him, but also to what He is establishing. Although He is the Almighty Son of God, although he is the King of Glory, although He is the beginning of the manifestation of the Kingdom of God, they needed to put their eyes on the thing He was bringing and not just on the person that He was.

A day was coming when Jesus would go back to the Father, but the thing He started—the Kingdom—would go on increasing throughout the earth. His activity on the earth was temporary, but the activity of that *something* would continue until it filled the whole earth. *The principle here is: We need to not only focus our eyes on the person, but also on the something He established, namely, the Kingdom!*

First, Jesus said that something is greater than the temple. If you have the Kingdom in your church, even though you are meeting in a small room at a shopping mall without a fantastic building or wonderful facilities, you are still more powerful than anyone who has the fancy buildings but is without the Kingdom. The best combination is to have wonderful buildings with the Kingdom operating! I am not against buildings, but I do say they are of no consequence by themselves. It is the Kingdom that is the power, not the building. You can have the greatest technical equipment and media techniques along with all the other advantages in this modern technical age, but the power of the Kingdom is the central issue. Those things are only useful to the degree that the Kingdom of God is present and active. It does not matter who you are or where you are, you can have the Kingdom! This Kingdom is far greater than the temple itself.

The temple was used for only one day for Kingdom purposes. At the beginning of Jesus' ministry, He cast out the money changers.

They put everything back the way it was after He left. When He came to the end of His ministry, He cast them out again. At the beginning He said, "This is a house of merchandise" (see John 2:13–17). But at the end of His ministry, He said, "This has become a den of thieves" (see Matt. 21:10–13). They practiced all kinds of wicked activity to make money. He cleared them all out, and for one day the temple experienced extravagant praise. For one day, all the sick and the lame came to receive healing. For one day, Jesus said, "This house is to be a house of prayer for all nations." In that one day, while Jesus was there, that great temple was used for the purposes of the Kingdom. Then it went back to being religious again. It was never used for the Kingdom after that. The Kingdom of God is far more important than any building.

Then, in Matthew 12:41, the second *something* greater is mentioned:

> The men of Nineveh will rise up at the judgment with this generation and condemn it, for they repented at the preaching of Jonah, and behold, *something* greater than Jonah is here (ESV).

Nineveh was a large city; it took three days to walk from one end to the other. Jonah came unwillingly to preach to this city, and God so anointed his ministry that the whole city repented, from the king to the common person. This city was dramatically changed from an incredible repentance that lasted nearly one hundred and fifty years. Jesus is saying that the Kingdom is more powerful than Jonah. Often we are looking for someone to come to our city and to have a Jonah-sized ministry to bring the nation to repentance. We are looking for the city to fall to its knees when this man comes to town. Jesus is saying, "When you get the Kingdom working in your city, it will be more powerful than Jonah."

Chapter 3 – Bringing the Kingdom

If the Kingdom comes to your city, it will have a more convicting effect and do more for repentance and changing the city than someone who has a Jonah-sized anointing. I would rather have the Kingdom than Jonah. When the Kingdom comes, it is the answer to bring cities to conviction of sin and to powerful and successful evangelistic ministry. The Kingdom can gather the whole city in repentance. The Kingdom will produce multitudes as followers of Christ.

The final *something greater* is found in Matthew 12:42. Something greater then Solomon has come. If you look around the world and consider the Middle East crisis, you might agree that Bill Clinton did his best to solve these problems. Few have been more successful in negotiations with the Palestinians, but he still could not make it work. The sore in Northern Ireland continues to this day. If you visit Rwanda and other African nations, you find incredible challenges. Just come to America and visit any downtown area. How in the world are we going to solve these problems? We need the wisdom of the Kingdom of God, where God speaks directly regarding many unsolvable problems. However, it will not be the wisdom of man, but the wisdom of the Kingdom. It will come through our corporeity. It is not one great genius who will save the world, but the power of the Kingdom can do it.

Solomon brought to his kingdom a time of unprecedented peace and prosperity. It was the conclusion of everything David had prepared. However, Solomon brought the kingdom to its full expression. David started it, but Solomon completed it. It was a time of unprecedented prosperity and economic success. There was incredible peace, law, and order. The fame of Solomon went out across the whole world. Even the Queen of Sheba came to see it for herself and said, "The half has not been told me." If America gets the Kingdom into its culture, economic problems, social challenges, racial problems, and other areas of seemingly impossible solutions, the answers will come.

Section 1 – Moving into Kingdom Christianity

The whole world will come running, asking, "How did you do it?"

If the Kingdom comes to San Antonio, to Houston, to Boston, or any other town of our nation, our problems can be solved. The drug problem can be solved. Violent crime will discontinue. "How did you do it? Was it the new police chief?" No, it was the Kingdom. Of course, having the right people in the right places is quite necessary for the Kingdom to come. There must be something behind these people in order to make their positions advantageous for the Kingdom.

If we can nurture the passion for the Kingdom to come, then I believe the outworking will be transformed cities. Without the Kingdom, we have no hope. It is not just intercessors, even though they have an important part to play. It is not simply the right political people in place, although they too have a part to play in the Kingdom. It is not one component, but all the components together that can change cities with the Kingdom as the driving force. We need a submission and harmony in our corporeity in the Kingdom of God. Then we have something that will break every chain and be irresistible as the Kingdom advances.

Jesus came to *begin something* and not just *be someone*. We need to see this. He was and is the Almighty King of the Kingdom. But He said, "Don't just look at Me as an individual. See what I am bringing in. I am bringing in the corporate power of the Kingdom." If the Kingdom comes, then this will make our king glorious. If we want to glorify our king, then we need to work together to establish and advance the Kingdom. This will set Him on His throne and magnify His name. This is not taking away from Jesus; it is actually magnifying Jesus. I hope you can see this.

4

MIRACLES REQUIRED

What is the difference between the John the Baptist anointing and the Kingdom anointing? The answer to this question is an important test for us and our churches. In John 10:41, people said about John, "John performed no sign, but all the things that John spoke about this Man [Jesus] was true." So, even though John did no miraculous signs, he did teach accurately about Jesus. *The second characteristic of the John the Baptist anointing is that it can accurately teach the truth about Jesus, but does not do anything miraculous. This is description without demonstration*, or John the Baptist Christianity.

I have cried out all my life for the miraculous. I had to move in the power of God because of the dark, hostile, and demonic environment of India. Otherwise, I had no chance. The circumstances of our ministry drove us to seek God for power. I have seen a flow of the miraculous through my ministry all the years that I have known Jesus Christ. I have never been set in the church as a worker of miracles, but it does happen on a regular basis. It is like an affirmation of the word I preach. Without that, I would feel like a fraud.

In my own family, we have experienced some incredible healing miracles. I've experienced incredible healings, along with my wife. My son, David, was congenitively deaf when he was born. He was gloriously healed when he was baptized in the Holy Spirit at age four. My daughter, Rachel, should have died in a hospital in Zimbabwe when the devil tried to kill her during a Reinhard Bonnke crusade. Now she is a walking miracle of God's power and healing. The miraculous runs right through my family. I expect God to do the miraculous.

As I have traveled the country encouraging pastors to become Kingdom-thinking people, it is amazing how many of them have been hit by the devil. It is amazing how many do not know how to respond to these attacks. When a leader begins to advance the Kingdom, there is usually a direct attack upon them by witches, or some other form of witchcraft, to strike them with various kinds of ailments and diseases. Frequently, the disease comes in the form of cancer. I feel righteous anger about this dynamic, which is more than coincidence.

If we go against the devil in the power of the Kingdom, the Bible says the following, "Behold, I give you the authority to trample on serpents and scorpions, and over all the power of the enemy, and nothing shall by any means hurt you" (Luke 10:19). I do not have time to tell all the stories of why some of these attacks were allowed to take place because of negligence or open doors. But as a result of these frequent occurrences, a militant spirit came into me, and I have said, "God, You must give us a breakthrough! I am claiming in Jesus' name that there will not be one pastor in Texas or anyone under my influence that will ever die through cancer! I want power over cancer."

In a meeting about six months ago, the power of God came to me in an unusual way. I knew a fresh anointing had come upon me, and I heard God say to me, "I'm answering your prayer, and I am giving you power over cancer that you have never known before."

Then He said, "I am giving you power over AIDS, because I want a powerful advance into the homosexual and lesbian community. If you have an answer for AIDS, they will come running to you. I will give you victory over AIDS."

I've had little experience with this, but quite recently in Poland powerful things took place in the AIDS realm. Something is going to break out in this nation, and we will see hundreds and hundreds of dying homosexuals and lesbians turn to Jesus and be powerfully healed. They will return to their community being more powerful evangelists than we could ever be. God will simply out-power the devil!

John did no miracles, but Jesus did, and all Kingdom Christians do as well! In Isaiah 8:18, which is linked to Hebrews 2:13, the Spirit of Christ says, "Here am I and the children whom the Lord has given me! *We are for signs and wonders....*" That is what we are for! Did Jesus do signs and wonders? Yes! Are we His children? Yes. Then we are also for signs and wonders.

In John 5:35, Jesus bore witness to John the Baptist, saying, "He was the burning and shining lamp, and you were willing for a time to rejoice in his light." People were willing to rejoice for a time in his light. Again, Jesus pointed to John and honored this great man of God. He referred to the mighty anointing on his life and the power of his ministry. He said, "He was a lamp that burned and gave light."

In John 1:4–5, John the apostle described Jesus in this way: "In Him was life, and the life was the *light of men.* And the light shines in the darkness, and the darkness did not comprehend it." Then, a few verses later in that chapter, John the apostle said of John the Baptist, "*He was not that Light, but was sent to bear witness of that Light. That was the true Light* [Jesus] *which gives light to every man coming into the world*" (John 1:8–9).

There is a clear distinction between the light of John the Baptist and the light of Jesus. John the Baptist was a lamp and gave light, but Jesus was *the* lamp that gives light. Interestingly, once the Kingdom came, Jesus began talking of His disciples in the same terms He used about Himself. He said of Himself, "I am the light of the world..." (John 8:12). Then He said to His disciples, "You are the light of the world..." (Matt. 5:14). He put His disciples in the same category as Himself. He never talked about John in this way, even though John was a burning light. Instead, we are told that John was not that light. The Kingdom, like its founder, is *the* light.

First John 1:5–7 tells us that the core of this light is the life we live. This is so powerful and so important. The whole burden of that letter is to get Christians to believe that the power of that eternal life is now in them, equipping them to live the same life as God Himself. That life was evident in the Lord Jesus Christ.

John the Baptist never manifested eternal life here on earth. Most of the evangelical Christian world expects to get eternal life when they get to heaven. They do not expect to manifest eternal life on earth. But this is where we need it. We need God's eternal life now in order to let the world see what that eternal life is like. This eternal life has many different dimensions, which we will look at in greater detail later in this study. I do not expect to live an ordinary life, but I expect to live a supernatural life that is just as much the light as Jesus was the light. That sounds like blasphemy for many people, but this is the solid truth. This is not only biblical, but it is also absolutely necessary so that this dark world will see *that* light.

The Double Portion Principle

In 2 Kings 2, we see that Elisha learned much from Elijah, but he discerned that he needed a greater anointing than Elijah to accomplish his task and succeed where Elijah failed. He asked for a double portion of the Spirit that was on Elijah, and he received it.

Chapter 4 – Miracles Required

This is a hard but not impossible thing.

In this passage, Elijah knew he would soon be taken away. He went to four different stops, and at each one he said to Elisha, "You stop here. I will go on."

But Elisha said, "No way. If you are going forward then I am going with you." Each time he said, "As the Lord lives, and as your soul lives, I will not leave you" (2 Kings 2:4).

When they crossed over the River Jordan, Elijah said to Elisha, "Ask! What may I do for you, before I am taken away from you?" (2 Kings 2:9). Elisha said, "Please let a double portion of your spirit be upon me" (2 Kings 2:9). Elisha's request came from a certain conclusion. He watched Elijah in his life and ministry. I believe they traveled together and came to a high level of intimacy. At some point, Elijah felt free to tell Elisha one of the most shameful moments in his ministry, the day when he ran away from Jezebel and hid in the wilderness.

Elijah didn't know what came over him. It was like a dark cloud that suddenly overshadowed him, "I was one moment on the Mount of Carmel, and all the prophets of Baal were slain. I prayed and the rain came down from heaven. I ran with supernatural power back to Samaria. I was on a roll, but suddenly, something came against me, and I went down fast. I ran like a scared chicken, and I don't know what happened to me. I cannot explain it. Since then, I have not felt the same fire or anointing. I don't feel the faith I once felt. Something was irretrievably damaged in me."

I know people in many countries to whom this has happened. Some of them are men I walked with forty years ago who would say the same thing to me privately, "The fire has gone out of me. All I am looking for now is retirement." This nearly happened to me, so I know what it feels like. When Elisha listened to Elijah's story, I believe he

Section 1 – Moving into Kingdom Christianity

discerned that if he wanted to succeed where Elijah had failed then he would need something more than what Elijah had. He loved what Elijah had. He admired it. He learned so much from what he had. Elijah had imparted so much to him, but Elisha saw that he must go beyond where Elijah was; otherwise, he would end up the same way.

I would suggest to you that the Pentecostal movement that began at the turn of the last century is a picture of this. Great men and women came out of these movements, including the incredible healing revivals of the '40s and '50s, the Jesus People movement of the '60s, and many others. Some of these individuals are still operating. Others have gone to be with the Lord. If you listen to them, however, and walk with them, seeing what has happened to so many of them, you are forced to one conclusion.

All through the twentieth century, despite all the great moves of God in the United States, socially, morally, and spiritually we have disintegrated rather than improved. Our cities are one hundred times more wicked today than they were before the Pentecostal revival. Whatever this outpouring has done for the church, it has not yet accomplished its purpose for society. Therefore, we need something more than what these great men and women had. We need double portion. We need to be able to heal like they did, but we need much more than that.

Elisha asked for a double portion of Elijah's spirit. He did not ask out of arrogance or bravado, but out of dire necessity. Elijah's response was, "You have asked a hard thing" (2 Kings 2:10). It was not an impossible thing, only a hard thing.

I wonder how many of us are prepared to develop the kind of discipline in our lives that is necessary so that the Kingdom consumes us, rather than being consumed by many other perfectly valid things that aren't sin, but aren't the Kingdom either. Some know more about the latest statistics of their favorite team than they do about the book of Ephesians. Are you prepared for the hard thing? Are you prepared for God to take your life and remove even legitimate things in your life in order to free you completely for the purposes of the Kingdom? I am prepared to pay that price.

Some people ask me, "What do you do for recreation?" I usually have to say, "I don't have time for recreation." They usually say, "That is not good for you." I keep remarkably physically fit, but I keep fit not by some exercise program, but by the power of God's grace. I live and work at a level that makes most people feel tired just reading what I do. This is not a burden to me. I am not lying to you.

I learned this several years ago when I read what Paul said in his letter to the Colossians:

Him we preach, warning every man and teaching every man in all wisdom, that we may present every man perfect in Christ Jesus. To this end I also labor, striving according to His working which works in me mightily (Colossians 1:28–29).

I learned that as part of God's grace I can access a physical energy that God provides to do His purpose. I came to America in the most amazing way to be a part of a team that God will use to bring revival to this nation. That is why I am here, and this is what consumes me.

Elijah's response was two-fold:

- You asked a hard thing.
- If you see me when I am taken from you, it shall be so, but if not, it shall not be so.

As Elijah ascended into heaven, it says in verse 12, "Elisha saw it, and he cried out, 'My father, my father, the chariot of Israel and its horsemen!'" (2 Kings 2:12).

Section 1 – Moving into Kingdom Christianity

Spiritual Vision

From that moment, Elisha walked with a consciousness of the power and glory of the forces of God that were with him. It is a great and a necessary part of the Kingdom to have human covenant relationships, but it is far more important to know that the heavenly hosts are with you! When you go to take a city, it is not just you and a few other Christians. There is an army of the Lord that is very aware of the battle, and they are very much involved in the battle. A similar experience happened to me in Mumbai shortly after I was baptized in the Holy Spirit. I did not see any visions, but in one moment my eyes were opened. As we will see in this study, the first prayer of the apostle Paul is focused on this issue. All this preparation is building up to this important reality. There is no way we will take cities with people who cannot see spiritually or supernaturally.

Later on, Elisha used an incredible word of knowledge ministry to tell the king of Israel what the king of Assyria was thinking in his bedroom. The king was frustrated, saying, "Who is the spy in our camp?" They said, "It is not a spy, but it is Elisha! He tells the king of Israel what you are thinking in your bedroom." The king of Assyria sent an entire army to go and get him. When the servant of Elisha woke up, he saw the vast forces rallying against them (without spiritual vision), and he said, "Alas, my master! What shall we do?" (2 Kings 6:15). But Elisha looked at the same scene and saw something completely different. He said, "Do not fear, for those who are with us are more than those who are with them" (2 Kings 6:16).

It is one thing to speak bravado in a prayer meeting, but it is another thing to see things with such clarity. This happened to me in the city of Mumbai (called Bombay at the time). I knew that the forces of God were with us in our little company that broke through in that city. It was the heavenly vision that gave us the power and authority to go and see a breakthrough.

All the way through Elisha's life and ministry, he was always seeing. Even on his deathbed something very interesting took place. In 2 Kings 13, while Elisha was on his deathbed, he looked for someone to whom he could pass on the fire and passion for God's Kingdom. He found Jehoash the king, who greatly respected Elisha. This man had learned the language of the Kingdom, but he did not have the burning faith-filled passion in his heart. Jehoash the king came to Elisha because he was dying. He knew how to say the right things, "O my father, my father, the chariots of Israel and their horsemen!" (2 Kings 13:14). But Jehoash could not see them. He only knew theologically that they were there. That was the right political thing to say when you were in the company of Elisha. It is very possible to bring a church to the language of the Kingdom without seeing the Kingdom.

Elisha was aflame with a passionate desire to pass on what he had received to the next generation. He wanted it to move from him in even greater measure than what he received. But he could not find the right instrument for it. This was the tragedy. When we read the story in 2 Kings 13, we see that Jehoash did not have the fire needed. He did not even have enough fire to bang the arrows on the ground five or six times as Elisha commanded him. What Elisha had established by his fire soon began to die out because the fire was not generated or transmitted into the next generation.

Jesus came as the great Elisha. He was the Kingdom fulfillment of all that is presented in allegory through Elijah and Elisha. The Old Testament lists seven miracles, including one person being raised from the dead, performed by Elijah. Elisha performed fourteen recorded miracles, including two people being raised from the dead. One of these resurrections happened well after Elisha was dead. Elisha's bones were still on fire with the Spirit, and when people threw a dead man into his tomb, the man was instantly resurrected by the fire that was still in Elisha's bones. That's the way I want live.

Section 1 – Moving into Kingdom Christianity

That is the way I want to die. I want to die in battle. I want the fire to be greater at the end than it was at the beginning. I am looking for young men to lay my hands on, saying, "Shoot those arrows. Bang them on the ground until you know God has given you the victory" (see 2 Kings 13:15–19).

5

FAITH, ANOINTING, AND SONSHIP

It's important for believers to actually know and manifest the very eternal life of God. Until we do this, we cannot be that light that Jesus says we are. John the Baptist did not experience this. He could not, because he was on the wrong side of the cross. Everyone in the Kingdom, however, is called to live this way.

Kingdom Faith

The third characteristic of John the Baptist Christianity is that John did not live by faith nor could he do the works of faith. As far as I can find, John did not mention the word *faith* even once. However, he used the word *repent* many times. With John, it is simply *repent*. With Jesus, it is *repent and believe!*

Much of the evangelical world teaches repentance and nominally teaches on faith. If you attend a theological seminary, you are not required to pass a course on faith, apart from a theological understanding of the subject. You are not required to do works of faith. Yet in the early church, they would not even let you wait at tables unless you were full of faith, full of wisdom, and full of the Holy Spirit. You can graduate seminary with a doctorate, yet have no faith to cure a common cold or believe God for a financial need.

Section 1 — Moving into Kingdom Christianity

That is simply not part of the training. Some Bible schools teach this and have this ministry, and I commend them for it. Generally speaking, the opposite is the norm.

If you are going to come into the Kingdom and advance the Kingdom, you must come into faith. Without faith it is impossible to please God. It says in Romans 1:17, quoting Habakkuk. 2:4, "The just shall live by faith." It is by faith that you access grace, and by grace, God supplies everything you need. Faith is so important to my life and passion. I have many years of experience to prove that faith works. This is another mark of Kingdom life.

Jesus and all the subjects of His Kingdom live by faith. Jesus lived by faith, and He taught His disciples that they must live by faith. Every time they failed, they asked, "Why couldn't we do this or that?" What was His answer every time? His answer was: "Because of your unbelief." No other reason is given for failure except unbelief. When they could not move the mountain, He said it was because they did not have faith. He tells us in Matthew 17:21 that faith goes out by prayer and fasting. *It's not the demon that goes out by prayer and fasting, but the faith.* If you live a life of disciplined prayer and fasting, one of the dimensions of that life is ever increasing faith.

If you pray in tongues frequently, the constant abiding in the Spirit does exactly what the scriptures say it will: It builds your spirit for ever increasing faith. Those who pray in unknown tongues edify themselves. This word *edify* is the Greek word *oikodomeo*, which means "to build a house." When you pray in an unknown tongue, you build a house for God's Spirit to increasingly live inside of you. I have spoken in tongues now for some thirty-eight years. It still makes no sense to me whatsoever. I am as clueless about what is going on as I was when I first received the Spirit, but I do have the fruit of this experience in my life. I realize more now than in the beginning what an amazing gift this really is.

If I constantly pray in tongues or frequently pray in tongues, then it constantly increases my capacity for God to live in me. My spirit is enlarged to become a larger and larger residence for God in the Spirit. As a result, God is more resident in me, and God can then move more powerfully through me. But this is a total faith issue.

Kingdom Anointing

The fourth characteristic of John the Baptist Christianity is that John was never baptized or anointed by the Holy Spirit. John had the Spirit, but he was never baptized in the Spirit for a ministry of power and supernatural works. It says in Acts 10:38,

> God anointed Jesus of Nazareth with the Holy Spirit and with power, who went about doing good and healing all who were oppressed by the devil, for God was with Him.

This is how Jesus' ministry was summarized. He was anointed with the Holy Spirit and power for the purpose of healing the sick and delivering those who were oppressed of the devil. And Jesus said, in John 14:12, "The works I do you better not try and do them, because I am God. We need to maintain a respectful differentiation between us." Is that what He said? No! He said,

> Most assuredly, I say to you, he who believes in Me, the works that I do he will do also; and greater works that these he will do, because I go to My Father.

The Holy Spirit gives the power, but it is the faith mentioned here that allows that power to be manifested. These two always work together: the anointing of the Spirit and the power of faith. Jesus said, "You will go out and do the works that I did. In fact, you will do greater works than these because I am going to the Father." This is said to anyone who is willing to believe, because that is the Kingdom! Kingdom Christians are anointed with the Holy Spirit just like Jesus.

Section 1 – Moving into Kingdom Christianity

They go out and do the works of Jesus.

All of this points to the fact that John was not functionally in the Kingdom. John could powerfully and convincingly preach about the Kingdom, but he could not forcefully advance it. We have said much about this already. Jesus began the Kingdom, and He forcefully advanced it. All Kingdom Christians do the same thing. According to Matthew 12 and Luke 11, a manifestation of the Kingdom must result in the displacement of demonic power. Jesus said in Matthew 12:28, "If I cast out demons by the Spirit of God, surely the kingdom of God has come upon you." He says almost the same thing in Luke 11:20, "If I cast out demons by the finger of God, surely the kingdom of God has come upon you."

In Matthew, it is the Spirit of God, but in Luke, it is the finger of God. There are only two places in scripture where this phrase "the finger of God" is used. The first place is in Exodus 8:18 when Moses was locked in conflict with the great demonic powers working through Pharaoh, the ruler of Egypt. Pharaoh was adamant that he would not let the people of God go. Moses was sent by God to confront that spirit. I suspect this spirit was none other than Isis, the great Egyptian supreme deity that ruled over the Egyptian Empire. This demon was worshipped and sought after right up until the late days of the Roman Empire. This was a powerful deity. According to their mythology, Isis was a goddess. Cyrus was her husband and was killed by another god. Isis, however, found the power to raise him from the dead. Cyrus became dependent upon her superior power. Then they had a son called Horace. This is a perverted holy trinity. Isis is often seen as holding baby Horace in her hands. She is the power, and she is the great authority.

That was the spirit that came against Moses and was working through the powerful magicians. Moses did a miracle; they did a miracle. He

Chapter 5 – Faith, Anointing, and Sonship

did another miracle; they did another miracle. Then he did another miracle, and they could not repeat it. They began to have a strange feeling. This happens several places in scripture, where they suddenly feel that the demonic power they are relying upon suddenly experiences a power outage. They simply hang on the edge with nothing. They were completely scared. Then they said, "This is the finger of God!"

Jesus was able to not only work miracles, but also to diffuse the power of hell so that it experienced a power outage. I believe God will bring us to a place where witches and warlocks, along with occult groups who do their wicked works, will find to their amazement that they are suddenly absolutely powerless. When the Kingdom comes, then we are able to move with the finger-of-God power.

Quite a few years ago, we had an event in England in the sphere of responsibility that God had given to us. We saw some wonderful things happen. We saw many different demonic activities shut down. We were really seeing the Kingdom come. One weekend, we saw an advertisement for a conference entitled, "A Weekend of Fascination!" They were inviting every kind of witch, sorcerer, fortune teller, tarot card reader, and worker in the occult. There would be many sessions to teach people how to move in these things with many different demonstrations. It would really be a weekend of fascination in the realm of the mysterious.

When we saw this advertisement, I was really mad. I saw what kind of damage this could do to our city and to people. It was a direct satanic attack against us after we had planted five churches in this region. I called the churches together and said, "This is what I believe we should do. I want three hundred people who are not afraid, and I want you to come with me. We will not stand outside and demonstrate. We will not lobby as politicians. Instead, we will go there and pay our entrance money. We will go inside and walk up and down this conference center.

We will pray in the name of Jesus, binding every spirit, and we will pull the fuses on all the demonic power so that they will not be able to do a single thing. We will invade that place with the authority of Jesus Christ and the Kingdom and see a power outage!"

Everyone was ready to go, and we had an army of three hundred. Then, three or four days before the event, the organizers cancelled the entire weekend. They learned of what we were going to do, and they did not dare face us in competition. They simply pulled out. We must reach the place where we are not mopping up after the devil has hit our cities. Instead, we must take out the fuses so he cannot do anything.

Kingdom Sonship

The fifth characteristic of John the Baptist Christianity is that John did not live or pray as a son of God. There are many words in scripture that describe the parent-child relationship. The particular word used for the Son of God is *huios*. This describes someone who is a grown up adult son who has come to the age of thirty and has now come into his father's inheritance. He can now access the inheritance and use it for his purposes. The age of maturity in biblical culture was thirty, at which point you were eligible for your inheritance.

At the end of Jesus' ministry, in John 13–17, we find Him teaching two important truths. The first was the coming of the Holy Spirit. If you were about to be executed the next morning for your faith, you would be concerned to leave with your disciples the most important things. You wouldn't say, "Don't forget to water the plants. Remember to take out the trash and feed the animals." This was Jesus' last chance to impart something to His disciples. In this period, He mentioned the Holy Spirit nearly one hundred times. More than sixty times He spoke about the Father. He talked about the great day when the Holy Spirit would come as *that day*. In John 16, He said:

> And in *that day* you will ask Me nothing. Most assuredly, I say to you, whatever you ask the Father in My name He will give you. Until now you have asked nothing in My name. Ask, and you will receive, that your joy may be full. These things I have spoken to you in figurative language; but the time is coming when I will no longer speak to you in figurative language, but will tell [show] you plainly about the Father (John 16:23–25).

In Luke 11:1, the disciples came to Jesus and said, "Lord, teach us to pray, as John also taught his disciples." In response, Jesus spoke out for the second time the prayer we have come to know as the Lord's Prayer. He began with, "When you pray, say, 'Our Father…'" This was an incredible revelation for a Jew. For a Jew to call God his father would be impossible, "How could I do that? That is almost blasphemy." Jesus would not teach them to pray like John the Baptist. Instead, He taught them to pray like sons. Sons pray to their Father. One of the great reasons the Holy Spirit has come, according to Galatians 4 and Romans 8, is that He might come into our hearts crying out, "Daddy, Father!"

Many Christians have an experience of Jesus as their Savior. They have an experience of the Holy Spirit as the baptizer. But many Christians have never had a revelation of the Father. They just believe in the trinity. It is something altogether different for the Holy Spirit to come and show you the Father and for your spirit to cry out with this wonderful sense of adoption, "Oh, Daddy, Father!" You know from that day by the sheer amazing grace of God that *you are as much God's son by grace as Jesus is God's son by nature*.

I know the day this experience happened to me. It was in 1965 in Mumbai, India. I have had an ever increasing enriching of that experience, but there was a point when the revelation became real to me. It is the most powerful and wonderful thing to walk around knowing the Father and living as the son in absolute revealed truth.

Section 1 – Moving into Kingdom Christianity

It changes your life in so many ways, including the way you pray. You must learn to pray as a son and not as a beggar.

I was in England in 1966, on furlough from India. A friend of mine was responsible for a large Christian charity doing much work in developing countries. He needed as much money as possible to do what he could to meet the incredible need in so many developing countries. He received the opportunity to appear before the Duke of Edinburough, who was the husband of Queen Elizabeth of England. He was not the king, but he was an incredibly influential person. The Duke often became the patron of a charity if he thought it was a good cause. If he became the patron of the charity, then you had access to all kinds of trust funds. My friend was very interested in obtaining the Duke's patronage for his charity in order to increase the financial flow. He received a fifteen minute interview at Buckingham Palace in London.

The great day came. He put on his best suit. He traveled down very early by train in order to not be late. He arrived in London and passed through the many different stations with permits and passes until finally arriving in the waiting room of the Duke's private quarters. At 4 p.m. precisely he was given fifteen minutes to present his need. The door opened at exactly 4 p.m., and the Duke's private secretary escorted the man into the Duke's presence. My friend had written down very carefully what he intended to say. He did not want to waste one minute of the Duke's time.

He was invited to sit down and present his need when suddenly the door flew open. In came Prince Edward, at that time, a small boy. He came in and said, "Dad, my toy is broken." The Duke said, "Excuse me. I must attend to my son." The Duke used nine minutes to fix the boy's toy. He sent the boy off to play with his toy, turned to my friend after looking at his watch, and said, "I'm sorry. You have six minutes to present your need. How can I help you?"

My friend had a simple revelation at that moment that he never forgot. He said, "In that moment I learned that there is all the difference in the world between being a petitioner and being a son." The son has rights and relationship. He didn't need an appointment to see the Duke. He came crashing through the door with his broken toy to be fixed. My friend was a petitioner.

When Jesus stood outside the tomb of Lazarus, He said,

> Father, I thank You that You have heard Me. And I know that You always hear Me, but because of the people who are standing by I said this, that they may believe that You sent Me (John 11:41–42).

Jesus wanted the people to know why He always received the answer to His prayers. The Father always heard Him because He was His son. Jesus wanted us to know why He had no doubt about getting His prayers answered. Jesus did not pray as a petitioner, but as a son. Essentially, Jesus did not teach His disciples to pray as petitioners, but as sons. When the Spirit comes, He will reveal the Father to you, and you will cry out with the same adoring, "Daddy, Father!" spirit. You will have the same access to the Father as Jesus did.

In fact, Jesus said that He would not pray to the Father for me, but I can go and ask Him myself. I have as much claim on the Father and the same rights of sonship as Jesus has. I can say with the same confidence, "Father, I thank You that You always hear me." He will answer me. Therefore, Jesus said with total confidence, "Lazarus, come forth!" Sons receive answers to their prayers, but petitioners might be fortunate to receive answers to their prayers. Sons have a relationship that always warrants a response from the Father.

John the Baptist never prayed as a son, because he did not have that relationship. Jesus did, and all Kingdom Christians who come to understand their adoption rights pray this way as well.

Section 1 – Moving into Kingdom Christianity

Jesus was so desperate for His disciples to get this revelation. This would affect their whole prayer life and confidence before any opposition. They needed the confidence that what they prayed for as sons would come to pass. You need this same confidence.

The day I saw this in the Spirit, I learned to pray as a son and not as a petitioner. When I first went to India as a faith missionary, trusting God for our finances, I did not write begging letters. I did pray hard, especially with our two young children by our sides. Then one day God spoke to me as Eileen was ironing one of our boy's shirts. The shirt was frayed and needed to be replaced. She said, "Duncan needs a new shirt."

I said, "Fine. Go and buy him one."

God spoke to me and said, "What kind of Father do you think I am?"

I said, "What do you mean?"

He said, "Here is your son, Duncan, and he does not even know that he needs a new shirt. He does not need to come to you every morning and say, 'Oh, father, I need a new shirt. Please give me a new shirt.'" God said, "You have already arranged to change it, because you are a loving father. How much more will I supply your needs before you ask for them?" God continued, "I don't want to hear you pray again, 'Oh God, please supply my need.' Instead, simply thank Me, because I will always supply your needs."

Since that day in the 1960s, I have never prayed a prayer asking God for things that I need. I simply thank Him that He will supply my needs, and I go about His business, confident that He will give what I need. I am a son, and sons have their needs met. A son has a relationship with the Father. A son has rights in prayer. A son has all the riches of his father available to him. When the prodigal son ran away from home, the older brother became upset when he came back.

The father came out to the older son, who said, "You never gave me a goat to make merry with my friends." The father said to him, "Son, all I have is yours. The problem is you never asked me for anything." It was not the lack of supply; it was the lack of believing in a favorable response to his request. Kingdom Christians pray like sons, not like petitioners.

SECTION 2
The Assault on Ephesus

6

FIVE STAGES OF PREPARATION

We have been dealing with introductory material until now. This is all very important in order to really appreciate the book of Ephesians. We have to know the setting in which the book was written. Only recently have I realized the amount of scripture that centers on the battle for Ephesus. The two letters to Timothy were written while Paul was in Ephesus. And all the letters of John and the book of Revelation were written while John was the apostle of Ephesus, having the oversight of the seven churches in Asia Minor. An enormous amount of scripture is devoted to winning the battle for Ephesus besides the letter to the Ephesians itself. We will briefly look at these materials, but we need a few more details regarding the background first. In Acts 16:6, it says:

> Now when they [Paul and his companions] had gone through Phrygia and the region of Galatia, *they were forbidden by the Holy Spirit to preach the word in Asia.*

Asia is the area where the seven churches mentioned at the beginning of Revelation were located. Ephesus, of course, was the major city of this area. They were forbidden by the Holy Spirit to preach the word in Asia. Then the scripture continues:

Section 2 — The Assault on Ephesus

> After they had come to Mysia, they tried to go into Bithynia, but the Spirit did not permit them (Acts 16:7).

This part of scripture puzzled me for quite some time. However, I realized that the Holy Spirit was not allowing the apostle Paul to get into a battle of the magnitude of Ephesus without making sure he was prepared to win that battle. We need to learn important lessons here. We must not have bravado without common sense and true spiritual preparation. Bravado without sense leads to casualties without victory. There is no point in fighting a war like that.

I also realized that it was almost twenty years after Paul was converted before he attempted to go into Asia. He was not a new convert. Instead, he had much experience and training. He saw amazing things happen. He was based in Antioch for many years. He completed his first missionary journey seeing many miracles, signs, and wonders. After Paul lived twenty years of experiential faith, the Holy Spirit finally led him into Asia for the fight.

We need to take these things seriously. These truths are written for our instruction. The Spirit saw that Paul was not yet ready for the fight in Asia. I wonder how many of us can hear the Holy Spirit that well to know when God says *no* and when God says *yes*. You must have the right kind of relationship with the Holy Spirit in order to receive this kind of instruction.

The next thing that happened is in verse 9:

> And a vision appeared to Paul in the night. A man of Macedonia stood and pleaded with him, saying, "Come over to Macedonia and help us." Now after he had seen the vision, immediately we sought to go to Macedonia, concluding that the Lord had called us to preach the gospel to them (Acts 16:9–10).

Chapter 6 – Five Stages of Preparation

After reading these things, I must say that I am much more careful about where I go and what I do. There is tremendous pressure to go in every direction. When you are acknowledged more and more as a man of God, then the propensity to go and go and do and do is much greater. But if you go to the wrong places and do the wrong things, you are not accomplishing anything for the Kingdom.

God planned a training program for the apostle Paul to equip him for Ephesus. Paul went through five stages of preparation in Acts 16–18. We need to ask ourselves whether we have passed through these five stages.

Stage 1: Philippi

First, in Acts 16:11–40, we find the story of Paul in Philippi. When he arrived, he found a woman named Lydia. She was a dealer in purple cloth from the city of Thyatira. She invited the apostle to stay at her house. Paul came to the riverside, where he found a prayer meeting happening. All he could find in Philippi was a ladies prayer meeting. Paul connected with the spiritual life in that city. From that position, he moved out into the city.

Paul was first assaulted by a spirit of divination in verse 16. A young girl was bringing much money to her masters. While following Paul, she said, "These men are servants of the Most High God, who proclaim to us the way of salvation" (Acts 16:17). There was nothing wrong with this utterance. It was absolutely accurate. However, Paul picked up on the spirit motivating this speech. He was not blessed by this girl's endorsement of his ministry. Instead, he recognized the demon. This ought to teach you something about the deceptive nature of demons. If a demon says the right thing, then you are hearing the right thing from the wrong spirit. The spirit in which the truth is said is as important as the truth itself.

Section 2 – The Assault on Ephesus

You can find people in the church to teach the truth; however, in what spirit will they teach it? You cannot fault them doctrinally, yet something bad comes across through them. We need to be people of the Spirit. We live in a day when very deceiving spirits have gone forth. The fact that what they say is doctrinally accurate is not sufficient reason to give them a clear bill to go and do whatever they like.

This event caused Paul to become very upset. I cannot tell you whether he was in the Spirit or not, but he was mad. Being greatly annoyed, he turned to the girl and said to the spirit,

> "I command you in the name of Jesus Christ to come out of her!" And he came out that very hour. But when her masters saw that their hope of profit was gone, they seized Paul and Silas and dragged them into the marketplace to the authorities (Acts 16:18–19).

Paul was thrown into jail and beaten. Having been secured in the innermost prison and fastened by their feet in stocks, at midnight, Paul and Silas began to pray and sing songs to God while the prisoners listen. When you are in the Kingdom, you handle imprisonment differently than John the Baptist. John the Baptist went into prison, and for some reason it so offended him that he fell into complete doubt and wondered if Jesus was the one. I guarantee that when you begin to affect the kingdom of darkness and seriously establish the Kingdom of God, then the demonic powers will come against you to shut you up in some kind of prison. It could be a personal prison. It could be a literal prison.

I know men from a particular national church denomination who began to really proclaim and advance the Kingdom. As a result, they were thrown out of their church. They were shut in some financial prison. They were rejected by their congregation. The demons were so strongly in charge of that church that the pastor left instead of the demons.

They ended up in a prison. It could be a financial prison or a prison of personal rejection and isolation.

Inevitably, at some point in your ministry, if you truly advance the Kingdom, you will go through a prison experience. I guarantee it! This will happen to you as an individual, and it will happen to you as a church. If you do not know how to handle the prison experience, you will end up like John the Baptist. You will ask questions like: *Is God with us or not? Did I make a mistake to come here? Did I really hear God about this assignment? Why would God let this happen to me if He sent me here?* All these doubts begin to rise up, and you doubt your calling, you doubt God, and you wonder whether you should look for something else.

I've seen many men leave the ministry to never come back. I know of two churches in the Church of the Brethren denomination, which is not known for its openness to the Spirit, whose pastors were baptized in the Holy Spirit. The people continued to receive their ministry. They started to proclaim the Kingdom. They invited Cindy Jacobs and Peter Wagner to come and conduct a spiritual warfare conference. The guests came to their region, and following that conference, everything exploded in their faces. The elder boards of both churches turned on these men like packs of wolves and ripped them to pieces.

The tragedy is that both of these men are now out of the ministry and want nothing more to do with the Holy Spirit or the Kingdom of God. They simply found it too much to handle. Those two churches completely disappeared. The witches who perpetrated this defeat gleefully rub their hands and arrogantly declare, "Let's wait for the next manifestation of the Kingdom, and we will kill it, too." This is real warfare, friends. If you are going to advance the Kingdom, you better learn how to praise your way out of prison!

Section 2 – The Assault on Ephesus

Let yourself feel what it must have been like for Paul and Silas to have done nothing more than cast a demon out of a demonized woman, and then they were beaten to a pulp and thrown in the lowest and darkest prison of Philippi. They could have said, "Where is God in all this?" But their response was to see the event clearly as spiritual warfare, as an attack of the enemy. Yet, God was with them, and they did not lose their faith. Instead, they used their faith to come back with a mighty and deliberate intention to praise and worship God. An earthquake occurred, they came out of prison, the jailor got saved, and they left behind a powerful impact of the Kingdom in their wake!

Eileen and I pastored in Mumbai, many years ago, with a church of forty people in a very demonized part of town. The devil came and attacked us in so many vicious ways. I don't have time to go into the details, but our church dwindled to eight people. I was particularly assaulted by demons. Demons came upon us, and the pressure upon us seemed totally unbearable. The physical assault upon our bodies resulted in a strange temporary paralysis so that I could not even open my mouth.

However, in the middle of this incredible conflict, God gave us the grace to continue. One day we saw the breakthrough. In a short time after this event, the Spirit of God visited our community in the most powerful way. We saw thousands and thousands of people saved and filled with the Holy Spirit, and hundreds of churches were established in the following years. The earthquake came because we prayed our way out of prison. We praised our way out of our prison. I felt black and blue all over. The last thing I wanted to do was praise God, but praise Him we did. Something in me was able to keep me going. I was not only in the Kingdom, but the Kingdom was inside me!

Chapter 6 – Five Stages of Preparation

When Peter was thrown into prison, he came out victoriously. When John the apostle was thrown into prison for fourteen years, he came out a thousand times more powerful than when he went in. In the Kingdom, even prison works for good. But this is something you have to learn. Your prison may not be literal or physical, but spiritual, mental, or emotional.

Quite recently I learned more about a small man named Reshin Rog Prudel from Nepal. This man was in prison in Nepal between 1970 and 1990. He was in and out of prison throughout this twenty-year period. He was in prison more than twenty-two times. He was beaten. His legs were broken. His ribs were smashed. He had been a Hindu priest and so passionate about it that his leaders commissioned him to read the New Testament in order to refute Christian teaching. When he read the New Testament, instead of finding fault with it, he discovered it was the truth. He became as fiery for the gospel of Jesus Christ as he had been for Hinduism. However, at that time in Nepal it was against the law to convert to Christianity. You could go to jail for one year just for becoming a Christian. You went to jail for six years for inciting others to become Christian.

They kept throwing him into jail and beating him up. He preached Christ in jail, and he preached Christ out of jail. After twenty-two years, due to the pressure of the world community, Nepal was forced to give a measure of freedom to Christians. This man came out of prison and traveled to the thirty-seven districts of Nepal, a population of approximately 35 million people. Between 1990 and 1997, he traveled to thirty-five of the thirty-seven districts, planting powerful churches and seeing more than five hundred thousand Nepalese saved and added to the churches. That man did more in seven years than missionaries had done for one hundred years. I once heard him say, "We are filling up the suffering that remains of Christ. By our suffering we have paid the price for Nepal. Nepal will be a jewel in the crown of Jesus!" This is Kingdom Christianity.

Section 2 – The Assault on Ephesus

Stage 2: Thessalonica

Second, Paul came to Thessalonica in Acts 17. You can learn much more about Thessalonica by reading the two letters that Paul wrote to that church. But what you see here is that this city was well known as an idolatrous city with incredibly perverted forms of religion and sexuality. It was very dark and demonic. The cultural divide between the educated, intellectual Jew and the demonized, idol worshipping cesspit of iniquity was incredibly wide. Paul's ability to even venture there and preach the gospel took some courage. He went and preached so powerfully that many in Thessalonica turned to the Lord.

The interesting thing is that Paul had only three weeks in this city. Then he was thrown out of the town. Those three weeks were so valued by the people, as we see in 1 Thessalonians 1:4–9:

> For our gospel did not come to you in word only, but also *in power, and in the Holy Spirit* and in much assurance, as you know what kind of men we were among you for your sake. And you became followers of us and of the Lord, having received the word in much affliction, with joy of the Holy Spirit, so that you became examples to all in Macedonia and Achaia who believe. For from you the word of the Lord has sounded forth, not only in Macedonia and Achaia, but also in every place. Your faith toward God has gone out, so that we do not need to say anything. For they themselves declare concerning us what manner of entry we had to you, and *how you turned to God from idols to serve the living and true God* (1 Thessalonians 1:5–9).

These people, who were once dark, demonic idol worshippers, had become some of the fieriest saints on the earth. I think the church in Thessalonica was always one of Paul's favorites. The church was so on fire, and they so absorbed his spirit and so received his faith that they imitated his example.

Paul learned in Thessalonica that however deep and demonic the situation is you can see the power of God transform it. But in that situation, you need the power to cast out demons and to bring people to a living faith in Christ. The power of God's Spirit can bring people out of the most incredible messes so that they become faith-filled, righteous saints. The transformation in this city was amazing.

In these days, if you go out and evangelize, you can guarantee that almost anyone you reach could have a problem with demons. That is the society in which we live. Nice, respectable families waiting to be saved are not so plentiful. Our society is so perverted and polluted and filthy with demons that if you are not equipped to deal with that situation in the power of God you can spend a whole lifetime trying to get one person sorted out. But the power of God can do something that counseling cannot accomplish. Paul had three weeks in this city.

We learned in India that when Hindus were coming to the church, they needed to be delivered. Hindus are idol worshippers, which automatically leads to demonization. We learned that if we did not get them clean at the door, then they caused trouble in the church. We were with Reinhard Bonnke on a number of occasions in his big crusades, and they had an area where all the demonized people would come to find deliverance. If you are going to take Ephesus or your city, then you better have this equipment.

In Acts 17:10 we see that wherever Paul went he ended up causing a riot as well as a revival. As a result, they usually had to leave the city, because they always stirred up a hornet's nest of demonic activity through their invasion of the territory.

Stage 3: Berea

Then, in Acts 17:10, they came to the city of Berea:

> Then the brethren immediately sent Paul and Silas away by night to Berea. When they arrived, they went into the synagogue of the Jews. These were more fair-minded than those in Thessalonica, in that they received the word with all readiness, and searched the Scriptures daily to find out whether these things were so. Therefore, many of them believed, and also not a few of the Greeks, prominent women as well as men (Acts 17:10–12).

Here is what I want you to see. *No matter how much revelation you receive and how much you hear and know things from God, you must be able to turn it into solid Bible fact before you start teaching it to people.* This is necessary for two reasons. First, it will help keep you on track. Paul instructed Timothy with an important admonition, "*Take heed to yourself and to the doctrine.* Continue in them, for in doing this, you will save both yourself and those who hear you" (1 Tim. 4:16).

Paul continued, in his second letter to Timothy, telling him to stay on track in his teaching and doctrine, knowing many others would not:

> For the time will come when *they will not endure sound doctrine*, but according to their own desires, *because they have itching ears, they will heap up for themselves teachers; and they will turn their ears away from the truth, and be turned aside to fables. But you be watchful in all things...* (2 Timothy 4:3–5).

Second, it will establish people firmly in the word of God and not in the power of your feelings, visions, and impressions. I am appalled at the level of Bible knowledge in many charismatic churches.

I was in a large church some time ago that was in the process of finding a new pastor. They had a pastoral pulpit committee that was responsible for finding the next pastor for the church.

Chapter 6 – Five Stages of Preparation

This is like a high school that needs a new principle, so they invite a child from each grade and one teacher to choose their next principle.

They tried to hear God about one man who was a complete mess. When the church was falling apart and in a great mess, they called me in to help. It was like a consultant surgeon being called in when the medical students had been playing all afternoon with a body. They are just about to lose the patient when they call the consultant and say, "Can you help us save this body!" I looked at this mutilated body, and I honestly did not know where to start. I thought, "If only you had called me earlier, before you started messing with this, we could have done something much better."

In the course of this event, I came into confrontation with a rather super-spiritual pulpit committee. These were the "prophetic" people who hear in the Spirit, and they were chosen to be the hearers for the next pastor. They were actually called the "Hearing Committee."

When I confronted them with some of the lunacy of their actions, which they had attributed to the Spirit of God, this is what one of the men said to me, "This is God's will for us. God is getting us down to the pure core."

The church was running approximately two thousand people before this man came; when they called me, they were down to four hundred. The man said, "God can now move us on as the pure church that will do something fantastic for God. Jesus did the same thing. Jesus took a multitude and cut it right back until all he had left were the seven disciples."

I said, "It was not seven, but twelve disciples."

The man retorted, "I'm not a theologian. Don't confuse me."

They trusted a man like this to hear the Spirit of God about the new pastor when this man did not even know how many disciples Jesus had.

Section 2 – The Assault on Ephesus

I said, "Please tell me what you know about the Bible." He gave me no evidence of having his roots in the word of God. Instead, he lived in a charismatic dream world. If we do not get solidly in the word and we do not get our revelation confirmed by scripture, then we are in trouble.

Many of you know that I deal much with what God has shown me by revelation, but you would agree that I go to the word and I search the word to make sure these things are accurate. This is being Berean! Paul was sharpened in his preaching and teaching by this experience. Paul saw things by the revelation of the Spirit that were not traditionally Jewish. But he had to go back to the scripture because he would be lynched if he could not prove his revelations by the word of God. We need to become Berean in everything we do. Are you Berean? Will you give yourself to become an ardent student of the word who has much revelation?

God unfolds new mysteries about the scripture that have been deliberately kept until this time, because this is the time when we need to know them. We need to be able to sort out what God is showing us, because there is no historical teaching to rely upon. You must be the kind of people who can ask, "Is this according to scripture?" We need leaders who are as Berean, and as solid in the word, as the apostle Paul was. Although he moved in tremendous new revelation and understood these mysteries, he always came back to the completely trustworthy foundation of scripture.

Stage 4: Athens

The fourth stage of Paul's development brought him to Athens, in Acts 17:13–34. Paul came to Athens following these incredible revivals. However, something changed in Athens. Look at his message, beginning in verse 22:

"Men of Athens, I perceive that in all things you are very religious; for as I was passing through and considering the objects of your worship, I even found an altar with this inscription: TO AN UNKNOWN GOD. Therefore, the One you worship without knowing, Him I proclaim to you: God who made the world and everything in it, since He is Lord of heaven and earth, does not dwell in temples made with hands. Nor is He worshipped with men's hands, as though He needed anything, since He gives to all life, breath, and all things. And He has made from one blood every nation of men to dwell on all the face of the earth, and has determined their preappointed times, and the boundaries of their dwellings, so that they should seek the Lord, in the hope that they might grope for Him and find Him, though He is not far from each one of us; for in Him we live and move and have our being, as also some of your own poets have said, 'For we are also His offspring.' Therefore, since we are the offspring of God, we ought not to think that the Divine Nature is like gold or silver or stone, something shaped by art and man's devising. Truly, these times of ignorance God overlooked, but now commands all men everywhere to repent, because He has appointed a day on which He will judge the world in righteousness by the Man whom He has ordained. He has given assurance of this to all by raising Him from the dead." And when they heard of the resurrection of the dead, some mocked, while others said, "We will hear you again on this matter" (Acts 17:22–32).

When the council heard about the resurrection, some mocked Paul. Others said they wanted to hear more on this matter. Paul departed from them with this following report, "*Some men* joined him and believed, among them Dionysius the Areopagite, a woman named Damaris, and others with them."

Section 2 – The Assault on Ephesus

We know from history that the church Paul established in Athens was of no consequence in that city. It was his disaster city in terms of having significant impact. I can see the apostle Paul walking away from Athens with no riot and no revival. Only a small number of people became believers. For the majority, Paul's message was just another nice philosophical teaching. It had no impact.

I can see the apostle Paul asking himself, "What went wrong? Why was there no breakthrough here?" I can't prove this to you from scripture directly, although there is good evidence for what I am about to say in his next letter to the Corinthians. I believe God said to Paul, "You did not preach Jesus and Him crucified. You tried to be clever. You tried to intellectually persuade them by using their philosophers and theories about God. You dodged around the cross and simply touched on His resurrection. There is no power in philosophy, but there is power in the message of the cross!"

We do know that when Paul came to Corinth, which was the next stop on his travels, he said:

> And I, brethren, when I came to you, did not come with excellence of speech or of wisdom declaring to you the testimony of God. For I determined not to know anything among you except Jesus Christ and Him crucified.... My speech and my preaching were not with persuasive words of human wisdom, but in demonstration of the Spirit and of power, that your faith should not be in the wisdom of men but in the power of God (1 Corinthians 2:1–5).

Paul learned that you cannot make a breakthrough with clever intellectualism. It is the foolishness of the cross and the power of signs, wonders, and miracles that makes people turn from their darkness to the light and glory of our Lord Jesus Christ.

Prior to my conversion, I was a research scientist with the Kodak film company. I called myself an atheist, because it was a convenient way to live. I could forget about God and concentrate on doing what I liked. In that period of research, I went to the city of Nottingham and was employed in full-time lecturing at the College of Advanced Technology. I really enjoyed lecturing. I loved exciting these students and seeing simple scientific principles come alive for them. While I enjoyed my lecturing, I discovered that this was not really what I wanted. By a series of events, I ended up back with Kodak.

I was being head-hunted for another job. Another man in the company called my former boss in Kodak with a particular offer. My former boss called me and said, "If you are interested in getting back into the industry, come and see me, because I have a very interesting offer for you." I went back to Kodak and received the leadership of a research team which was called the Blue Sky Team. We were a group of inventors. I was paid incredible money to do what I absolutely loved. In those years, I found no Monday morning blues. In fact, I could not get to work fast enough.

When I left Kodak, I had left as a scientific atheist. However, I came back as "a nutcase" for Jesus! From day one, I decided to preach Christ and led an organization within the company designed to evangelize the factory. I would go into the men's work canteen and preach to them during lunch time. We had permission to do these things.

You can imagine that some of my colleges in the scientific realm thought I was completely bizarre. One of them was a famous scientist in our narrow field of expertise. His name was Dr. Stevens. At that time, he was the greatest living authority on what happens when a ray of light strikes a silver halo crystal. This man wrote great scientific books on these mysteries. Dr. Stevens worked in the laboratory next to me.

Section 2 – The Assault on Ephesus

One day, Dr. Stevens called me into this laboratory and said, "Alan, I want you to see this incredible new find in filming." Although the Doctor was sincere, he was also playing a joke on me. He put it under a microscope and said, "Take a look." When I looked down the microscope, I saw this fantastic new fine grain, but in the middle of it was a naked woman with some rude words that I don't want to repeat. He mocked me for my new prudishness as a born-again, unashamed Christian.

I tried to win these men with clever arguments for some time, while they ridiculed and mocked me. I was a little upset at this event. I remember turning around to Dr. Stevens and saying, "You are recognized as the world's leading authority on what happens when a ray of light strikes a silver halo crystal. You are a famous and well-known scientist, but inside you are a dirty old man who needs a savior!"

I gave him fifteen minutes of the cross, and he simply stood there in stunned silence. I could see powerful conviction coming upon him. I decided that day not to preach clever scientific arguments. I would not try and prove evolution verses creation. Instead, I would preach the foolishness of the cross of Jesus Christ.

When Eileen and I went to Mumbai, we saw many students come to Jesus Christ during my lecturing there. Many people would ask me, "What is your approach to the Hindu?"

I would say, "Jesus Christ and Him crucified."

"What is your approach to the Muslim?"

Again, "Jesus Christ and Him crucified."

I am not ashamed of the gospel of the Jesus Christ, because it is the power of God unto salvation. If we are going to take our cities for God, we must step down from our intellectual high horse and get down to the foolish yet incredible power and simplicity of the cross.

When I became a Christian, the person who talked with me did not talk about clever arguments. Instead, he said, "Alan, the reason Jesus is not real to you is because of the sin in your life."

I was a very respectable, self-righteous individual. I even drove at the speed limit before I was converted. I paid my taxes honestly. I didn't need God, because I was so self-sufficiently righteous. When the man preached the cross of Christ to me, in all its simplicity, I became convicted. He said, "You do not need to understand it; you simply decide to believe it. Then it will begin to work in your life."

That is how I began as a Christian, and that is how I am forty-two years later. There is a power in the cross of Jesus Christ, and we need to let it work in us and through us to the saving of people.

Stage 5: Corinth

The fifth stage occurred on Paul's way to Corinth. He was determined to know nothing else except Jesus Christ and Him crucified. His conclusion was to preach the power of the cross in the demonstration of the Spirit's power. When he arrived, Paul linked up with Aquila and Priscilla, which became very important later. Then he began to reason in the synagogue. He testified that Jesus is the Christ. When they opposed Paul by abusing and ridiculing him, he left the Jews and went to the Gentiles to preach Christ. Then it says:

> Then Crispus, the ruler of the synagogue, believed on the Lord with all his household. And many of the Corinthians, hearing, believed and were baptized. Now the Lord spoke to Paul in the night by a vision: "Do not be afraid, but speak, do not keep silent; for I am with you, and no one will attack you to hurt you; for I have many people in this city." And he continued there a year and six months, teaching them the word of God among them (Acts 18:8–11).

Section 2 — The Assault on Ephesus

In all the places where Paul went and preached, apart from Athens, he caused a group of people to respond to him with an overwhelming response to the powerful preaching of the gospel. At the same time, a vicious counter attack always drove him out of the city. Paul had revival and riot everywhere he went. He could not stay in a city for very long because he was driven out.

He finally came to Corinth, and as the gospel began to spread, people began to be saved. But you can sense a building up to the same conclusion: *Paul's departure.* However, this time Jesus appeared to him in the night and said, "Do not be afraid; keep on speaking, do not be silent. For I am with you, and no one is going to attack and harm you, because I have many people in this city."

In verse 11 it says something very important, "And Paul *continued* there a year and six months, teaching the word of God among them." The word *continued (kathizo)* is an often mistranslated word. In Luke 24:49, where Jesus commanded His disciples to wait in Jerusalem until they are clothed with power, He said, "Wait." I meditated on this word, *kathizo*. The 120 who obeyed became a city-taking community as far as Jerusalem was concerned. This is when the breakthrough came. When they came out of the upper room, within two years one third of the city was converted.

In both Luke 24:49 and Acts 18:11, we find the same word: *kathizo*. This word comes sixty-five times in the New Testament. Nowhere else in the New Testament is the word translated with the same meaning as in Acts 18:11. I went through the New Testament and looked through some of the Greek Classics and discovered a contextual definition for how this word was used at that time. I discovered that *kathizo* has a meaning very different from the way it appears to be translated. I feel that these are two unfortunate translations. This is how the word is used everywhere else: *"To sit down with certain connotations. First, you sit down comfortably. You sit down as if you belong there."*

The word *kathizo* is linked between eighteen and twenty times with the word *throne* in the New Testament. So, it is not just sitting, but sitting on a throne. There is a second word that *kathizo* is connected to, a particular kind of seat called a *cathedra*. We also get our word *cathedral* from this word. Moses, for example, sat down to give directions concerning the law. Even to this day, when the Pope gives a Papal statement, he speaks ex-cathedra, which means "speaking from the throne." According to Catholic dogma, when he speaks from the throne, he speaks the infallible word of God and must be obeyed by all Catholics. There is a submission required by the authority of that throne.

Throughout the New Testament, that is how this word is used. It is very interesting to see where and how it is used. *It is used again and again of Jesus sitting upon His throne for the purposes of exercising rule, authority, and judgment over His enemies.* Again and again, *we are put there together with Him for the same purposes.*

If I could summarize all this and give you a definition, I would say that the use of the word *kathizo* in the Bible means to sit down comfortably upon a throne with the sense of the right to be there. You have a right to sit there. From that throne, you exercise rule, government, and authority over all your enemies. I do not believe that any of us will be effective city-takers until we have learned this principle. That is why Jesus said, "Don't leave Jerusalem until you have this principle firmly in you."

In addition to this, you must be clothed with power. Power flows from the throne, and it is the power of the Kingdom in signs, wonders, and miracles. This is the word that is used in Acts 18:11. I believe Paul did not just wait passively for something to happen in Corinth. Instead, he said, "Yes, I have your word, Lord. This city belongs to Jesus. He has many people here. I am here as His authoritative representative.

Section 2 – The Assault on Ephesus

I will sit on the throne with Christ, and nothing will move me from here until I have reaped the harvest Jesus has promised."

When you read on, you will see there were several attacks against Paul in Corinth. However, Paul had learned to sit upon the throne and rule. Therefore, the attacks were neutralized and never had effect upon him. They did not succeed in throwing him out of the city this time. Instead, he was more effective in throwing his enemies out of the city. Sometimes I have wondered, "Paul, did you not know how to do that in Philippi? Did you not know how to do that in Thessalonica? Is this something that you learned later?" I suspect this is what happened. Paul adopted a totally new position as an ambassador, as the apostle of the Lord Jesus Christ, to bring the rule of the Kingdom and reap a mighty harvest. "No stinking demon who thinks he owns the city will stop me, in Jesus' name. I am not moving, and there is no room for the both of us! So either I go or you go. However, I am not moving, so there is only one other alternative. You are leaving!" A whole new authority came to Paul on this occasion.

God placed us in the city of San Antonio, along with other anointed men and women of God, to enforce the establishment of the Kingdom of God. In our case, the demons must leave, because we will not! You will see this breakthrough. We can begin to feel it happening. I am sure the same is true for the city you represent. You must come to a Corinthian attitude! You must know that God has placed you there! You must hear what Paul heard, "I've put you here. I have many people in this city." You have the utter assurance of the placement of God and of the definite harvest He has called you to reap.

Ever since I have been converted, I have lived by the principle in John 15:16:

> You did not choose Me, but I chose you and appointed [ordained] you that you should go and bear fruit, and that your fruit should remain, that whatever you ask the Father in My name He may give you.

The Greek word for *appoint* has the idea of placing something. I could take a chair and place it in a specific geographical location. Jesus said, "I will place you somewhere." The purpose of placing you is that you should go, bring forth fruit, and that fruit will remain. Everywhere Jesus places me I expect to be fruitful. I have no desire or will to be any other place than where God has placed me. I have seen consistent fruit through my life, not because I am some clever guy, but because I've had enough sense to let the Lord place me and then believe that the placing is of God. Therefore, I have seen fruit, and that fruit still remains.

If you return to Mumbai, India, you will still see the fruit of God's placing. We left there in 1976, and the churches have grown to thousands of churches. The young men we led to Christ are now apostles and powerfully moving in ministry. They are far beyond where I was at their age. The work has simply multiplied. This is fruit that remains. This is a lesson we must learn. It says in Acts 18:11 that Paul sat on his throne for many days. He reaped a harvest. Then it says, "So Paul still remained a good while. Then he took leave of the brethren and sailed for Syria, and Priscilla and Aquila were with him. ...And he came to Ephesus..." (Acts 18:18–19). Paul was now ready for Ephesus. He picked up his throne, and he travelled off to Ephesus. He will sit down there at Ephesus and see the Kingdom come to that place as well!

7

PAUL'S FIRST ENCOUNTER WITH EPHESUS

I want to have a quick look now at the assault on Ephesus. We need to see the demonic assault against this city, since the Kingdom comes to displace an already hostile kingdom that is set up in defiance of God and His rule. To understand that, we need to look quickly at the spiritual history of Ephesus.

Ephesus was the major city of Asia Minor. Asia Minor is an area represented today by Turkey. Ephesus was one of the seven churches mentioned in the book of Revelation. This was the fourth largest city in the Roman Empire. It had a population of 250 thousand people. In those days, it was a major city. The city was most famous as the seat of the Greek goddess Artemis. She was the great deity of the Greek Empire. Alexander the Great built a great temple to her which was one of the Seven Wonders of the World. Artemis was prayed to and glorified all over the Greek Empire.

When the Romans came to power, they recognized Artemis as their own goddess, but gave her the name Diana, which is Latin. These two different names represent the same spirit. If you take the trouble, which I have done, to trace this deity back, you'll find that the same

Section 2 – The Assault on Ephesus

properties, qualities, and images appear for the deity Isis, and you can even trace Isis back to the Babylonian deity Baal, which worked through Jezebel. The same evil spirit that ruled the Egyptian Empire through Isis also ruled the Greek empire as Artemis. It had already ruled the Babylonian, Persian, and Assyrian Empires as Baal. Now, during the time of this letter to the Ephesians, the same deity was ruling the Roman Empire as Diana. It is the same spirit manifested under different names.

If you see the pictures and images of this deity down through the centuries, you cannot help but see the similarities. Isis, Artemis, and Diana all have similar titles. These titles include: the Queen of Heaven, the moon goddess, and the goddess of nature and the animal kingdom. So much of what is called New Age is really represented in these deities. Each of them was also a fertility goddess, which brought about obscene sexual festivals and immorality. The idols and images also have many similarities. Archaeologists have recently found an ancient Egyptian image of Isis and Horace, which looks nearly identical to the modern Black Madonna.

This image of Isis and Horace was discovered through a new form of ultrasonic equipment which is far more sensitive than earlier models. This new equipment was used recently in the ancient port of Alexandria, a major city of the Egyptian Empire from which ships traveled to transport goods across the empire. It continued to be a powerful center during the Roman Empire. Artemis, Diana, and Isis were worshipped in Alexandria. An incredibly large earthquake happened in that region during the seventh or eighth century, and it reshaped the entire harbor of Alexandria. Many ships went down, many of them known treasure ships, but they had never been found or explored.

However, this new equipment was able to locate these ancient ships deep beneath the ocean floor. They were able to dig down and begin pulling up this ancient harbor's treasure. Some of the first things they hauled to the surface were statues of the goddess Isis in black marble holding baby Horace in her arms. I've seen a picture of one of these idols from the seabed placed next to a black Madonna, and you cannot tell one from the other. Secular archaeologists concluded that these idols are the same thing. This is where the worship of Mary originated. It came from the worship of Isis, the sun goddess, and her baby son Horace. The Roman Catholic Church continues to argue in defiance against it, but the evidence is irresistibly convincing.

This spirit ruled over the center of military, political, and economic power in all the empires where she was found. That was what was waiting for Paul when he came to Ephesus. This explains why there had to be a preparation for such a confrontation in Ephesus. God took Paul through a series of training steps before he allowed him to come to Ephesus, as mentioned previously. And when this thing was successfully dethroned, the whole of Europe and Northern Africa was released into a great advance of the Kingdom.

In our modern world, this spirit has taken root in Free Masonry and in Islam. Free Masonry has its roots directly from the worship of Isis. Its symbols and signs are the same. Free Masonry is one of the biggest strongholds in the United States, holding most major cities in its power, including the nation's capital. Also, nearly all of the presidents of the United States have been Free Masons. It is also very easy to trace the beginnings of Islam to this same source. Diana, Artemis, and Isis all had a fine crescent-shaped necklace that hung around their necks. This is identical to what you see on the Muslim flag today. We can learn from the battle of Ephesus how to deal with these things in our day. This was no minor confrontation, as we see in Paul's first encounter with Ephesus.

Section 2 – The Assault on Ephesus

Before Paul's arrival in Ephesus, he knew how to break a place open for the Kingdom, but he did not yet know how to deal with the demonic forces that came against him. This happened after twenty years of apostolic ministry. Please do not think you know everything. Paul was a continual learner. On previous occasions, Paul was driven out of town by the opposition. The church had to struggle. In some cases, it struggled powerfully and successfully, but in other cases, it struggled with great difficulty. It was in Corinth that he learned the important principle of taking his authority in the heavenly realm and ruling over demonic principalities and powers.

God's Secret Weapon

Once he had learned this lesson, the Spirit of God said to him, "You are ready now to take on Ephesus." We find the following description of his first encounter with Ephesus:

> And he came to Ephesus, and left them [Priscilla and Aquila] there; but he himself entered the synagogue and reasoned with the Jews. When they asked him to stay a longer time with them, he did not consent, but took leave of them, saying, "I must by all means keep this coming feast in Jerusalem; but I will return again to you, God willing." And he sailed from Ephesus (Acts 18:19–21).

I want you to see the strategy here. When certain people have a reputation in the Kingdom, they are as known in hell as they are in the Kingdom. When the seven sons of Sceva tried to cast out a demon in Ephesus, the evil spirit said, "*Jesus* I know, and *Paul* I know; but who are you" (Acts 19:15). So Paul was on their fear list, and as a result, he was also on their hit list. Sometimes it is not always wise for the big guy to go into town, because the moment he goes into town and begins working, all hell is immediately on the defensive.

If you think about missionary stories, you will find that God often uses a secret weapon. It was Mr. and Mrs. Nobody who never had their name in Charisma magazine and no one knew who they were. However, in the spirit they had as much authority as some of the big guns. You may ask, "Why doesn't anyone recognize me? Why don't I have fame?" Maybe it is because you are one of God's secret weapons who will do much more for the Kingdom than always having public prominence. *I want us to agree that we will allow God to give us the profile that He wants us to have. If we are invisible all our life, it might be for a very good reason.*

How many of you have heard of Jackie Pullinger? She was a small, respectable, middle class English lady, yet she went to the Forbidden City in Hong Kong in response to God's leading. There were two main sources of the drug trade in the world. One is in the north of South America. God is dealing powerfully with that area right now. The other source comes from the Triad gangs who are Chinese. Their base is in Hong Kong. The Triad gang has done more to bring the curse of drug addiction across the world than any other. Their stronghold was called the Forbidden City, within the city of Hong Kong. It was so bad that even the police did not venture into that part of the city. If a high profile person tried to go in and do something for that city, he would not have lasted one day. They would have killed him immediately.

Little Jackie Pullinger went into the Forbidden City, and all she could do, it seemed, was speak in tongues. She started reaching out to Triad gang members and many other people on drugs. She revealed her method to us one day, "All I do is try to get them to speak in tongues, and sooner or later they get filled with the Spirit and the demons leave them." I can't tell you the whole story, but her book, *Chasing the Dragon*, is worth reading. Today, the Forbidden City does not exist, because one little lady went in there and knew how to speak in tongues. I do know that over three thousand former Triad gang members are now in full-time Christian service. These men and women are most responsible for shaking the nation and establishing the church in China.

You don't have to be a big name to take a city. In fact, God often uses the small names to break the ground. I believe the apostle Paul was hearing God when he decided not to stay in Ephesus, instead, he left Priscilla and Aquila there. They had been with him during his journey, facing these different situations. They were as spiritually equipped as he was, but they did not have the same profile as Paul. So Paul left them there in Ephesus. This couple is mentioned no less than six times in scripture. They had churches in their house. Not all apostles have blinking lights around their names. However, they are just as powerful in the Kingdom. They are doing a devastating work at a foundational level that will only be fully recognized in heaven. We must agree together that we want to please God rather than be concerned about our reputation among people.

Priscilla and Aquila came into Ephesus, and the first thing they noticed was a certain Jew named Apollos. Listen to this man's qualifications. Apollos came from Alexandria, which was the second largest city in the Roman Empire. It was the former center of the Egyptian Empire. It had a strong and powerful Jewish community. We assume Apollos was Jewish, although he could have been an African proselyte (convert to Judiasm) who later converted to Christianity, like Simon of Cyrene (see Acts 13:1).

Apollos was an eloquent man, mighty in the scriptures, having been instructed in the way of the Lord. He was fervent in spirit and spoke accurately about the things of the Lord. What a fantastic man, right? Notice what it says at the end of Acts 18:25, "This man had been instructed in the way of the Lord, and being fervent in spirit, he spoke and taught accurately the things of the Lord, though he knew only the baptism of John." Apollos was a John-the-Baptist Christian.

When Priscilla and Aquila sensed this, they felt it was necessary to instruct him in the way of God more perfectly.

I am convinced they introduced him to the Kingdom. They introduced him to the power of the Holy Spirit and all the gifts of the Spirit. In this way, God was preparing the task force that would take Ephesus. Although Apollos was a well-equipped, informed, eloquent, and educated man, he had not yet transitioned from John-the-Baptist Christianity to Kingdom Christianity. Priscilla and Aquila helped him make that transition.

Becoming a Kingdom Team

Finally, in Acts 19 we read:

> And it happened, while Apollos was at Corinth, that Paul, having passed through the upper regions, came to Ephesus. And finding some disciples he said to them, "Did you receive the Holy Spirit when you believed?" So they said to him, "We have not so much as heard whether there is a Holy Spirit" (Acts 19:1–2).

I believe Paul listened to those disciples pray and picked up on a deficiency in the way they prayed. Their whole approach to God was intellectual, ordered, safe, petitioning like a servant. I believe these disciples lacked fervency, a Father-son relationship, a confidence in prayer born out of knowing the Holy Spirit.

So then Paul asked them:

> "Into what then were you baptized?" So they said, "Into *John's baptism.*" Then Paul said, "John indeed baptized with a baptism of repentance, saying to the people that they should believe on Him who would come after him, that is, on Jesus Christ."

Section 2 – The Assault on Ephesus

> When they heard this, they were baptized in the name of the Lord Jesus (Acts 19:3–5).

Here are three things: They were baptized in water, they repented, and they believed in Jesus. For 90 percent of the evangelical world, this is enough. But I want you to see that this is John's baptism, and that baptism does not empower you for city taking. It only ensures your own eternal salvation. But this is not enough for the task God has for us. Paul laid hands on them, and they had a mighty encounter with the Holy Spirit. They were baptized in the name of Jesus, the Holy Spirit came upon them, and they spoke in tongues and prophesied. The total number of them was twelve.

I am not advocating re baptism, but what I am saying is that if you had a traditional baptism as a child and you've never had a powerful encounter with Jesus Christ, then I recommend you go and get baptized again into all His fullness life and power.

We will see what this means when we come to the book of Ephesians, because it talks about being *in Him* throughout Paul's epistles more than eighty times. I have met countless people who were baptized years ago, and they confess that it meant nothing to them at the time. But now they see what it means, and they long for the power of that prophetic act, the impartation that takes place through faith-filled water baptism. They ask, "Would it be possible for me to be baptized again?" Personally, I have always said yes to this request. I believe something happens in the act of baptism.

I learned how powerful water baptism is in the nation of Nepal. From the early '70s, I would sneak into Nepal where it was forbidden to preach the gospel. You received a one year jail sentence for converting to Christ, and you received six years in jail for proselytizing. Missionaries in that country could not do much, because they were marked. But I could sneak in on two or three week journeys and keep moving.

Chapter 7 – Paul's First Encounter with Ephesus

The communication was so bad in the country that by the time the police caught up with me, I was already in the next town.

In 1972, we had our first nationwide gathering of Christian leaders, with approximately eighty people, in the capital city of Katmandu. I was speaking the word, and the power of God fell on them while I spoke. It was like the book of Acts all over again. At that time there were only four hundred believers in the whole of Nepal gathered in sixteen little groups of secret Christians. Many of them were never baptized, because it meant going to jail. This event marks you as a follower of Jesus, and the devil sees it as your threshold where you become irretrievably Christ's follower. These believers went back to their homes in the power of the Holy Spirit. Now there are hundreds of thousands of Nepalese following Jesus Christ. It all began then, and I saw that baptism is a tremendously important issue.

We need to think over whether we are proclaiming and practicing water baptism properly. In our church in England, baptism was one of the most powerful evangelistic tools we could ever use. We had a tank in the floor. All the children would sit around it like it was a swimming pool. We were seeing many people saved, so one Sunday a month we declared a baptism night. The candidates would bring all their relatives and friends. Most thought it was a religious ceremony equivalent to Christmas or Easter. We didn't misinform them, but we wanted to get people to church by any means, and water baptism was an excellent opportunity. Each candidate gave their testimony. I preached for about ten to fifteen minutes, and then I gave an invitation for people to be saved. The power of God came every time. We would see dozens and dozens of people convicted and converted.

On some occasions, someone new was baptized right on the spot. We had spare sets of clothes available. The spontaneity of the event is incredible, provided the power of God has really hit them.

Why make them wait years? This is a power we have lost in the church in America. Baptism is usually done on a Sunday afternoon with a few friends and perhaps only once or twice a year. Most churches are missing their evangelistic opportunity. We need to do this publicly and declare the power of baptism. These believers in Ephesus were properly baptized. They received the Holy Spirit, spoke in tongues, and prophesied. Now Paul had a team to work with. He had a Kingdom preacher in Apollos. He had a Kingdom community in this group of believers. He was now equipped to take the city.

The Assault on Diana Begins

Paul started to work in the city, and the assault on Diana began. Acts 19:11 tells of a strong power encounter: "Now God worked unusual miracles by the hands of Paul." *When the devil gets rough and tough, God likes to come back at him with mighty signs and wonders.* God loves a fight, and I like to be with God when He is in a fighting mood. There is nothing like it. I have been in such situations in India with my precious brother John Babu, who is now with the Lord. He and I went to these Hindu villages where the witch doctors were stirring up the people, and they challenged the power of the name in which we came. I love to hear this challenge, because I know God will show up.

In one village they brought a highly demonized woman to the place where we were, and they said, "Let's see if there is any power in this name of Jesus." As they brought her to the door of the building, she fell down on the ground, screamed, and all the demons left her. She was suddenly in her right mind! As a result, everyone in the village was delivered, and everyone who was ill was healed. That village went to its knees and honored the power and glory of Jesus Christ. I like this kind of thing! This is where we are going.

Chapter 7 – Paul's First Encounter with Ephesus

There is no other way to take a city except being ready for a sustained fight. At the end of Paul's ministry, he said, "I have fought the good fight..." (2 Tim. 4:7). He said to young Timothy, "You have to learn to fight the good fight of faith." *There is no other way to forcefully advance the Kingdom without having a permanent attitude of war.* If you do not have this attitude, you won't do anything other than take good notes. The Kingdom will not significantly advance in your sphere. However, if you let this power come upon you, and if you let the warrior spirit come upon you, then God will use you as powerfully as He has used anyone else.

The assault on Artemis began with mighty signs and wonders. Then Acts tells us about some Jewish exorcists who tried to cast out demons. They used the right formula, "We exorcise you by the Jesus whom Paul preaches" (Acts 19:13). They felt they had the right formula, but they lacked the anointing. We must be careful in these days, because we have so much instant information. We know what is going on around the world. When people have success somewhere, they are invited other places to share their methodology. When the methodology is put into practice in other places, it often does not work. We need to hear God for our cities. I am not saying there won't be similarities in methodology, but the important thing is to have the same powerful anointing that comes from the Holy Spirit.

When the anointing is there, the city must reckon with the power of God's Kingdom. Paul stayed in Ephesus for the longest time, approximately three years. We read in Acts 19:21 that Paul was already prophesying in spirit to go to Macedonia and Achaia and then on to Rome. You can see that this man had the world on his heart. As he thought about leaving, the demons said, "If he is leaving, this is our chance to hit back!" In verse 23 it says, "About that time there arose a great commotion about the Way."

Stirring-Up Opposition

Despite these great miracles and great breakthroughs, and although a powerful and living church had been established, a greater opposition arose. Within just two or three years, the first attacks began on the emerging church. These attacks took several forms that are important for us to understand.

1. Disturbing Economic Gain

In Acts 19, we find a man called Demetrius who became a gate for hell's activity. He was an instrument of Satan that viciously attacked the church of Jesus Christ. His argument was an economic argument, because he was making a fortune by selling silver idols of Diana. He saw that if people gave up worshipping Diana then he would lose his income and livelihood. His motivation was totally economic, but he was used by Satan to stir up a great assault against the apostle Paul and the emerging church in the city.

In Acts 19:25, Demetrius said, "Men, you know *that we have our prosperity by this trade.*" Would you not say that the Mafia would say the same thing about drugs? They have their prosperity by this evil trade. If we begin to really deal with drug addiction and begin rescuing countless young people from this trade, so that they do not want drugs anymore, how do you think the Mafia will think about this? This is already happening in Cali, Columbia. Some of the key drug lords who could not survive the changing spiritual atmosphere in that city have moved to Bogotá and Median.

We need to be involved in the world scene and know what is happening worldwide. What happens in some of these places deeply affects the places where we live. The Demetriuses of these places will stir up trouble; they do not want the church to progress, because it affects their income. You will be in the same kind of warfare as the apostle Paul when you really go after your city by advancing the Kingdom of God.

We need not be scared of these things, but we must be prepared for them.

2. Disturbing Patriotic Loyalties

The second attack in Ephesus is the attack of patriotism. Demetrius also laid out this argument in his speech against Paul:

> Moreover you see and hear that not only at Ephesus, but throughout almost all Asia, this Paul has persuaded and turned away many people, saying that they are not gods which are made with hands. So not only is this trade of ours in danger of falling into disrepute, but also *the temple of the great goddess Diana may be despised and her magnificence destroyed, whom all Asia and the world worship*. Now when they heard this, they were full of wrath and cried out, saying, "Great is Diana of the Ephesians!" So the whole city was filled with confusion..." (Acts 19:26–29).

In many cultures, if you reject the cultural norms by becoming a Kingdom person, you will come under fire. Many people pay a heavy price to come out of their cultural norms. To be a loyal Indian, you must be a Hindu. If you convert to the foreign religion of the Christians, then you are regarded as non-patriotic. This is the weapon used in many Islamic nations. To be an Iranian is to be a Muslim. The same is true for many Catholic nations. To be Croatian or Slovenian is to be a Catholic. To be truly Serbian, one must be Orthodox.

We must make sure we do not allow a wrong loyalty in our lives. We must know that we will be attacked when leaving our cultural norms to embrace the Kingdom. There is a price to be paid. Paul said to Timothy, "...Share with me in the sufferings for the gospel according to the power of God" (2 Tim. 1:8). If you go out powerfully, then you will be attacked. We need to decide that we will not pull back or retreat in the face of opposition.

Section 2 — The Assault on Ephesus

In the case of Ephesus, the city elders quieted the uprising, but that was the end of the breakthrough. After stabilizing the church following these first attacks, in Acts 20:1, Paul left and moved on to Macedonia. We must conclude that Paul knew what he was doing, although it did not seem like a strategic time to leave the city. He left in AD 59 and urged Timothy to stay behind and strengthen the church.

8

A LIVING CHURCH IN A DEMONIZED CITY

So in Ephesus now, they had a living church, powerfully founded on signs, wonders, and miracles, that was situated in a city still controlled by the great goddess Diana. *They had not won the war. Instead, they had simply started the war.* I suggest to you that planting a living church is where we found ourselves in Mumbai all those years ago. Planting a living church in a demonized city is a good start, but it is not the end. God wants the city!

For quite some time in Ephesus there was a living church. However, that living church was under great pressure, suffering many attacks. If you asked someone in Ephesus, "Who is the god of Ephesus?" they would say, "Diana is the god of Ephesus!"

The church in Ephesus was established in approximately AD 56. Paul stayed there for three years and left in AD 59. He came back to Ephesus in Acts 20 while traveling on his way to imprisonment in Jerusalem. He knew this would happen, since it was prophesied to him in several places. In Acts 20:17 it says, "From Miletus, he [Paul] sent to Ephesus and called for the elders of the church." Miletus was a coastal city, and Ephesus was approximately twenty miles inland.

When they came, Paul said to them:

> You know, from the first day that I came to Asia, in what manner I always lived among you, serving the Lord with all humility, with many tears and trials which happened to me by the plotting of the Jews; how I kept back nothing that was helpful, but proclaimed it to you, and taught you publicly and from house to house (Acts 20:18–20).

Two Ways of Establishing the Kingdom

Notice the different ways in which Paul proclaimed the Kingdom. He proclaimed it publicly and from house to house. Paul had two levels of establishing people in the truth. If you study revival, you will discover that the most successful revival was the revival that struck England under the ministry of John Wesley. Interestingly, the combination of these two elements was also found in Wesley's ministry. He publicly proclaimed the Kingdom everywhere he went. It was considered a great humiliation to go out of the church building and stand in a field to preach the gospel to a crowd of ordinary people. If you read Wesley's diary and other people's writings of the time, you find that this was a great humiliation for his religious respectability. It cost him much to do that, and it made him many enemies at the same time.

But John Wesley wanted to get out to where the people were. They were not coming to church, even in those days, so John went out to where they were. In a number of the major revivals of the world, those who were most affected and had the most powerful impact on the nation were the common working people. The Wesleyan revival transformed the nation. It took about seventy years to do it, but it happened. All major social services, including nursing, childcare, and care for the orphans and the elderly, were radically affected during this time. The trade unions started at this time as Christian movements trying to get some decent working conditions for men and women.

The revival powerfully affected society.

John Wesley publicly proclaimed the word, and he also had class meetings, which are like our modern home groups. They taught the people in this smaller setting until the truth of God was put into them by repetition. They asked questions, and people had to give the answer. They were determined that every Christian who came into the revival was personally tutored into a foundation in the word of God and a practical life of holiness.

These were the two aims of these groups. There was constant accountability and constant meeting. Wesley simply followed what Paul had done in Ephesus. Paul publicly proclaimed the word, but he also went from house to house. He did this for three years. As a result, the full revelation of God was imparted to the people.

From my earliest day in Mumbai until now, I have always believed in powerful public proclamation along with some system of small groups where people are established in the word of God. These smalls groups become very powerful evangelistic tools when they are led well. I never have and never would have a church that does not have both dimensions functioning. I do not believe home groups alone are enough. I feel that powerful public proclamation is necessary, and congregational life with two hundred or three hundred people is important to church life. We need both of these dimensions to grow people to full spiritual maturity. It's all here in scripture.

Paul continued his message to the Ephesians by saying:

> And see, now I go bound in the spirit to Jerusalem, not knowing the things that will happen to me there, except that the Holy Spirit testifies in every city, saying that chains and tribulations await me. But none of these things move me; nor do I count my life dear to myself, so that I may finish my race with joy, and the

> ministry which I received from the Lord Jesus, to testify to the gospel of the grace of God. And indeed, now I know that you all, among whom I have gone *preaching the kingdom of God*, will see my face no more (Acts 20:22–25).

Notice again that Paul went about preaching the Kingdom. Paul gathered those elders one more time to challenge them to step up to the plate so they could be as powerful and effective in their ministry as he was in his.

The Kingdom is by nature generational. You will never accomplish in your lifetime the full purpose of God. One of your primary callings is to successfully impart to the next generation. In the spirit, generations do not take that long. I am a great, great, great, great grandfather of wonderful men and women of God in Mumbai. Generational transmission can take place within five to six years. Paul was able to do it in Ephesus within three years. He produced another generation who from raw conversion were now ready to move out in the power of his full apostolic revelation. That was some accomplishment.

When I saw that, I determined to teach the whole counsel of God to any church I lead within three years. That has been my target, and we worked out a system in my church in Great Britain where we had this as our goal. I love shepherding a church, because you can take whole books of the Bible and go right through them teaching the whole counsel of God. Pastors have opportunities that other ministries do not have. I know I am doing what I am called to do, but I envy pastors who can take a group of people and transform them by the consistent week-by-week ministry of the word. Do not give them dry old bread! Please feed them with fresh bread from heaven. Have it as your goal that within three years you produce another generation of warriors for the Kingdom of God. Can you impart everything God has taught you to a group in three years?

Chapter 8 – A Living Church in a Demonized City

God said to Timothy, "The things that you have heard from me among many witnesses, commit these to faithful men who will be able to teach others also" (2 Tim. 2:2). This was Paul's generational passion. The plurality of the Kingdom is accomplished without losing the power of the Kingdom, providing there is full generational transmission. The spiritually young we impart to should go as far as we do.

When I see where some young people are today, at seventeen or eighteen years of age, it amazes me. I had a visitation from a whole new leadership of young people who came to me in Graz, Austria. I've been imparting to that church for many years now. They have taken what I taught and imparted it to each other and exported it into all the new Balkan countries that are emerging like Slovenia, Croatia, Serbia, Bosnia, and Macedonia. I discovered that many people there are living on my teachings. When they discovered that I was coming as close as Graz, they jumped into their cars and traveled for nine hours to meet me. I was amazed at their hunger for the word and their desire for apostolic input.

While meeting with them, I heard all the terrible stories of warfare and destruction. There is much carnage and wrecked homes in these areas. Many went through last winter with broken windows and no heating. They lived in unheated buildings at minus 20 degrees. But the joy and fire in these people is absolutely incredible. These groups of leaders represent a leadership that is rising up across these nations. I discovered that more than half of them were under seventeen years of age. They knew things in God and experienced His power in ways that astonished me. They hunger for God and His word. They had known nothing except communism for so many years. Now, the real Jesus meets them.

I was shown pictures of people who were unable to come.

Section 2 – The Assault on Ephesus

I saw a young girl of six. She was gloriously saved and had such a powerful encounter with God that she just lived in His presence all the time. The parents were very disturbed, but they were not cruelly vindictive. They were very concerned because their daughter had forsaken Islam. They went to the local Imam, and he instructed them to put her into a local school for the Koran where she would be re-trained to become an orthodox Muslim. The parents followed this instruction, and she was immediately cut off from all Christian influence. She was put into the school full-time. However, the Holy Spirit had such communion with this girl that He told her what to do. He gave her a strategy and said, "You obey your parents in everything they tell you to do; even be respectful and obedient to the Imam. But you must start a fast. You must wage war against the demonic principality that is holding your parents and your city in bondage." This little child began waging warfare against this principality. She fasted for nine days. The power of God broke that city open, with the result that her parents converted. The Imam was converted, and the power of God is shaking that city.

There is also an eleven-year-old girl who is a powerful evangelist. She came from a Muslim background. She is marked as dangerous. The Muslims have threatened her. They've had prophetic words that she will die as a martyr, and many believe they are true. She said, "As long as I am on this earth and as long as God spares my life, I will preach the gospel of Jesus Christ and get as many people saved as possible." She is not trying to be a martyr, but neither is she afraid of martyrdom. What will we produce if we can impart to our spiritual children the reality of the Kingdom?

An established Pentecostal church has existed in this region for many years. In their own way, they fought a good fight, holding on to the truth through all the vicious days of communism. However, those circumstances have hardened them in a certain mindset so that none of the truths they were willing to die for could possibly be changed or improved upon.

They are frozen in a time warp of fifty-year-old Pentecostalism. They simply will not move into the new thing that God is doing.

God is using a woman to break open the city of Sarajevo. She is a powerful evangelist. She is an apostolic leader. One year ago, the temperature dropped to negative 20 degrees Celsius in her apartment, where she lives in the most primitive of conditions. To keep from freezing to death, she put on two pairs of pants. When the Pentecostal leaders heard that she was walking around town in pants, which are men's clothing in their minds, they kicked her out of the church, even though she had seen more than two hundred Muslims saved. Can you understand such lunacy? She is on her own without any support except that Almighty God is with her! This is not a bad exchange.

Paul spoke to the elders from Ephesus and said:

> So now, brethren, I commend you to God and to the word of His grace, which is able to build you up and give you an inheritance among all those who are sanctified. I have coveted no one's silver or gold or apparel. Yes, you yourselves know that these hands have provided for my necessities, and for those who were with me. I have shown you in every way, by laboring like this, that you must support the weak. And remember the words of the Lord Jesus, that He said, "It is more blessed to give than to receive" (Acts 20:32–35).

I don't know why, but these elders never rose to the same spiritual authority in the city as Paul had. I have never quite found out the reason, but they did not have the spiritual clout in the city that they should have had. We have a tremendous responsibility to get elders, our next level of leadership, into the full revelation of where we are. I go to many churches where I see a wonderful man of God with possibly one person with him, and then there's a large gap before you come to the next level of leadership. That is a precarious way to build a church.

It certainly will not be a city-taking church. You need to look at your situation and find out what you are doing.

Many leaders know how to get people to work for them. When God calls people to serve you, it is a two-way street. They are there to serve you. This is correct, and they should honor the gift and anointing that is upon the leader. But the leader also has a responsibility like a father or mother to bring other people to the place where they are supposed to be. The serving of the leader should bring emancipation, not domination.

When I see people join with me to help fulfill the vision God has given me, I earnestly seek to pour into them what God has given me. If I don't give more to them than what they have given to me, then I am short changing them. We must adopt this as a principle in our ministries.

Troubles from Without and Troubles from Within

All of these events were part of the preparation for the takeover of Ephesus by the Kingdom of God. Paul warned the leaders about troubles that would occur:

> Therefore take heed to yourselves and to all the flock, among which the Holy Spirit has made you overseers, to shepherd the church of God which He purchased with His own blood. For I know this, that after my departure savage wolves will come in among you, not sparing the flock. Also from among yourselves men will rise up, speaking perverse things, to draw away disciples after them. Therefore watch…" (Acts 20:28–31).

What the devil cannot prevent from without he will pervert from within! Paul essentially says, "When I leave, the devil will take opportunity to come and wreck the church. It will start with savage wolves from the outside, but also people from within will cause trouble.

Their ambition for themselves is greater than their ambition for the Kingdom." This is where we need to examine our own hearts. We need to ask, "What is my primary ambition?"

Paul says, in another place, that we should make it our ambition to have no ambition, except to please Him who called us to serve (see 1 Thess. 4:11). There is no greater success than pleasing the Lord. I am prepared to take any place in God's pecking order in fulfilling His purpose for the Kingdom. God must raise people to places of prominence in order to achieve His purposes. That does not make them fantastic. In fact, they are in more danger than people who are more hidden. But I am content in the state I find myself. We simply need to learn to be content. I have passion and ambition for the Kingdom, but I am not striving by any degree for self-promotion. I was driven by this for almost twenty years, so I know what it feels like.

When I returned to England, I had developed quite a reputation in India. I was known all over the nation and was in much demand for conferences. I came from obscurity to become a main leader in the nation. Then, when I came back to Britain, I was totally unknown. I didn't know I was doing this, but after several years God revealed to me that I was moving around trying to make the right contacts in order to give myself a high profile in the nation. I was seeking to promote myself.

When this was revealed to me, I was absolutely disgusted. I repented of it. *I am not saying it is wrong to have a high profile, but it is wrong to seek a high profile.* If God gives you one, then God bless you. That is your calling and place. If God does not give you one, then God bless you. That is your calling and place. In either state, we are still nothing without Him. In either state, we are more valuable than anything, because we are precious to the Lord. *Our value must be in our Father, not in our ministry.*

The Ravenous Wolves Stage

These elders in Ephesus did not rise to the occasion for a forceful advancing of the Kingdom. Paul left Timothy behind in Ephesus, according to 1 Timothy 1:3, to address this issue: "As I urged you when I went into Macedonia–remain in Ephesus that you may charge some that they teach no other doctrine." Paul wanted Timothy to be there, because he did not have total confidence in the ability of the elders to hold the fort and advance the Kingdom. We will see how carefully Timothy is instructed by Paul in these two letters. It only dawned on me quite recently that these two letters were written to Timothy while he was in Ephesus. They were written to instruct him on how to hold a church that is under fire. This is right where we are in many places.

The church in Ephesus had a glorious start, but then came a massive counter attack. Many leaders have experienced the same thing. Very often the trouble begins with a church split. Someone you thought was a covenant brother goes off and starts another church. That is very painful. Or the extended leadership might rise up against you, because you are not remaining orthodox in their view. They won't make any change, but you want to make changes, and a collision happens between you and the elders. This happens again and again in churches among the deacons or elders. The leadership begins to believe that the leader is there to do their wishes. This is a misuse of church government. The leader ends up either leaving or getting kicked out and then wonders where to go from there.

You are bruised and wounded, and you wonder, "What's next?" If you handle these events correctly, then God will use it to make you more powerful in the next thing God has for you to do. But you must get it right. This is a phase we all go through. I've been through it, and any person in the nation or world who has broken through to do something significant can remember the days when all hell came against him or her. The same happened in Ephesus.

Chapter 8 – A Living Church in a Demonized City

The church that was doing so great was suddenly ripped apart by ravenous wolves. We need to learn the lesson of how to hold a church through that phase, because we cannot move on to city taking without moving through this stage successfully. The ravenous wolves phase is an inevitable part of taking a city. There may be exceptions, but I believe this is the general rule.

I remember hearing about when Dr. Cho stood on the tenth floor of a new half-finished church building, totally out of money and having no reputation. He said, "I thought the best way out of that situation was to simply jump." He came that close. He somehow held on during that crisis. The church had been sentenced to lose all their property due to debt. All the money providers turned against him, because he would not jump through their spiritual loops. He was very alone at that time. He put his own savings on the line. He sold his house and put the money into the new church building. He was sleeping with his family on one of the half finished floors of this new building. He thought he had missed God, because everything seemed to be going wrong.

He went to a church meeting where they tried to raise some money to clear the debt and keep going. The breakthrough came when a precious lady, known as the poorest woman in the church, offered the only property she had, which was a bowl from which she ate her daily portion of rice. That was all she had. She made it an offering. That event triggered something in the church. Some of the rich businessmen in the church were convicted, and very soon the money began to flow in, and the crisis was over. But he came that near to quitting. I've talked to him about these things. Behind these great works of God are tremendous costs and crises that almost ended their ministries. If you are going to take a city, you will pay something for it.

Section 2 – The Assault on Ephesus

Apostolic Authority in the City

Paul left Timothy in Ephesus as an apostolic presence for that city. After that, Paul never came back to Ephesus. He was thrown into prison and got a temporary release, but he was finally executed around AD 64 under the persecution of Nero. That was the end of Paul's influence on this church. The city was not taken. From AD 59–64, the church was under tremendous pressure. Then in about AD 68, the apostle John came to Ephesus and lived there. God saw this city as very strategic. Certain strategic cities need heavy weight apostolic input to see the breakthrough.

I believe there is a principle here we need to understand. God gives an authority to apostolic ministry that must be recognized and valued. Apostolic ministries need to be surrounded by a grace-filled community so that they can function at their full level. God chooses to use certain men and women to spearhead assaults, yet at the same time, they need a corporate community working together with them. The apostle Paul was anxious to see apostolic ministry remain in the city of Ephesus. Timothy's appointment to Ephesus happened in AD 59.

The apostle John came to Ephesus in approximately AD 68 and remained there for the rest of his life. He finally died there around AD 100. For fourteen of those years, he lived in exile on the island of Patmos during the terrible persecution under the emperor Domitian. Apart from that time, the apostle John was in Ephesus. During John's exile on the Island of Patmos, Jesus wrote to the church at Ephesus through the apostle John. This is one of the seven letters in the book of Revelation. It happens to be the first letter, because Ephesus was the key city in that region. All seven churches in the book of Revelation were overseen by the apostolic ministry that flowed out from the city of Ephesus. The apostle John was the key to that ministry.

God gave a priority to this key city by placing strong apostolic ministries there. There are certain key cities in the United States of America and in countries around the world where we need to recognize certain strongholds that prevent the advance of the Kingdom.

Over the next thirty-five years, the church at Ephesus experienced many attacks and simply maintained their ground with no significant advance. I am not saying we will experience the same historic lengths of time as Ephesus, but I do want you to understand that there is no "one moment" when a city is suddenly taken for God. When a principality topples from his throne, it does not mean he ceases to exist. Instead, he is furious to be off his throne, and he manipulates by every possible means, attempting to stop the movement that has deposed him. This is where the war really begins. Whether it takes five years or thirty-five years, we must stay in the fight. If we cannot accomplish it in our lifetime, then we must prepare the next generation to do it.

When we were in Mumbai, no one really understood the dynamics of spiritual warfare. We simply stumbled through trying to hear the Spirit of God and do what He said. We saw the breakthrough. But the huge city of Mumbai is still not taken, although it is vastly different from when we went there. At that time, there were no effective churches seeing any breakthrough or growth in the city. Now, there are at least three thousand who are experiencing breakthroughs and advances continually. They are militantly evangelistic, and I know the day is coming when India will bow the knee to Jesus Christ. This will happen. Therefore, the warfare is fierce right now. People are paying a heavy price for the Kingdom; they are being attacked so fiercely by the Hindus because of the success they are having. Hinduism has never felt as threatened as it does now, because the church has never been as powerful as it is now.

9
PAUL'S LETTERS TO TIMOTHY

Paul wrote his two letters to Timothy while Timothy was doing his best to be the apostolic ministry in the city of Ephesus. The instructions Paul gave in these letters were given to a man who had responsibility for a church that started off with a powerful impact and was at the height of spiritual warfare. I want to list a few things of importance regarding Paul's instruction to Timothy.

Watch Your Doctrine

Timothy was forced to deal with all kinds of false doctrine, including Gnosticism, myths, and endless genealogies. In every truth there is a danger of error. Let's take spiritual mapping for example. This is a valid and powerful tool provided it is used in the right way. Some things historically are significant, and they need to be powerfully and decisively dealt with, while other things are not significant. If you simply become a historian praying over everything then you have been subtly diverted off track. You cannot do these things without the constant Spirit of revelation showing you the truth. That is why we have an anointing that teaches us all things.

Watch out for people who come into your church and pass out materials of a certain ministry, taking people off to conferences and getting them infected with doctrine that is in opposition to where you want to take the church. If the doctrine is erroneous or out of balance, then you must deal with it. That is part of being a good shepherd. We need to watch out for wild and unbiblical teachings, fruitless discussions, and misusing the law.

The two safe guards that keep us on track theologically are being in tune with the Holy Spirit and staying continually imbedded in scripture. I have watched many people become weird and go off into error in many different directions. We need to stay on track and scripturally sound.

Promiscuous Dress and Teaching

In 1 Timothy 2:1–15, Paul addressed the issue of promiscuously dressed women and teachers. It talks about women adorning themselves in modest apparel. This may seem strange, but we need to understand the context in which this was written. In these great cosmopolitan cities like Ephesus and Corinth, women often used their physical charms seductively. Particularly within Gnosticism, many women teachers taught the word with background music and gyrations of their bodies that made their teaching more delicious to men who were filled with lust, enticing them to come and listen. It was important that those in the church should leave such worldly ways behind.

This is what Paul was striking at when he talked about the way women taught. He was not saying that women should not teach, but they must not teach in certain ways. The word *usurp* that is used in verse 12 is not used in other places in the New Testament. It was a rude or vulgar word. I can't think of an equivalent today. Imagine Madonna becoming a believer yet using that same power she used to sway crowds for Satan to sway crowds for Jesus. She attempts to influence people for Jesus using the same techniques, same clothes, and other methods.

This is what Timothy was dealing with.

If we are going to come to the right interpretation of scripture, then we must ask ourselves certain questions. First, why was this person moved by the Holy Spirit to say that particular thing at that time? Knowing the cultural and historical setting helps you enormously in understanding what was said and why it was said. Once you discover this, you find the principle of the matter. The principle is eternal, but the cultural problem is negotiable.

Let's look at the question of women and head coverings in 1 Corinthians 11 for example. Paul says something in verse 10 and 11 that has been distorted by the translators because they wanted to make it fit their doctrine. They say, "A woman ought to have a sign of authority over her head." Thus, a whole movement and culture of head coverings was developed. But it does not say this. It says in the Greek, "A woman should have authority over her head." The subject of the sentence has the power to exercise authority over the object. Therefore, the woman has authority over her head. Men do not have this. If you walked the streets of Corinth with your head loosed, your hair flowing, you were basically advertising yourself as a prostitute. This was a powerful sign of provocation for men.

When I was a young man in England, a woman wore a gold chain around her right ankle to tell everyone that she was a loose woman looking for a man. Today, it is only a decoration, but it still makes me shudder if I see it because of my youth. Culturally, things have changed, so there is no reason for a woman not to wear it now if she pleases. However, in 1945 through 1950, that same gold chain in Britain said, "I am available. Do you want me?" This is exactly what is being said with a woman who wore her hair loose in Paul's day in Corinth. Therefore, she always covered her head and kept her hair hidden except before her husband.

Section 2 – The Assault on Ephesus

The only created being in all of creation that can stand before God uncovered is redeemed humanity. Even the cherubim and seraphim cover themselves and cry, "Holy, holy, holy." But redeemed humanity, the darling of God's heart, stands before the Father uncovered. That is what redemption has done for us. When this dawns on you, you realize how wonderful this is:

> *But we all, with unveiled face*, beholding as in a mirror the glory of the Lord, are being transformed into the same image from glory to glory, just as by the Spirit of the Lord (2 Corinthians 3:18).

In that day, men covered their heads, whether they were Jewish or Corinthian. It was a simple part of their religious culture to humble themselves before their deity by covering themselves with a shawl. The Jews still use coverings today. They were saying, "I am a miserable unworthy sinner. But by this covering, please give me protection from your wrath." People crawled into their deity's presence like worms. But if we go into God's presence like that, we are insulting His Saviorhood. Paul said, "You men, don't wear a head covering. You are insulting the Savior by saying you are unworthy to come into His presence when the blood of the cross says you are worthy!"

A woman, however, had another complication. She had the right before God to be uncovered because of His incredible salvation for men and women, but the trouble was that society would not understand her freedom. If she walked out of the house uncovered, people might say, "There goes the prostitute," or, "There goes a loose woman." This would insult both the Savior and her husband. Therefore, the woman had the right to decide about her head according to her cultural circumstances.

In many Indian villages to this very day, it is the same dynamic.

If a woman walks down the road with her hair loose, even in a Sari, she can look very appealing. She is advertising herself in the wrong way. How could a humble, godly woman of God walk down the street looking like a prostitute just because she has freedom before Christ? She must think about her husband and the name of Jesus, and she must not send the wrong signals into the culture around her. Where the culture does not say, "To be uncovered is to be a prostitute," you don't need to cover your head. This makes glorious sense to me. All these knotty tangles in scripture about women regarding what they can or cannot do have similar answers when you dig down deep enough to find out what Paul was really saying.

Part of Timothy's role was to get these recently saved women out of Gnosticism, prostitution, and other entanglements. If you start gathering the world into your church, you will need to bring in a few regulations about dress. Most people have no idea what is proper and what is not proper. This applies to the men as well as to the women. When I see a man come to church, lounging back with his baseball cap on, I want to say, "Take that cap off!" This is not right. When you have a woman who has a beautiful voice in the worship team, and she has a skirt ten inches above her knees, I don't think this is the way our worship teams should appear. We do not have this kind of freedom. The apostle Paul was telling the apostle Timothy, "You set things in order in all these respects." We must not be afraid to do the same, because this is protection for our communities. Many confusing spirits come through the doors of our churches, and they need to be met with clarity and godliness.

Work and Give

The next issue Paul addressed for Timothy concerned people who wanted to live off the church and not work properly. I am sure you are familiar with this as well. To be a full-time ministry, for some people, means they don't work anymore.

Section 2 – The Assault on Ephesus

The ministry is never intended to be a haven for the lazy. When my youngest son went to school, the children were asked what their fathers do. My son said, "My father doesn't work. He is a pastor!" Children may think that, but our dedicated lives must prove to be different.

I want you to simply note Paul's words to Timothy in 1 Timothy 6 regarding the erroneous prosperity teaching. It says:

> But those who desire to be rich fall into temptation and a snare, and into many foolish and harmful lusts which drown men in destruction and perdition. For the love of money is a root of all kinds of evil, for which some have strayed from the faith in their greediness, and pierced themselves with many sorrows. *But you, O man of God, flee these things and pursue righteousness, godliness, faith, love, patience, gentleness* (1 Timothy 6:9–11).

I believe that we should have sufficiency for ourselves, but I am always looking to God for abundance for the Kingdom of God. Just as I have been given ministry gifts, other men have been given the gift of making money for the purposes of the Kingdom. I may have met one man in America who has this message clear. Jesus said it is hard for a rich man to enter the Kingdom (see Matt. 19:24). This means that all your financial resources come under the direct rule and government of God. He may tell you to live on 2 percent and give 98 percent away. You must have the same enthusiasm to make money for the Kingdom as you would for yourself, even though you are not personally benefiting from it.

Twice Paul urges people to work for the purpose of having enough to give. That was the only purpose for making money. He said, "Work hard so that you will have plenty to give away." I don't know many people who have said, "I took a second job because I didn't have enough money to give for the purposes of the Kingdom."

Many might get a second job for a larger house or second car, or to get the children through college, but to find someone who would do this simply for the Kingdom is very rare. When this day comes, then we will have the resources to get the job done.

I met a man in Zimbabwe who is under some challenge right now because of the political and economic hardship in the country. Several years ago, he was an entrepreneurial businessman powerfully born again. However, any time he tried to do something more with his business, the communication between the rest of the world was difficult because of the antiquated government phone system. He tried to bring in modern telecommunication systems, but as a result he was banned by the government, because they did not want any competition for the antiquated, worn out, inefficient government phone system. In the end, the Spirit of God told him to fight it in the courts.

To take the government on in the courts is a very dangerous thing to do in Zimbabwe. He did it anyway. He was arrested several times. He was threatened and beaten up. They said, "Withdraw your case or else." Legally, according to the law of the land, he had a case against the government, but the political forces were not going to let him plead his case. God gave this man grace, and he finally came to court and won the case. He received the freedom to import modern telecommunications systems into the country. He was the first one to introduce cell phones to his nation. He was the first to bring internet capabilities to his nation. He has made millions and millions of dollars. He also had franchises into other African nations.

At the moment, he is in hiding, because the ruling political party is out to ruin him. However, this man's business has mushroomed. He told me a few years ago that in one year he made 20 million dollars in profit. He put 17 million into the church. The rest of the money he has used strategically for the Kingdom. If this man meets with you, he will do so in a very ordinary restaurant wearing very ordinary clothes. He drives an ordinary Toyota five or six years old. You would never know he is the man that he is. He does not live as a rich man in regards to himself. However, when it comes to the Kingdom he is very rich. I've had this man come to several other African nations to conduct business seminars on how to be a Kingdom businessman. Other businesses throughout Africa are shooting into power and prosperity because of his teaching.

If we had one hundred men like that in America, think what we could do for the world. Timothy had to deal with a false prosperity message without losing the true prosperity message of the Kingdom. We must do the same.

Be an Example: Flee and Pursue

Paul then called Timothy to be an example. He was to remain in holiness and purity of life. He was to flee what is harmful and pursue what is profitable. In 1 Timothy 6:11, it says, "But you, O man of God, flee these things and pursue righteousness, godliness, faith, love, patience, and gentleness." I want us to agree together that the ministry you have responsibility for will never be known for any kind of financial mismanagement. We must encourage and teach people to give, but we must not use that place as an advantage for ourselves. We want to teach them for God's sake, so that they may come into God's glorious prosperity lifestyle. We are not there to rip them off. We want all of our financial dealings to be conducted with the highest integrity.

Paul told Timothy to flee from these things. This is a powerful word and very important injunction. If you are facing a few financial crises, then that is the time for you to hold course without taking any shortcuts. You don't write begging letters, and you do not manipulate people for your advantage. This is so easy to do and is often accepted as normal practice in many Christian circles.

I do not make my decisions regarding conferences or speaking engagements because of the size of the offerings or honorariums. One place might offer a five thousand dollar honorarium and another a three hundred dollar honorarium, but that in no way influences my decision on where to go. I say, "God, where do You want me to go?" I will go wherever He tells me to go, whether it costs me money or not. Sometimes, I have been sorely tempted. It is not always easy to stay on track regarding these things, but that is the reason for Paul's instruction to Timothy. If we want to be city-taking people, then we must heed these warnings and instructions.

In 1 Timothy 6:11, Paul talks about fleeing certain things, but there is another side to the coin. He also says we must pursue other things. What should we pursue? Should we pursue a first-page article in Charisma magazine? Should we pursue the right conferences to meet the right people in order to get our name known? Paul says, "But you, O man of God…pursue righteousness, godliness, faith, love, patience, and gentleness." As part of this, Paul told Timothy to rebuke, to exhort, and to be particularly careful in how he handled older men and women. Most of all, he was to be an example to the believers.

Make Progress

Paul gave another important instruction in 1 Timothy 4:13–15:

> Till I come, give attention to reading, to exhortation, to doctrine. Do not neglect the gift that is in you, which was given to you by prophecy with the laying on of the hands of the eldership. Meditate on these things; give yourself entirely to them, that your progress may be evident to all.

As a leader you must be seen making progress. Even at my age of 71, I must be making progress in these things. I do not want people to meet the same Alan Vincent at the end of the year as they did at the beginning of the year. I am always on the search for new things from God.

Section 2 — The Assault on Ephesus

I want new revelation and new encounters with the living God.

Paul continued in 1 Timothy 4:16, "Take heed to yourself and to the doctrine. Continue in them, for in doing this you will save both yourself and those who hear you." Notice how many times the words *doctrine* and *teaching* occur in 1 and 2 Timothy. We must lay a sound foundation in the word for our people. We must continue in these things. If you do not make progress, then you will stop the church from making progress. If you make progress, then you will drag them along in the wake of where you are going.

No Place for Fear

Paul also instructed Timothy to deal completely with any fear operating in his life. This is found in 2 Timothy 1:7, where he is told, "For God has not given us a spirit of fear, but of power and love and of a sound mind." This is in connection with verses 8–9, where it says:

> Therefore do not be ashamed of the testimony of our Lord, nor of me His prisoner, but share with me in the sufferings for the gospel according to the power of God, who has saved us and called us with a holy calling..." (2 Timothy 1:8–9).

If you start shaking cities, then you will be attacked. You can almost see Timothy looking at Paul saying, "I am not sure I really want to follow you. You are in jail, and you have suffered much. Maybe I could find something more comfortable and less harmful." Timothy could certainly find something more comfortable, but he wouldn't shake cities or plunder hell. Through warring faith, Timothy was to grasp the things that were prophesied over him. This instruction appears several times for Timothy. In 1 Timothy 1:18 it also says, "This charge I commit to you, son Timothy, *according to the prophecies previously made concerning you*, that by them you may *wage the good warfare*."

We must understand that prophesy is weaponry for warfare.

Prophetic words do not ensure your victory. They simply announce that the war has begun. Those prophetic words must be diligently pursued, while you follow the Spirit, in order to bring them to pass. It is not the end of the fight, but only the beginning.

Appointing Proper Eldership

Lastly, an important principle in the letters to Timothy, as well as Titus, is that when a church is being rocked and attacked, the right response is to establish a strong eldership and strong deacons. I believe establishing proper eldership in the church is one of the most important foundational things you can do. If you get it right, you will see blessing. If you get it wrong, you have scheduled the church to blow up at one time or another. Elders and deacons are the biblical government that God has established for the local church under apostolic or pastoral headship.

In 1 Timothy 3 and Titus 1, Paul gave the qualifications for these people. He made the same demanding requirement for deacons. The only difference in the two lists is that an elder must have the ability to teach and refute those who oppose. I do not believe this means getting up and preaching publicly. Instead, when dealing with people, you must be able to bring them to the foundation of scripture. You say, "Don't argue with me about my opinions, but let's look at the word." The right way to pastor people is to bring them up in the power of the word. Let the word of God confront them and change them. You can say, "You are not arguing with me, but with God. I did not write the Bible. I am simply pointing out to you what it says." The elder must be able to teach and correct in this sense. The same is not required of a deacon.

This second aspect of an elder's ability to refute people who oppose is in Titus 1:9, "*Holding fast the faithful word as he has been taught*, that he may be able, by sound doctrine, both *to exhort and convict those who contradict.*"

Notice that the elder has first been taught. You cannot teach if you have not first been taught. The elder obviously has a teachable spirit. He has been brought up in sound doctrine and has been willing to learn. Who teaches the elders? What did believers devote themselves to in the early church? They devoted themselves to the apostles teaching. If you do not have apostolic input into your church, then you will have elders who can go off into all kinds of different directions. They and the entire flock can go off into error.

If you get under genuine apostolic instruction, then elders will be stretched to think bigger, to think wider, and to become more receptive to the whole truth of God. Apostles do not narrow you down to a particular view of doctrine. This is one of the reasons you need apostolic input. Elders must be taught sound doctrine, and they must be skilled in upholding it before others. I have been called into many needy church situations. Foundational to all of them was the ability to appoint sound elders.

The deacon's job is to serve a particular task, but their character requirements are just the same. If you go through the list of elder requirements in 1 Timothy 3, then you will find that of the sixteen requirements, fifteen of them are character requirements. If you go through the list in Titus 1, you will find in the seventeen requirements that fifteen of them are character requirements.

I have learned to my own cost that if you overlook these requirements you are doing a disservice to the church and yourself. Don't think, "He's pretty good in many areas, but his finances are in a mess. He had significant debt, but we will work on that." The choice to appoint such a person has always produced significant regret. The elder must be an example in all things. I have a list of twenty-two things that I look at when I have the responsibility to discern who the Holy Spirit is appointing for this task. If you want to establish churches that will stand the kind of warfare a city-taking church encounters, then you need a solid base of elders who know how to honor the head of the house that God has appointed.

SECTION 3
Ephesians Chapter 1

10

THE GREETING

Finally now we come to Paul's letter to the church at Ephesus. Paul wrote this letter in AD 64. He was in jail for approximately four years before writing the letter. The letter was probably written from Rome. The church had been under fire for several years. It was making little progress after a glorious start because a major principality known as the goddess Diana, or Artemis, was stubbornly resisting any advance of the Kingdom. Paul wrote to the church in Ephesus to establish principles by which they might fight effectively and win the battle that was raging all around them. This is the complete manual for city taking. If we follow the progression that is given to us in this letter, then there is no doubt that we will shake cities with the power of His Kingdom. I have no doubt they would have taken the city had they followed his instruction.

When Paul wrote the book of Ephesians, that church had never become the full manifestation of what he saw in the spirit. In my opinion, no church has yet lived to the full revelation of what Paul wrote to the Ephesians. Therefore, the book of Ephesians is a prophetic book waiting to be fulfilled. It is a step-by-step manual for how to take a city. I do not believe any scripture from God will fall to the ground without being fulfilled.

It must be fulfilled. Churches must rise up to fulfill these prophetic scriptures. I am inviting you to believe God with me that the cities we represent will experience the power of what Paul wrote to the Ephesians.

Many Christians are trying to live in Ephesians 6 when they have not traveled through chapters 1 through 5. That is why there seems to be so many spiritual casualties. When the apostle Paul was anointed by the Holy Spirit to write this letter, he was writing to a church under tremendous attack and opposition. The church, however, had the commission to take the city with the task of dealing with the largest and most powerful demonic principality over the earth. We need to take this seriously. We need to see where the letter begins and how it progresses.

Apostolic Leadership

> Paul, an apostle of Christ Jesus by the will of God, to the saints in Ephesus, the faithful in Christ Jesus: Grace and peace to you from God our Father and the Lord Jesus Christ. Blessed be the God and Father of our Lord Jesus Christ, who has blessed us with every spiritual blessing in the heavenly places in Christ (Ephesians 1:1–3).

This is not just a flowery introduction. Let's begin with this phrase, "Paul, an apostle of Christ Jesus by the will of God...." In earlier generations, we may have been forgiven for not clearly understanding the role of apostles. However, we do not have that excuse anymore. What I find so distressing is that when people have seen the truth but are not prepared to pay the price of the truth. While all my being cries out for a unified body, you must not produce unity at the lowest common denominator. This will totally paralyze the body from doing anything. If unity becomes your god over truth and the will of God, you will not go anywhere.

You find again and again in churches across a city that leaders come together at the lowest common denominator. They will be completely egalitarian so that no one is allowed to lead or emerge as a leader of leaders. Instead, such a group meets together for years without going anywhere, because we can only go somewhere when we are apostolically led. I say that without compromise. I do not believe any city anywhere will be shaken and changed unless there is a coming together of leaders who recognize and receive apostolic leadership.

Paul was very candid about his apostolic leadership. He did not call himself a bishop. Instead, he called himself what he biblically was, an apostle. I believe I am called by God to contend for that title. I will not budge on this issue at all. Of course, apostolic leaders must work in right relationship to prophets. If we can get the apostolic and prophetic partnership together, which is a recurring theme in the letter to the Ephesians, then we will be on the right road to city taking. Paul was not ashamed about his apostleship.

At the same time, Paul spoke candidly about his humility. True humility is not self-effacement, but it is the denial of self in order to fulfill the purposes of God. Pride is the exaltation of self against the will of God. Humility and pride must be measured against the criteria of our relationship to God. We are told that Moses was the meekest man on the face of the earth (see Num. 12:3). Yet, Moses was a very powerful and strong leader. He was used in the New Testament as a type or shadow of the apostolic ministry that was yet to come. Moses was a model of what apostolic ministry looks like. He was not afraid to be zealous for the will of God and was self-denying when it came to his own will. That is what marks true humility.

Sanctified and Set Apart

Paul wrote to the saints in Ephesus. The word *saint* means to be set apart exclusively for a particular use. It has nothing to do with looking like a saint on a stained glass window. Instead, to be holy is a decision we make. The word *saint* or *sanctified* is the same Greek word used for *holy*. If you are called to be holy, then you are called to be sanctified. If you are sanctified, then you are holy. The word literally means to be set apart exclusively for a particular use. In the biblical context, that use is always for the use of God.

We are commanded to be holy. The Lord says, "Be holy, for I am holy" (1 Pet. 1:16; see also Lev. 11:44; 19:2). We are not emphasizing the glorious character of God here, because it is the decision to be sanctified which produces the character we call sanctification or holiness. The heart of the Kingdom is God's will being done. We are taught to pray in the Lord's Prayer, "Your will be done on earth as it is in heaven" (Matt. 6:10). That is what defines the Kingdom. The Kingdom is wherever God's will is done perfectly.

As you may know, the Kingdom is referred to as the Kingdom of God or the Kingdom of heaven. For many years, I pondered these expressions, trying to find out what the differences are, and I have concluded that there is no difference. They are two dimensions of the same reality. The Kingdom of God emphasizes that we are submitted to God's rule. Heaven is what is produced when God's will is perfectly obeyed. If we perfectly obey God, then the automatic result is heaven. It is impossible to have heaven without God being perfectly obeyed. The moment God ceases to be obeyed is the moment heaven disappears. As a result, hell comes in its place. That is the difference between heaven and hell. The difference is how much and to what degree the will of God is accomplished.

I believe some Christians will have a problem. Many want to go to heaven, yet they do not want to live the only way you can in heaven, which is in total obedience to God. When we start to practice this on earth, heaven comes. This is how heaven comes to earth. It first starts in an individual. That is why Jesus was the personification of heaven on earth, because of His perfect obedience. That is what made Him so heavenly. The command to be holy is nothing more than the command to become a perfect Kingdom person by obeying the will of God. This is a decision you can make. You can say, "Lord, I choose from now on to be available exclusively for You. I will only do Your will." This is the decision to become holy.

Let me explain this in terms of power assisted steering. Imagine getting into a large truck and putting a small lady behind the wheel. Although she has all the traits and beauty of feminism, when she gets behind that wheel, she can turn that big truck with one finger. Those enormous wheels move with just the small exertion of her little finger. Someone might think she is a bionic woman. In reality, however, a power mechanism allows the simple touch of her finger to move those enormous wheels. This is a great picture of what happens when you decide to be holy. Our job is to put our finger on the steering wheel of our lives, saying, "I want to go in this direction." Once we make that choice, all the power of God closes around that choice to make it possible.

We are actually made holy by the power of God, but we are also made holy by our decision to want to be holy. The two flow together. It says this in Philippians 2:12–13:

> Therefore, my beloved, *as you have always obeyed*, not as in my presence only, but now much more in my absence, work out your own salvation with fear and trembling, *for it is God who works in you both to will and to do for his good pleasure.*

Section 3 – Ephesians Chapter 1

I am sanctified by the power of God, but I am also sanctified because I choose to be. I made the decision to be holy. It is my will being enclosed with all the power of God to ratify my decision. I have made this decision. I am exclusively and entirely available for God's use on earth. I have only one passion and one ambition–to do His will. That is entire sanctification.

The fruit of that decision is a quality of life that has all the fruit of the Spirit and loveliness of holiness. Many people try and counterfeit the fruit rather than digging to the root, which automatically produces the fruit. You end up producing plastic pears and apples. In reality, you must plant the real seed of the Kingdom, and that fruit comes automatically. It says in Romans 4 that when we are joined to Jesus, married to Christ, then the fruit of that relationship is all the loveliness of Christ. We must concentrate on the relationship, not the fruit of the relationship.

In John 15, this relationship is described in terms of a branch that has been grafted into the vine. The sap of the vine flows into the branch and produces the fruit. The grafting of the branch into the vine produces the fruit. No branch by itself can produce fruit. Cut off from the vine, you cannot produce anything. This is total Christ dependence, yet at the same time, the choice to live this way produces the fruitfulness. We need to unashamedly teach these things. We also need to be a good example of these things we are teaching.

The apostle Paul said in Philippians that he was still grasping for that which he was grasped by Christ. He was not there yet, and his passion was not to be the most well-known ministry in the church. Instead, he wanted to know the power of His resurrection, having been made conformable to His death. He did not grasp it fully yet, but he was still grasping those things for which he was grasped by Christ. He was not ashamed to say, "Imitate me, just as I also imitate Christ" (1 Cor. 11:1).

Chapter 10 – The Greeting

Imagine taking a long journey using Interstate 75, which runs from South Florida all the way to upper Michigan and the Canadian border. I could start driving in southern Florida and successfully arrive to Atlanta, Georgia. If I have completed this journey, then I can help other people get to where I am. But if I have never completed that journey, then I am in no position to help them. I can say, "Follow me, because I know how to get to Atlanta from where you are. By the time you get to Atlanta, I will be on my way North to Toledo, Ohio." If I stay where I am, then everyone will drive past me. I need to be on a road that leads to the perfection of Christ. I know this is an obtainable goal, and I know the end of the road really exists. The road does not end in a mist in the heavenlies. It is a reality. I am on my way there.

God knows I can tell you that I am much different now than I was ten years ago. I am much farther down the road, but I have not yet arrived. I can say to many young men, "I was like you twenty years ago, so I do not condemn you. I was like that forty years ago, so I do not condemn you. But I can say that you need God to deal with this and that in your life." I can speak from experience, because it has happened to me. Many things no longer trouble me, because the Spirit of God has trained me along the path of following Christ. This is the role we have.

We are called to be saints. Paul wrote to the saints who are at Ephesus and to the faithful in Christ Jesus. Paul tells us a number of times that God put Paul into the ministry because of one reason, "And I thank Christ Jesus our Lord, who has enabled me, because *He counted me faithful*, putting me into the ministry" (1 Tim. 1:12). These words that appear in the beginning of Paul's letter are not just a flowery greeting. Instead, each one of them is a powerhouse of revelation for us.

Section 3 – Ephesians Chapter 1

A Grace-filled Church

Then, in Ephesians 1:2, it says, "Grace to you and peace from God our Father and the Lord Jesus Christ." You will never find Paul starting a letter without this exhortation or desire for his readers: grace and peace. He frequently said, "Grace and peace be multiplied to you…" In some of his letters, he said, "Grace, peace, and mercy be multiplied to you…" He often ended his letter with, "Grace and peace be multiplied to you…" Peter did the same thing. They first talked about faith, and then they talked about grace and peace. At the end of Peter's second letter he said, "Grow in the grace and knowledge of our Lord and Savior Jesus Christ" (2 Pet. 3:18).

We must have a real understanding of what grace is. Grace is used in the evangelical world quite frequently. It is used as a word for salvation. This is certainly true. However, 98 percent of the power of grace comes after we clearly know we are saved by grace. Most Christians are living on the 2 percent and have never really entered into the remaining 98 percent. The power of the early church was that everyone in the church was full of grace (see Acts 2:33). Great grace was upon them all.

I want to give you the briefest definition I can for grace. *Grace is all that God is in character, person, and attributes, and all that God has in terms of resources made available to us as a free gift through faith in Christ Jesus.* It's as if God takes a large treasure house and puts all the vast resources of Himself and what He has created into that treasure house of grace. Then He gives you the key, which is called faith. The tragedy is that most Christians never go there and never learn to access what has been made available for them.

In John 1:14, we are told that the power of the life of Jesus in His humanity was the power of grace. It says, "…We beheld His glory, the glory as of the only begotten of the Father, full of grace and truth."

Chapter 10 – The Greeting

The life that Jesus lived in His humanity was the perfect example of what grace-filled humanity looks like. All the time that Jesus lived on earth as a man, for the sake of righteousness, He never once drew on the power of His own deity. Instead, He drew on the resources of His Father through the channel of grace. All He needed from God to live that amazing human life He drew from what the Bible calls grace.

We see in Jesus the fullness of grace manifested in human life. The next amazing thing comes in John 1:16, "And of His fullness we have all received, and grace for grace." This is an incredible statement. *All the fullness of grace that Jesus knew how to access is made available to us.* His life was so amazing, because He knew how to access the grace of God. The same deposit of grace that He received is deposited in our spiritual bank account, if only we would believe it.

I am saying this because the thrust of these first few verses of Ephesians 1 is to get us to see that we are sanctified, set apart, grace-filled, and completely blessed. Paul says in Ephesians 1:3, "Blessed be the God and Father of our Lord Jesus Christ, who has blessed us with every spiritual blessing in the heavenly places in Christ." In other words, everything you could possibly need or want is already credited to your bank account, but the account is in heaven. *The problem with so many Christians is not the problem of supply, but the problem of access.* I have used an illustration again and again to highlight this point, but I cannot find a better one.

Imagine that John Brown goes home tonight, and there is a letter waiting for him. It is addressed to the Reverend John Brown. It has come from Switzerland, more specifically, from Bank Swiss. It says:

Dear Mr. Brown.
We have had some trouble tracing you over the last several months. But we are now completely satisfied that you are the person we have been trying to trace for a period of time.

> *Unknown to you, a relative of yours amassed a large sum of money in this bank. He was a very successful businessman and acquired a vast fortune. He recently died, and in his will he made this whole fortune completely available to his nearest surviving relative.*
>
> *We are now satisfied that you are that surviving relative. We are happy to inform you that in this Swiss bank account there are 850,000,000 USD.*
>
> *We are waiting for your instructions!*
> *Sincerely,*
> *Wolfgang Hermann*
> *Swiss Bank*

Imagine that John received such a letter. At first he thinks it is a friend playing a joke on him, but then realizes it is absolutely genuine. He shows the letter to his wife. He says, "Look at this letter! It looks like I have become a multi-multi-multi millionaire! But I have a problem. I have no idea how to access this money."

John takes the letter and puts it in the trash saying, "We will just have to manage on my salary." Would you not say he is absolutely crazy! I can assure you that John would be motivated to find out how to access that money. He may not have the knowledge when the letter arrived, but he would certainly be motivated to find out what was necessary to come into those funds.

The vast majority of Christians behave just as foolishly. The riches that God has made available for us in Christ are laying there in our heavenly bank account, totally useless to us, because we do not take the effort to access our inheritance. Having my sins forgiven is only .05 percent of the total value of the bank account. But that is the way most Christians live. Through ignorance, they never access the vast treasure that is waiting for them.

Chapter 10 – The Greeting

There are some who believe it is there, but they do not believe it is available now. But, God *has already* blessed us with every spiritual blessing in the heavenly places in Christ Jesus. The tense of the Greek in Ephesians 1:3 is what is called the past-perfect tense. In other words, it is a past event having continual present impact. So the problem is not God's supply, but our inability to access what He has made available.

As leaders, we must access these resources of God, because by doing so we will encourage other people to go and access those resources for themselves. Each of us has received a deposit. Draw on it richly. The more you draw upon it, the more you encourage other people to go and get it. I don't expect us to go from our present level of financial management to managing vast amounts of money. If I received a check tomorrow for 1 billion dollars, the interest alone on such a vast sum of money would be approximately 3 million dollars a week to spend. How many of us would know how to spend that much money? Wouldn't you like to learn to try? I would be a quick learner. But to go from spending a few hundred dollars a week to suddenly administering several million dollars a week would mean large leaps in wisdom, faith, and organization.

Let this message strike into your heart for yourself and for your church. Say, "We will go for it. We want to make progress by accessing everything God has for us." I am determined by this time next month to be more into grace then I am this month. This time next year, I want to be much farther down the road. I have a whole set of teachings called "The Power of a Grace Filled Church," which describes this in much more detail. It also describes seven ways the power of grace can begin working in your life. It also gives five or six reasons for why we often come short of the grace of God. If you can get a grace-filled church and your whole congregation working and moving in the power of great grace, then you have a city-taking church.

Section 3 – Ephesians Chapter 1

The Power of Peace

Following grace comes the word *peace*. Again, this is the word that brings about the kind of reconciliation that brings about true unity. This is a very powerful word. The Greek word for *peace* is *Eirene*, and the Hebrew word is *shalom*. In both languages, the word has approximately the same meaning. In English, however, the translation is totally inadequate to convey the meaning of both of these languages. Here is a quick definition of biblical *peace*. It is essentially a relational word. To get the full value of biblical peace, you must think of two people who hate each other. They are at war with one another, trying to kill each other. But suddenly something happens. They stop fighting each other; they lay down their weapons, and the war ends. But, it is not enough to simply end the war. Instead, they must fall in love with each other and change their hostile relationship into a relationship of loving intimacy. Only then have you come to biblical peace.

If you go through scripture, the words *peace* and *reconciliation* are found together again and again, because they are both part of the one truth being conveyed. It tells us in Colossians 1:19 that God made peace through the blood of Christ on the cross. Humanity rebelled against God and stepped into disobedience. Humanity was 100 percent guilty, and God was 100 percent innocent. But it was God who came running after humans to die on a cross so that they might be fully reconciled. *God is not interested in saving sinners, but He wants sons and daughters to fall in love with Him!* God is a relational God, and He wants loving relationships!

The Greek word *Eirene* was also used in the medical profession. When a bone fractured and the broken bone came back together, the marrow squeezed out and formed a strong bond between the broken parts. When it became completely healed and completely hard, the point of fracture became the strongest part of the bone.

That is a medical fact. When a bone is fractured, the point of fracture actually becomes stronger than its original condition when the mending is properly completed. At the point of fracture, it has now become unbreakable! During the time when the Bible was written, this word was used in the Greek medical profession when a fractured bone was completely mended and now unbreakable. They would say, "The bone has come to peace."

When Adam walked with God in innocence, he had a relationship with God, but the relationship had never been tested. The devil tempted Adam, and he stepped away into independence. The bone was broken. The relationship was fractured. But then God came running, looking for sinful humanity. He gave His life on the cross to pay for our sins so that He might make peace with us. I have a relationship with God now that is like the mending of the broken bone. It cannot be broken! My relationship with God through Christ is stronger than what Adam had before he fell.

It says in John 16 and again in Psalm 34:20 that He keeps all His bones, and not one of them shall be broken. If we get all the believers in a city to come together in unbreakable relationships, then we have made peace in a biblical sense. The power of that peace gives us the authority to trample all over the devil. It is the God of peace who crushes Satan under our feet (see Rom. 16:20). There is a tremendous message here that I cannot fully develop now, but this must be part of our obedience.

What would happen if we started to apply these truths racially? Suppose we never had the ghastly background which we have in the United States. Terrible things happened that make me feel ashamed when I study the history of the United States. Imagine that we had never done anything wrong, and we were able to walk together in the same nation in a relationship of innocence.

Section 3 – Ephesians Chapter 1

Something might have happened down the road that could have broken the relationship. After having had the most awful break in relationship with wicked and evil things done in the natural, it seems impossible for a mending to occur. If they now come together in the power of grace, then you can see that it is a more glorious relationship than when the relationship was untested. In a way, to be broken and put back together makes it more powerful than if we had never been separated by evil activity on one or both sides. Can you see this? This is where God wants to take us.

It is not enough to end the war. That is not complete biblical peace. We must fall into one another's arms and absolutely love each other, being completely reconciled. This is biblical peace. When the Hispanics, blacks, whites, and Asians in our country achieve this, then we will have something far more powerful than if we had never done any harm to each other. That is where I believe we are headed. I will give my life joyfully to be a peacemaker in this respect. We will see later on in the Ephesian letter that this is a vital part in preparation for city taking. We will never take a city in our ethnic diversity, even if we do not fight each other anymore. We can live in tolerant isolation, but that is not the Kingdom.

Paul says again in verse 3, "Blessed be the God and Father of our Lord Jesus Christ, who has blessed us with every spiritual blessing in the heavenly places in Christ." This is in the tense called the past-perfect tense, which means something is completed in the past with a continuing effect up until the present time. The event is history, but the consequences of the event are a very present now reality. Those consequences will also continue on into the future. There is a vast treasure in heaven that was deposited to my account in the past, and it is there right now, and I can have free access to it by faith.

11

OUR DIVINE IDENTITY

In the next few verses of Ephesians 1, we find these tremendous words:

> Just as He chose us in him before the foundation of the world, that we should be holy and without blame before Him in love, having predestined us to adoption as sons by Jesus Christ to Himself, according to the good pleasure of His will, to the praise of the glory of His grace, by which He made us accepted in the Beloved (Ephesians 1:4–6).

This is how the apostle Paul began the letter on city taking. He needed to establish in the people who will be the city-taking community a sense of destiny, uniqueness, importance, and understanding of divine election and God's divine planning.

You are more important to God than the moon, stars, sun, and all the heavenly bodies. This is incredible, if you let the Spirit of God teach you. You will sit there in silent amazement thinking, "Lord, how could You do it?" Your worth, value, and purpose are completely changed in light of these truths. In a totally new way, you become aware that you are called literally to be a worker together with God.

Section 3 – Ephesians Chapter 1

When God made you uniquely, like no one else, He broke the mold and said He would never make another person like you. In the infinity of God, there is a part of Him that I was created to be that no one else can be.

Some of you have several children. You know that every child is unique. Children from the same parents are very different. Each one gives you pleasure, but each in his or her own way. They are all fantastic, unique, and wonderful. You can't say, "I have thirteen children, so if one dies it really doesn't matter." You cannot talk like that about precious children. God is the same in His regard for us, but on a much larger scale. There is something in God that is aching for Alan Vincent. I will gladden God's heart in a way no one else can. When we see these things, then our insecurities and competitiveness are washed away. The unworthiness and fears are swept away in the power and glory of our divine election.

Important Words in Ephesians

Here are some important words and concepts that Paul highlights for us to consider:

- election
- acceptance
- forgiveness
- redemption
- holiness
- blamelessness
- wisdom
- adoption
- family
- sonship
- inheritance
- citizenship
- rule and authority with Him on His throne

Chapter 11 – Our Divine Identity

If we can get these realities into our spirits, so that we are eternally alive, then we will be like a glowing truth that never ever dims.

I have spent time with Reinhard Bonnke on several occasions. The beautiful thing about Reinhard is his exuberant delight when someone gets saved. It is incredible to watch. I am privileged to be on Reinhard's mailing list, where he pours out his heart on what God is doing in many places. What is happening in Nigeria right now is absolutely incredible. During his last crusade in that nation, approximately 3.6 million received Christ as their personal Savior.

I boarded a plane in Nairobi where Reinhard was conducting a crusade, and he was already on the plane. We were able to talk all the way to London. He had just completed a very demanding crusade, and his main administrator was fast asleep in his seat behind us. But Reinhard was on fire, whispering to me all the incredible stories of people who were saved and healed. By the end of that journey, I was glowing from the impartation of this man.

I have watched him when someone gets healed, and he reacts like it is the first time he has seen such a miracle. When someone gets saved, the reaction is the same. There seems to be an eternally fresh excitement about the event. I believe this is one of the qualities that makes him so fantastic. It is a part of God's infinite glory being expressed through a person who has given God total liberty with his life.

I want the same eternal fire to burn in each of us. There is an eternal fire of thanksgiving and passion. These words are not just theological concepts; they are alive in us to the glory of God. We will never have dull meetings with people glowing with the revelation of God within them. You will not have flat praise, because the reality of what is burning inside of us must be expressed.

Section 3 – Ephesians Chapter 1

This is how the Spirit of God, through the apostle Paul, chose to prepare this great treatise on city taking. We must not pass these realities in order to get to the methodology. The methodology is people with the right fire in them. These are the city-takers, even if they do something wrong. It is good to have the right methodology, but a mistake in methodology is easier to overcome than having things wrong with the people.

Let's look now at Ephesians 1:13. We have listed some incredible words, each one worth one hour of explanation. Several of these words are used throughout the letter. It says in verse 13:

> In Him you also trusted, after you heard the word of truth, the gospel of your salvation, in whom also, having believed, you were sealed with the Holy Spirit of promise.

This important verse explains to us how teaching becomes life and power. First of all, it says, "You heard the word of truth, the gospel of your salvation." Jesus again and again gave us an important admonition to be careful how we hear. Every time we hear the truth, we have a responsibility. He said *that the value of the word and what it does in you will be determined by the value you place upon that word while you are hearing it.* He says this in Matthew 13 and Mark 11. Then He goes on to say that to those who value the revelation, more will be given, but to those who do not value it, even what they have will be taken away from them. Therefore, the warning comes again and again, "Take care how you hear!"

The word *trusted*, sometimes translated as *believed*, here means "to cling to; to cast yourself in reliance upon." I like the following phrase, which has become my translation: "to stick to like glue." There is a way we can stick to God's word like glue and, therefore, bring about the full dimension of fruit in our lives. Following *belief*, it says that we were then sealed (or marked) with the Holy Spirit of promise.

Chapter 11 – Our Divine Identity

This seal is the guarantee of our inheritance. In other words, all that is promised to us through this letter is our inheritance. All that God is and all that God has is ours in Him. We are now of the household of God. We are citizens of heaven. All these tremendous phrases are used.

When you received that word and believed it, you were sealed with the Holy Spirit. He is the guarantee of your inheritance. If God had not given you the Holy Spirit, then you would have no guarantee. But because He has given you the Holy Spirit, this is your guarantee that everything is yours. God does not give His Holy Spirit to people in whom He will not fulfill His word. If you are filled with the Holy Spirit, then it marks you out as genuine. It is like a stamp. You are marked. God says, "You and I have made a covenantal transaction. Here is the Holy Spirit who will guarantee for you our transaction."

We find another important word used in verse 14, which says, "Who is the guarantee (earnest) of our inheritance until the redemption of the purchased possession, to the praise of His glory." This word, *guarantee* or *earnest*, was used in the same way that we use *down payment*. If you go into a financial transaction saying, "I want to buy your piece of land and house," there comes a point in those negotiations when the contract becomes legally binding. Once the contract is made, you are committed to it, and it is totally legal.

In order to make this transaction clear, a down payment or earnest money is required. It might be 10 percent of the full value. Once that money is handed over, it is like the buyer is saying to the seller, "Here is 10 percent. I will go to the bank to receive the rest of the money to complete the deal. I won't give you the 10 percent without the intention of giving you the full price." If you fail to give the rest of the money, then you forfeit the 10 percent. You don't give those kinds of deposits lightly. If God has given you the Holy Spirit, He is saying,

Section 3 – Ephesians Chapter 1

"I would not give you the Holy Spirit without the intention of giving you the full inheritance. The fact that you have the Holy Spirit is the guarantee that the whole package is coming. The full grace of our Lord Jesus Christ is for you to use. The sonship of the Lord Jesus Christ is now your sonship." This is staggering.

I have the same sonship with the Father by grace that Jesus has with the Father by nature. The same prayer life that Jesus had with the Father, I now have with the Father. The apostle John makes this incredible statement in the beginning of his letter, "…Truly our fellowship is with the Father and with His Son Jesus Christ" (1 John. 1:3). The word *fellowship* (*koinonia*) means we are joined together in a common life and joined together in a common purpose. John says that the triune God has taken me into fellowship with Himself. He has made me a joint heir with Christ of all the unsearchable riches of God. We are on the same footing. These statements in scripture are mind blowing if you let the full weight of them hit you.

The Holy Spirit is not the end of the deal. Instead, He is the earnest and down payment of the deal. If you have the Holy Spirit, then the guarantee of the full package is there in the giving of the Holy Spirit. God is saying, "I wouldn't give you the Spirit without committing myself to the whole package." He who has begun a good work in you will complete it until the day of Jesus Christ. God starts a work by saying, "Here is my earnest on the deal." When you are dealing with a totally righteous person, then the earnest money is as good as the whole sum. God will not go back on His word. He will not short-change you or try to negotiate another deal. He will give you the full value of what that earnest represents.

If we have the Holy Spirit, then all these other great words and truths are to be fulfilled in us. Paul continued with the most incredible prayer:

> Therefore I also, after I heard of your faith in the Lord Jesus and your love for all the saints, do not cease to give thanks for you, making mention of you in my prayers: that the God of our Lord Jesus Christ, the Father of glory, may give to you the spirit of wisdom and revelation in the knowledge of Him, the eyes of your understanding being enlightened; that you may know what is the hope of His calling, what are the riches of His glory of His inheritance in the saints, and what is the exceeding greatness of His power toward us who believe, according to the working of His mighty power which He worked in Christ when He raised Him from the dead and seated Him at His right hand in the heavenly places, far above all principality and power and might and dominion, and every name that is named, not only in this age but also in that which is to come. And He put all things under His feet, and gave Him to be head over all things to the church, which is His body, the fullness of Him who fills all in all (Ephesians 1:15–23).

In the middle of verse 18, we find the sequence of this letter. In the first part of Ephesians, the whole emphasis is on being seated (*kathizo*) with Christ. I was first made aware of this progression back in Mumbai, India. A wonderful foreign missionary from China was the first to translate Watchman Nee's material, and the printing press where I served was the first to produce Watchman Nee's materials on a large scale; including *The Normal Christian Life*, *Normal Christian Church Life*, and other materials. Watchman Nee was the first person to point out the order of Ephesians, which is: *sit, walk, and stand.*

I have added one more phrase to this order: sit, walk, stand, and fight. This is the order of the book of Ephesians. If you have not learned to sit, then you don't know how to walk. If you don't know how to walk, then you don't know how to stand. If you don't know how to stand, then you will not win the fight. I want us to look at these things progressively.

Sitting in Our Identity

In verses 4–16, we have a list of incredible words. I want to include a few phrases here. The first thing we need to do is learn to sit on our throne. This is where the word *kathizo* is used. You sit down in a relaxed way, sure of your right to be there. You sit in the incredible revelation and truth that was obtained for you by the power of the cross. You don't do anything at all except receive them. The first thing you learn to sit in is the state of holiness and blamelessness in love, as it says in verse 4:

> *He chose us in Christ before the foundation of the world to be holy and blameless before him in love.* He destined us for adoption as his children through Jesus Christ, according to the good pleasure of his will (Ephesians 1:4–5 NRSV).

I have a series of messages that speak about our adoption and sonship entitled, *Sons Can Change Their World; Babies Can't Do Anything*. This series explains what sonship is all about. It means that, by the grace of God through faith, we become God's sons in every sense of the word and to the same degree that our Lord Jesus Christ enjoyed as the first human son that God ever had. I explain how the eternal Son of God in His deity became the first human son of God. That is why He had to fulfill the just requirements of the law. That is why for thirty years He didn't do anything except wait for his thirtieth birthday. He lived in perfect, obedient submission to the Father during that time.

According to Jewish culture, a son came into his functional sonship if he served his father faithfully for thirty years. On a son's thirtieth birthday, a father was legally required to give him all the treasure of his inheritance. Sons inherited when they came to their thirtieth birthday, not when their father died. That is why the thirtieth birthday is an important event in scripture. Jesus had to wait until his thirtieth birthday before He could begin drawing on the resources of His Father to attack and destroy the devil and all the forces of that kingdom.

Chapter 11 – Our Divine Identity

For thirty years, Jesus watched the devil do his devilish things and could not do anything, because He did not yet qualify as a man to be God's son, although He was eternally God's son by nature. Jesus could not use His divine nature on earth without disqualifying His humanity.

Jesus was the first man to ever fulfill the conditions of sonship by perfectly obeying His Father for thirty years. During Jesus' baptism, the Father conveyed upon the son the full rights of sonship. The Father cried from heaven, "This is My beloved Son, in whom I am well pleased" (Matt. 3:17). From that moment, the man Christ Jesus (not the divine Son of God, who we know was the Son from eternity) became qualified to be the first human ever to have the full rights of sonship conferred upon Him by God the Father. From that moment, He began to move out in the power of sonship.

We see Jesus in those three and a half years functioning as the first human son that God ever had. However, He would not be the last. It says in Hebrews 2:10 that His purpose was to bring many sons to glory. We are also told in Galatians 3:26 by the apostle Paul, "You are all sons of God through faith in Christ Jesus." In verse 27, he says that baptism is a significant event where we put on Christ. And in verse 28, he says sonship is not a matter of social standing, gender, or nationality, "There is neither Jew nor Greek, there is neither slave nor free, there is neither male nor female; for you are all one in Christ Jesus" (Gal. 3:28). Incidentally, the Greek word for sonship has no male connotation to it. A prefix must be added to the word in order to make it male or female. Therefore, God is speaking equally to women as He is to men.

Jesus fulfilled what God's law required for sonship by thirty years of obedience to Him. The great theme of Ephesians is that we are in Him. Because we are *in Him*, all the benefits of being in Him now flow powerfully through us. Everything He was, we are. This is the principle of heredity that we will look at later. The rights of sonship come to us through inheritance.

Section 3 – Ephesians Chapter 1

We must understand the law of heredity because it is the only way to understand these great phrases like "in Him," "together with Him," "raised with Him," and "seated with Him." These phrases come again and again in scripture. We must understand that this is not just a theological concept, but they are practical realities that will change our lives.

Jesus blazed a trail for us on our behalf. That is the language of Hebrews 12. Jesus was a pioneer. He is the author and completer of our faith. Jesus hacked a trail through the jungle and said, "All you need to do is walk in what I have accomplished and prepared for you. You must come into what I have obtained on your behalf. I didn't do what I did simply for Me, but it was for you." Therefore, I come into the same functional sonship by faith, which Jesus obtained by obedience to the law. He was born of a woman and born under the law that we might receive the full rights of sonship (see Gal. 4:4).

His purpose was to bring us into the full rights of sonship, not when we get to heaven, but now. It would be too late to wait for heaven. It's too late to get the world saved when we are in heaven. Sonship is not a matter of time, but a matter of faith. Jesus had to wait thirty years. You don't have to measure time to come to sonship. You must come to faith. Some people have been Christians for forty years and have never come to sonship. They never believed for it. Their church does not teach it. Others have come to sonship in a matter of one or two years.

I was in Hungry just a few days after communism collapsed. I used to travel to Eastern Europe on a regular basis in the bad old days of communism. When communism collapsed, there was a building used for lecturing on communist issues that was completely empty in just about every city. Everyone was obliged to attend these meetings for indoctrination before the collapse. Suddenly, these buildings were no longer needed. However, they were just what we needed for what I had in mind.

The people I worked with in Hungry were born and raised under communism. They had no idea what free society was like.

I said, "Let's go and evangelize."

They said, "How do we do that?"

I said, "Let's rent the former communist lecture hall and use it for evangelistic meetings."

I went to this particular town and was given the opportunity to speak to a large gathering of students. They asked me to come and do two things. First, they wanted their students to hear real English. Second, they wanted me to teach them the first principles of Christianity, which was never permitted before. They called the whole student body together, along with all the staff, and for three hours I was free to speak to them about the foundations of Christianity. As a result, we invited them to attend our evangelistic meetings in the evening. I was free to preach totally uninhibited. I gave my testimony of how I converted from scientific atheism. That was very relevant to them at the time.

People came out in the hundreds to our evening evangelistic meetings. I remember one eighteen-year-old young man in particular. We had three nights in this hall. On Wednesday night, this young man was gloriously saved. On Thursday night, he was powerfully filled with the Holy Spirit. We were seeing healings and many miracles taking place. There were so many people pressing forward for healing that I could not get to them all. I discovered that communist society was desperately sick in so many ways. I was at my wits end on how to pray for all these people. This same young man was with me, and I said to him, "You start praying for people." On Friday night, this young man was laying his hands on people and miracles were taking place. So Wednesday, he was saved. Thursday, he was filled with the Holy Spirit. Friday, he was moving in the miraculous. This is how it should be.

Section 3 – Ephesians Chapter 1

This young man came into his inheritance very quickly. It is not a matter of time, but a matter of faith. When you come to live in the full rights of sonship, then your relationship with the Father is identical to the relationship Jesus has with the Father. They are identical. There is no difference whatsoever. This is one of the laws of sonship in action. In biblical times, a father could designate his own natural children as his *huios*, his grown-up, mature adult son. This was not automatic. Instead, the father bestowed this relationship on his children. The children knew that if they pleased him for the first thirty years of their lives, then on their thirtieth birthday the father could designated them as his *huios*, meaning they would inherit all that the father was and had.

A father also had the right to go outside the family and choose a child that was not his naturally. By a special ceremony of adoption, requiring several witnesses, he could take that child and adopt him. The condition was that if this adopted child was made a *huios*, he must receive the same rights as the natural *huios*. The adopted child would not be treated any differently than the natural child. What a glorious picture that is! The Father will not treat us any differently than He treated Jesus. Otherwise, the Father would not be acting righteously. I can stand before God with the same rights of sonship as His own natural son. But I did not do one thing to earn it. Rather, I simply believed in what Jesus did for me. This is amazing grace.

We could go much deeper into each of these fantastic words to discover their depth, but we don't have the time. The tragedy is that most of the Christian church has no understanding of these things. The tragedy is that many leaders have no comprehension of these things, so they cannot teach it to their people. These are the foundations the Spirit of God moved upon the apostle Paul to establish in Ephesus. The Spirit said, "You must establish these truths in the people before they start going off into war. This is the power and authority by which they will be victorious in that war."

I have great delight in teaching these foundational things, because I know the power of them. What happened to me in Mumbai continues to burn in me until this day. We had 40 percent unemployment in Mumbai. I taught them the same principles of prosperity that I teach here. In Mumbai, they are living out the fruits of that revelation contrary to the economic norms of the city. No one in our church was unemployed, because we prayed them into work. If we could not find the right job, then we created industry of our own. I was involved in a large and successful company that is now worth millions of dollars. We saw a flowing prosperity in the Kingdom even in a city like Mumbai. The giving of that church is phenomenal. Even though we are on the fourth and fifth generation of spiritual inheritance, they are moving forward. It is in the culture of the Kingdom now.

If you go to Mumbai to minister the word of God, they will give you an honorarium that makes you believe you are ministering in America. If you go to some of the new amazing faith-filled works in Nigeria, the prayer and healing camps, they never ask for offerings, but their prosperity is abounding. All these things are possible when sons come into their inheritance, even in poor nations. Sons are not short of money when they have a rich Father. If you have a multimillionaire in your town and one of his children is walking around in rags, what would you think about that father? I am not suggesting extravagant living. I hate extravagance to indulge selfish desires and tastes, but I do believe in living in sufficiency. My Father takes care of His sons.

12

THE SPIRIT OF REVELATION

In Ephesians 1:17, Paul prays "that the God of our Lord Jesus Christ, the Father of glory, may give to you the spirit of wisdom and revelation in the knowledge of Him." One of the difficulties in all that we are talking about is that no matter how well I put these truths, your mind will not be able to receive it. But if there is a spirit-to-spirit transfer, then you will get it. Jesus was well aware of this dynamic, because He said to His disciples, when talking to them about the Father, "I have spoken to you in figurative language. I've tried to find the best illustrations I can. But I know that until the day the Spirit comes you will not understand it. When the Spirit comes, He will show you all the things I have taught you. He will lead you into all truth. He will show you the Father. Then you will be absolutely excited about these things" (see John 16:13–25). Jesus filled them with teaching that went into their heads, but none of it had come alive in their hearts. They had to wait for the Spirit to come.

The apostle Paul was in travail praying for these Ephesians to get the revelation. He taught in Ephesus for three years, but his concern was the same as the Lord Jesus Christ. Jesus taught for three years, yet nothing went off in their hearts until the Spirit came.

Section 3 – Ephesians Chapter 1

They were totally ignorant of the things He taught them, although they knew them intellectually. Spiritually they were not yet alive with the truth He taught. These truths were not yet birthed in them in the only way it can happen, which is by the revelation of the Spirit.

When the Spirit came, Peter was suddenly made alive with all kinds of revelation. The things Jesus taught him before were suddenly life and spirit. Things started to make sense and click together, and he started to live these incredible truths, because the Spirit revealed things to him. One of the things they saw was that they were true sons of God, and God was their Father. They could pray the right way. They could believe the right way. They could heal, deliver the sick, and raise the dead. It had to come by revelation.

As far as Jesus was concerned, this was the main theme of the upper room. Jesus said, "I will be praying for you." It says in scripture that Jesus ever lives to make intercession for us (see Heb. 7:25). I believe His primary intercession is, "Oh Father, open their eyes!" In the gospel of Luke, you will find eight occasions when Jesus was at prayer. This gospel particularly emphasizes the humanity of Jesus. It is very interesting to see when He prayed, what He prayed, and what happened because He prayed. One of His major burdens in prayer was that His followers might have their eyes opened to see what He had taught them.

Of course, until the Spirit came, His prayer could not be answered. One of His great yearnings was that they might know who He was. In Matthew 16:13, Jesus asked them, "Who do men say I, the Son of man, am?"

> They replied, "Some say John the Baptist, some Elijah, and others Jeremiah or one of the prophets" (Matt. 16:14).
> Then Jesus looked at them and asked, "But who do you say that I am?" (Matt. 16:15).

> Peter said, "You are the Christ, the Son of the living God" (Matt. 16:16).
>
> Jesus said, "Blessed are you, Simon Bar-Jonah, for flesh and blood has not revealed this to you, but My Father who is in heaven" (Matt. 16:17).

Just before this event, Jesus had spent all night in prayer. It is likely that Peter received this revelation because of Jesus' prayers that God would open his eyes.

Once people start getting revelation by the Spirit, their potential in God is unlimited. Jesus told Peter, "Once you have had revelation by the Spirit, the Father showing you things spiritually, then I can take you and I can use you as living stones to build a church against which the gates of hell cannot prevail" (see Matt. 16:18). You cannot begin to build a church that can deal with the gates of hell until the people have had supernatural revelation. It is not enough to be informed about it, but we must see it by the Spirit. If we are only informed, then we are not rooted in such a way that we become the unshakeable church. Instead, a deficiency still exists to advancing the Kingdom until we begin seeing things by the Spirit.

As I have led churches, my cry increased more and more, "Oh God, open their eyes to see!" I want you to see by the Spirit. I know I am not using even a fraction of the eloquence of Jesus to teach these things, but I am comforted to know that Jesus said about Himself, "You are not going to get this stuff until the Spirit shows it to you." I could use the most wonderful figurative words and most fantastic illustrations, but until something happens in your spirit because of His Spirit, then this teaching simply remains a nice teaching. But when the Spirit comes, things will begin exploding in you to make you powerful in Spirit to advance His Kingdom.

Section 3 – Ephesians Chapter 1

The apostle Paul cried out for a spirit of revelation and wisdom in the knowledge of Him for a specific purpose:

> The eyes of your understanding being enlightened; that you may know what is the hope of His calling, what are the riches of the glory of His inheritance in the saints, and what is the exceeding greatness of His power toward us who believe, according to the working of His mighty power (Ephesians 1:18–19).

I want to look at three purposes of revelation from this apostolic prayer. Paul was in travail that the saints would see what he saw. We saw how Elisha had to see. Elijah said, "If you see me when I am taken up, then…" The ability to see in the spirit distinguishes a son of God from an ordinary person. There are three things we need to see.

1. The Hope of His Calling

First, we must see what is the hope of His calling. I am called in this life to receive a measure of grace and the holy blamelessness in the presence of God that makes me realize that my sins have been totally washed away by the blood of Jesus. All that offended and offends God has now been removed so that I am reconciled to Him in an amazing relationship. I have become as much God's son by grace as Jesus is by nature. I have the full rights of sonship to walk on earth the way Jesus did. That is what Jesus obtained for us. All of heaven's treasure is mine just as it was His. I have the same access to the Father in the one Spirit. I can pray to the Father. All the things that Jesus was able to do, I can do. He obtained it for me. He has given it to me as a free gift. When this becomes revelation, then we begin to live this way. This is a whole other dimension of living. But you must see it. This is the hope of His calling.

2. The Riches of His Inheritance in the Saints

Second, we are called to see the riches of His inheritance in the saints. This word *inheritance* comes several times in Ephesians. I was hit like a thunderbolt a few years ago when I saw that God has chosen the almighty, risen, ascended Lord Jesus Christ to so identify with humanity that He made humans the instrument of bringing Him where He ought to be as the King of Glory, ruling over all the creation of God without any dispute. You could say, God put all of His eggs in one basket. We are all that God gets out of the deal. We are His total treasure. We are His inheritance. We spend much time dwelling on what God has done for us and this is rightfully so. But there is one thing I can do for Him. *I can be, along with my brothers and sisters, passionately committed to seeing that He comes into His full inheritance as speedily and as powerfully as possible.* I am the means of bringing Jesus into His inheritance. Is that not staggering?

I want you to see what the riches are of His inheritance in the saints. The sanctified ones will drive the devil off the face of the earth. They will repossess the world for Jesus to come as the glorious King, and we will worship Him and praise Him, throwing down our crowns before Him saying, "What a privilege to be alive as a participator in making all this happen!" I become a participator with the Holy Spirit, with the Father, and with the angels in bringing Jesus into His full inheritance.

John said, "…Truly, our fellowship is with the Father and with His Son Jesus Christ" (1 John 1:3). One dimension of the word *fellowship* (*koinonia*) is to be joined together in a common life. Another dimension is to be joined together in a common purpose. I am joined together in a common purpose with God the Father, with God the Spirit, and with the heavenly hosts to exalt and magnify the name of Jesus Christ on the face of the earth. I am a worker together with the Father, with the Spirit, and with the angels to this end. It has become the passion of my life.

Section 3 – Ephesians Chapter 1

When I hear about the Spirit breaking out in other places, about Jesus being honored as demon powers come crashing down, I get excited. I don't care where it is or through whom it occurs.

When I saw this, something dramatically changed in me. I thought, "He has given me this responsibility. He risked Himself for such weak nobodies like us to work together with Him, with the Holy Spirit, with the angels, and with each other in a unity with the Spirit." He did all of this in order to enable us to accomplish this purpose of giving Him His inheritance in the saints.

Some people want city transformation because it would be nicer to live in nice cities than in the bad cities we are living in now. You can actually want city transformation selfishly. "I want nice public schools for my kids to go to. I don't want them to be tempted by drugs. I want the whole place to be cleaned up." When you come to the bottom of these things, you see that there is much self-motivation in them. It is another thing altogether to absolutely want this for Jesus' sake. There is a personal benefit and goodness in it that comes as a byproduct, but it is all for Him.

3. The Exceeding Greatness of His Power

Third, we need to see the exceeding greatness of His power. This is an incredible statement. Immediately following this phrase comes the Greek preposition *eis*. Certain prepositions in the Greek language have movement. This preposition has the idea of moving from one place to another. We should translate it "into." This means that *there is nothing that God is and can do that can't flow through me when I have learned to be an effective conductor or channel.* Paul is saying, "I want you to see the immeasurable greatness of His power *into* us who believe."

There is so much silly talk about who can address demons. Some teach that you must be a general in the Lord's army to tackle a general in the devil's army. Imagine you have a private and a general in combat, and

Chapter 12 – The Spirit of Revelation

they both put a bullet up their gun and aim it at the person on the other side. When they shoot, which bullet will be more deadly? Obviously, it is not the person firing, but the bullet, that makes the difference.

The only thing I must be sure of is that I do what I do in the will of God. He is the power, not me. I don't have any power. I couldn't command a mouse to move in Jesus' name. But when the Spirit of God chooses to use my humanity through my person, my spirit, and my audible voice to display the exceeding greatness of His power, then that demon spirit trembles and flees–not from me, but from the One who moves through me. I can be a vehicle because I am human. That is the only requirement necessary.

I can be a vehicle of His exceedingly great power. I provide the connection between the power of almighty God and the object to which His power is being directed. It might be the power of healing. It might be the power of casting out demons. It might be speaking an authoritative word that commands a principality to flee. It could be a prophetic word that causes something to move powerfully for the purposes of God. There are many ways God can use this power. The only thing I must be sure about is that I am there as the obedient conduit of His Almighty power. It does not matter who I am or who I am not.

There are many different qualities of paint brushes, but when you see a fantastic Picasso, you don't say, "This fantastic paint brush was used to paint this painting. Let's worship the paint brush!" He could have used any paint brush to accomplish that work. The power was not in the brush, but in the one who used the brush. We are not stupid enough to give credit to the paint brush in the natural, so why can't we see the same principle working in the spirit. The almighty God, the exceedingly powerful One, is so amazingly powerful that it is no handicap to Him to take a little paint brush like me and do marvelous things with it. The glory belongs to Picasso, not the paint brush.

Section 3 – Ephesians Chapter 1

In the same manner, the glory belongs to God, not the vessel He uses. Even handicapping God with people like us, He still accomplishes His purpose, which is a testament to His exceeding power. The fact that He uses us shows how exceedingly great His power is. In situations like these, I think about the Old Testament example of Moses. When he went to Pharaoh's court to be the instrument of God's power, something significant happened. The film *Prince of Egypt* conveyed this very accurately. They portrayed Moses as a little man totally out of his level of competency, yet he was willing to say to the boss, "Yes, Sir!" Almighty God flowed through him to do amazing and phenomenal things. All the glory rightly goes to God and His power, not to His instrument.

This exceedingly great power is again and again measured in scripture. It is the power that He worked in Christ when He raised Him from the dead and seated Him at the right hand of God in the heavenly places. I must spend some time on this truth.

When the early church went out into the world, they went everywhere preaching the resurrection of Jesus Christ. They never went anywhere preaching the raising of Lazarus from the dead. In fact, that event was never mentioned again. Yet, in terms of a miracle, the raising of Lazarus was a greater physical miracle. He was in the tomb for four days. His body was stinking and rotten. Jesus was in the grave for three days, and His body was preserved from decay. Jesus simply disappeared. Here is the point. In His death, Jesus took all the sins of Adam's race upon Himself. He even took the very nature of sin upon Himself. The human Christ became more loaded with sin than any other man as He was crucified. He took the totality of sin from Adam's race, from beginning to end. If there was anyone who should have never risen from the dead it was Jesus Christ.

Chapter 12 – The Spirit of Revelation

Jesus descended into the depths of death with the load of billions of sinners on His shoulders. Think about the weight and burden that must have been on Him. Think about what the Nazis did. Think about all the ghastly things that have happened throughout humanity's existence. Think about all the blood-stained soils of Europe and the United States of America. Think of all the atrocities around the world. Think about the worst, foulest, and most obscene sex offenders of our day. Think about all the sexual perversions and obscenity of just one major city, not to mention the world at large. All of that was laid upon Him. When I saw these things, I shuddered in amazement.

I still remember spending one night with a demon possessed man who got gloriously saved. He was the most filthy, foul sex pervert I had ever met in my life. He had had innumerable encounters with women. He had also had numerous relationships with men. Then he began having sex with animals. This demonized man cried to Jesus to save him. I labored with another brother for several hours, and the demons eventually came out of him. At one point, Jesus Himself came and helped us in the fight. It was a magnificent victory.

While I was ministering to him and the demons were manifesting, it was like the filthiness of his condition came upon me to some extent. I felt what it was like to be homosexual. I felt the foulness of the perversion coming upon me, and I revolted against it, "This is terrible!" When all the demons left and the man was delivered, in the early hours of the morning I went back to my room. I had a long shower, trying to wash the perversion off of me. That man's filthiness did not really come upon me, but it came near me. This was the sin and demons in only one man, and I am not pure and perfect like Jesus, either. But the filthiness of that experience left me shuddering. Then I thought, "What must it have been like for Jesus? He tasted death for every person."

Section 3 – Ephesians Chapter 1

As Jesus died on the cross as the great sin bearer, the last Adam, He became the garbage can for humanity. The cup Jesus drank was the concentrated filth of obscenity, violence, and perversity of the whole of Adam's race from beginning to end. It was concentrated in that cup, and He took it into His body on the tree. He became more filthy with sin than any other man a million times over. Death had more claim on Him than on any other man because of the sin He was carrying.

The Bible says that the sting of death is sin. In Hebrews 5:7 it says:

> In the days of His flesh, when He had offered up prayers and supplications, with vehement cries and tears to *Him who was able to save him from death*, and was heard because of His godly fear.

I could not make any sense of this verse for years. But once again, here is a Greek preposition with movement. This time it is the preposition *ek*. This little preposition has the idea of being inside something and then you come up out from within what you were formerly inside. Jesus did not say, "Father, I don't want to die." Instead, He prayed a much more powerful prayer, "Father, when I am offered up on the cross, *I am praying that you will deliver me out from within death*." Or, said another way, "When I have taken all this sin upon Me and have gone down into the depths of death, I am praying that You will raise Me up out from within death by the power of Your Spirit!" And He was heard!

In His prayer, Jesus declared, "I will not be held by death!" He was going to come up out from within death to the glory of the Father. He tasted this on behalf of every person. Because He did this, death is a non-event for us. The sin is already dealt with. We simply pass from one wonderful life to another more glorious life. He obtained not only His resurrection, but also our resurrection. He had the resurrection by faith even before He went to the cross.

Can you see now what we are being told here in Ephesians? Paul cried out for those believers that they might know the exceeding greatness of power that raised Jesus Christ from the dead. When Jesus was raised from the dead, from that unbelievably deep dying in sin, something was completely broken in the spirit realm. Death said, "There is no way we will let this man go!" They thought there was no power that could deliver a man from this degree of bondage to sin and death.

But hell started to shake. The power of God, which is called the glory of the Father, raised Jesus from the dead. This is more than a dead body being resurrected. That is what happened to Lazarus and that is wonderful, but it is nothing compared to what happened with Jesus. When Jesus came up out of the grave, of all those 10 billion lustful, wicked, perverted, corrupt, evil, foul, filthy sins, not one of them was sticking to Him. He left it all behind. In fact, He was a completely new man who rose from the grave.

In Matthew, we are told that He is the beginning of a new genealogy. The risen Christ is something completely new, and that is who we are related to in the spirit. Because I have changed my genealogy and hereditary line, I do not belong to Adam's race anymore. I belong to this new man, the man from heaven, the Lord Christ Jesus who rose up out of that grave totally triumphant and completely victorious over sin, the devil, and death itself.

That is the power Paul is talking about. He wanted this church to see it. When you have seen it and you walk into a demon infested city, you know that demon infestation is nothing compared with the grave that Jesus rose up out of. Every demon in hell was gathered together against the Christ to say, "Don't let Him rise!" Yet the power of God–the glory of the Father–was greater. And this same power flows through us. No demon has the power to compete with the power of God at work in us.

In the jungles of northern India, leeches often attack and hang on to a person. It is hard to get them off. I picture Jesus rising from the dead with demon leeches trying to hang on to Him as He said, "Get off, you filthy things!" He stripped Himself of anything and everything that tried to stick to Him. This is what charges me with unconquerable victory in our Lord Jesus Christ. This is what God showed me when I was first baptized in the Holy Spirit as a Baptist minister. I came from an old, stuffy British Baptist background. But God broke me open and transformed me. That led to a mighty revival in our city. I began to see these things. Paul the apostle saw these things. He prayed that the Ephesian church would see these things. How about you? Will you see these things?

At the end of Paul's prayer in Ephesians 1, it says:

> ...according to the working of His mighty power which He worked in Christ when He raised Him from the dead and seated Him at His right hand in the heavenly places, far above all principality and power and might and dominion, and every name that is named, not only in this age but also in that which is to come (Ephesians 1:19–21).

This passage has five superlatives, one right after another. The word *principality* is the Greek word *arche*, meaning "top dog." Jesus is far above the top dog demons. I don't care how high that demon is in devilish ranking, my Jesus is far above him. He is far above all *power*. This is the Greek word *exousia*, which is the word for authority. There is no authority like the authority of the risen Christ sitting upon His throne. He is far above any authority. He is far above all *might*. This is the Greek word *dunamis*, which is like raw power and strength. Again, Jesus is far greater and more powerful than any power or strength. He is far above all *dominion*. This is the Greek word *kuriotes*, which the word *lord* comes from. Jesus is far above all lordship. If there is a lord, then He is so much more lord.

He is also far above any other name. This is the Greek word *onoma*, which means to have a reputation. We use it in modern language by saying, "Oh, that man is a big name." We might ask, "Who is the big name in football?" If you mention someone's name, then everyone knows him. That is the idea behind this word. Anyone who is on this earth with a name has a rival who is far above. Jesus has a name that is far above any other name, not only in this age, but also in the one to come.

His Fullness Fills Everything

I can feel Paul grasping for superlatives to try and capture the grandeur of this glorious one upon His throne. Let this soak in:

> And He put all things under His feet, and gave Him to be head over all things to the church, which is His body, the fullness of Him who fills all in all (Ephesians 1:22–23).

Jesus did not do all of this just to sit in isolated glory while we are down here somewhere. That might be our rightful place, but that is not where He put us! He is not there just to be glorified and worshipped in isolated majesty. The amazing truth that we must see is that He did all of this on behalf of the church. Everything He entered into and pioneered, He did so that He could bring us to where He is. He tasted death on behalf of every person so that we might come into all the benefits of that death. He became the son of glory so that He might bring many sons and daughters to glory.

He who sanctifies and all those who are sanctified come from the same origin. The word literally says that they are from the same womb. I am from the same spiritual womb that Jesus came from. That is why He is not ashamed to call us brothers and sisters. If we are from the same womb, then we are brothers. This is not a theological lie, but a glorious eternal truth. God does not look at us with rose-tinted glasses, saying, "Pretend to be something you are not."

Section 3 – Ephesians Chapter 1

Instead, He says, "You better believe who you really are!" We will see later that by participating with Him in all these glorious things, we are also participating with Him now in everything He is accomplishing.

In the last phrase of this first chapter of Ephesians, Paul says that Jesus "fills all in all." Jesus saw the days of His flesh as the days of His constriction. He was limited to one human body and could not be in many places at the same time doing different things at the same time. He could only be in Judea, Jerusalem, or Galilee. He could not be everywhere at once. There was a certain limit to His human energy, although He pushed His body to incredible lengths. An average day for Jesus makes you feel faint. He was up early in the morning praying. He healed many people. He traveled from one place to the next. People were out to kill Him. He spent nights in prayer. He ministered the word all day, healed the sick, and then walked great distances. He was incredible in His humanity. But even so, there was a limitation on what He could accomplish.

In Luke 12:49–50, He cried out,

> I came to send fire on the earth, and how I wish it were already kindled! But I have a baptism to be baptized with, and how distressed I am till it is accomplished!

In other words, He was saying, "I've come to cast fire upon the earth, and how I am constrained and restricted and shut in until that baptism of death on the cross is accomplished. Only when I release many more men and women into this same life, where I can come and live in them the way I have lived in this body temporarily, will My Kingdom advance. This new body, the church, will be available to Me so that then and only then will I be seen in all My fullness." This is the fullness of Him who fills all in all. This is not some pale, insipid imitation of Him, but it is the fullness of Him who fills all in all. This is glorious.

This is Paul's apostolic prayer for the Ephesian church, "Father, do this for the church in Ephesus. If they get this, if they see it, and it becomes a burning fire in them the way it is a burning fire in me, then we will have a church that can take a city!" This was his prayer for them, and it should be our prayer for ourselves and our churches.

SECTION 4
Ephesians Chapter 2

13

THE POWER OF THE CROSS

Let's begin now to look at Ephesians 2. I want to establish a principle regarding the power of the cross that made one new man. There are two things we need to understand. First, we must understand what it really means to be *in Him*. This is a phrase that is used by many Christians and frequently repeated in scripture, so I want you to be sure that you understand what it means. We need to get hold of this truth. Therefore, I must explain to you carefully what I call the *law of heredity*.

Please open your spirit wide while putting your intellect on sleep mode. Your spirit will receive this. Then your spirit can gradually educate your intellect on what this fantastic truth does to transform you. Bible logic is not the same as natural logic. We are told in the Corinthian letter that by the wisdom of this world people never come to know Jesus. Paul said, "We do preach wisdom, but it is not the wisdom of this world" (see 1 Cor. 2:6). We are also told that the wisdom that comes down from above has glorious qualities. It is peaceable, open to reason, easy to be entreated, not jealous or envious, yet it is unwavering. I want us to look and receive from that wisdom in order to understand this important truth.

Section 4 – Ephesians Chapter 2

I find this law of heredity working in a number of ways. Hebrews 7 is the chapter where we are introduced to the great theme of the book of Hebrews, which is the Melchizedek priesthood. The beginning of chapter 8 tells us that this is the most important thing being said in the book of Hebrews. Here in Hebrews 7, Melchizedek is being introduced. He is called the king of Salem. He is called the Priest of the Most High God. We also read that Abraham met him when he returned from the slaughter of the kings in Genesis 14. About Melchizedek, Hebrews 7:2–3 says:

> ...First being translated "king of righteousness," and then also king of Salem, meaning "king of peace," without father, without mother, without genealogy, having neither beginning of days nor end of life, but made like the Son of God, remains a priest continually."

When I read this passage of scripture to my daughter Rachel when she was seven years old, I said, "Tell me who this is talking about?"

She said, "That is Jesus!"

I thought, "You know more than most theological seminary professors." It really is that simple. This is what we call a theophany. This is a pre-incarnate manifestation of God in human form. Abraham met God as a triune person. The one who stood outside Jericho was another theophany. There are many of these appearances throughout the Old Testament.

The second person of the Godhead, who we now call Jesus, the Son of God, was the one standing there before Abraham. He administered to him the elements of the new covenant, giving Him bread and wine. This occurred two thousand years before it happened in time, when it was ratified at the cross. We must see that the cross is an eternal event as well as happening at a specific point in history.

Chapter 13 – The Power of the Cross

The cross reaches into eternity. We have many references that confirm this. In Hebrews it talks about Jesus being slain in a new way. This does not mean we are going into the Catholic error of taking communion believing he is re-crucified.

What Jesus did on the cross had the power of an eternal now. Therefore, the event never needs to be repeated. It is as powerful at this moment as it was when the blood first gushed out of His quivering body on Calvary. The blood is as powerful today as it was when He took sin upon Himself, paying the full penalty for it. Abraham could grasp for it two thousand years before the event took place in time, because it is eternal. You and I can grab hold of it two thousand years after the event. It is just as powerful for us as it was for Abraham or any other person in time.

Abraham was a new covenant believer. King David also lived in the new covenant approximately one thousand years before it was ratified in time. He erected a tabernacle that was totally illegal. He did things as a priest and king unto his God that only new covenant believers can do. The theology of most of the Psalms, which were written in David's tabernacle, is the theology of the New Testament, not the theology of the Old Testament. You must not make a hard and complete division between the Old and New Testaments. That divide is not there in scripture.

Abraham had an encounter with the glorified high priest. Jesus was not yet incarnate in time. He had not yet died upon the cross in time. However, in eternity it already was an eternal event. We must allow our spirits to be instructed in this way. We cannot be prisoners of time.

Then it says in verse Hebrews 7:4, "Now consider how great this man was, to whom even the patriarch Abraham gave a tenth of the spoils." If someone gives a tithe to someone, we are being told that the receiver of the tithes is clearly greater than the one who gives the tithes.

Section 4 — Ephesians Chapter 2

This is the first principle we are being shown. By this first argument, we are told that Abraham is inferior to Melchizedek. Therefore, Melchizedek is superior to Abraham. The purpose of this argument is to prove that the Melchizedek priesthood is superior to the Levitical priesthood. You must see, however, how the argument flows.

A few verses later, we are told:

> But he whose genealogy is not derived from them received tithes from Abraham and blessed him who had the promises. Now beyond all contradiction the lesser is blessed by the better (Hebrews 7:6–7).

This is the second argument. The fact that Melchizedek reached out and blessed Abraham tells us again that Abraham is recognizing his inferiority to Melchizedek. We presume that Abraham knelt down before Melchizedek and received the blessing. Therefore, by two things Melchizedek is shown to be superior to Abraham.

The Law of Heredity

Now we come to the law of heredity. Look at Hebrews 7:8–10:

> Here mortal men receive tithes, but there he receives them, of whom it is witnessed that he lives. *Even Levi, who receives tithes, paid tithes through Abraham, so to speak, for he was still in the loins of his father when Melchizedek met him.*

Levi was not yet born. He did not exist yet. In fact, Isaac and Jacob had not yet been born. The generations were Abraham, Isaac, Jacob, and then Levi. So, there were three generations before Levi came into existence.

We noticed earlier that God had already formed me before He created the world. Although I did not exist physically, I did exist in the plan of God, and my days were already numbered.

Chapter 13 – The Power of the Cross

This is how amazing our God really is. We are not an accident, but we are part of His eternal plan.

It was God's plan to bring forth Levi in the fourth generation after Abraham. Levi was in the body or loins of Abraham. Therefore, in good Bible logic, Levi was participating with Abraham in what he did to Melchizedek. It was not simply Abraham submitting to Melchizedek, but Levi participated in that act of submission. It was not simply Abraham being blessed by Melchizedek, but Levi was also blessed.

As Abraham bowed and submitted to the superiority of Melchizedek, Levi was *in him* participating with Abraham in that act of submission. Therefore, according to the writer of Hebrews, Levi was clearly inferior to Melchizedek, because he came out from the loins of Abraham. This is the principle of the law of heredity. This great truth is used to explain many important things from scripture.

In Romans 5, we are introduced to two people who represent two different genealogies. There is a genealogy after Adam, and there is a genealogy after Christ. All of us by natural birth have a genealogy after Adam. Adam's decision to sin by disobeying God deeply affected the genealogy after him. The Bible tells us that we were in the loins of Adam, participating with him in that act of disobedience. I was in Adam when Adam decided not to obey God and do his own thing. I was there, and therefore, I participated with him in his rebellion against God. Therefore, I suffered the consequences of that decision.

When I was born, I already had the Adamic nature inherently part of me, because I was born of him. You might say, "That is not fair!" We are not talking about fairness. Instead, we need to see the importance of these mighty spiritual principles. When I was born, I did not have to learn how to lie. It was in me. The Bible tells me that Satan is a liar, and he is the father of all lies. That shows me the satanic activity that was able to enter Adam the moment he stepped away from God.

181

Section 4 – Ephesians Chapter 2

As a result, it has been passed down to every succeeding generation since.

The reality of the Adamic nature is very real. I was never taught by my parents to be angry, but I was very good at it. A six year old child is pretty good at showing his anger when he does not receive what he wants. The child is a beautiful creation, but if you cross the will of that little one, he is capable of letting you know his displeasure. We can see this in absolute reality. This is not simply a theological concept, but a reality.

The fruit of sin that comes through Adam has come to all of us because our roots are in him. As a result, every one of us expects to die. Death can only come to human beings who have sinned. I often use this as an argument to people.

They say, "I don't need God. I am living a righteous life."

I say, "Do you expect to live forever, or do you expect to die?"

They usually say, "Don't be silly. Of course I expect to die."

That proves that sin is working in a person; otherwise, we would not die. Jesus said, "No one can take my life from Me…" because He was the only man who never sinned. He said, "I have power to lay it down, and I have power to take it up again, but no one can take it from Me." Only when Jesus joyfully and voluntarily became the garbage can for Adam's race and all humanity was it possible for Jesus to die.

A New Genealogy; A New Man; A New Creation

Romans 5 tells us that many things happened because of Adam.

> Therefore, just as through one man sin entered the world, and death through sin, and thus death spread to all men, because all sinned…. Nevertheless death reigned from Adam to Moses, even over those who had not sinned according to the likeness of the transgression of Adam, who is a type of Him who was to come (Romans 5:12, 14).

Chapter 13 – The Power of the Cross

Adam is described here as a type of Christ who was to come. Both Adam and Jesus Christ are heads of a genealogy. We all receive an inheritance from one or the other. It further tells us:

> For if by the one man's offense death reigned through the *one*, much more those who receive abundance of grace and of the gift of righteousness will reign in life through the *One, Jesus Christ*. Therefore, as through *one man's offense* judgment came to *all men*, resulting in condemnation, even so through *one Man's righteous* act the free gift came to *all men*, resulting in justification of life. For as *by one man's disobedience* many were made sinners, so also *by one Man's obedience* many will be made righteous (Romans 5:17–19).

God is dividing all humanity into two genealogies–the genealogy of Jesus Christ and the genealogy of Adam. By nature we are all born of Adam. We all have a responsibility with the way we live our lives. We will produce a family line, assuming we have children. I can either set up a genealogy of righteousness, or I can produce a genealogy of sin. What I do with my life will powerfully affect my children, my grandchildren, and my great grandchildren. I will start something in my family line that will either result in blessing or cursing. Tragically, an alcoholic father usually produces alcoholic sons. This trend continues until the curse is broken in Jesus Christ.

My great grandfather was a dock worker in a port in Bristol, England. He had a son who became my grandfather. This grandfather of mine went into the British Army and became an officer. He was a regimental sergeant major, which was the highest rank he could receive without being an officer. My grandfather had a son, my father. He was an engineer. My father had me, and I became a research scientist.

Section 4 – Ephesians Chapter 2

Imagine for a moment that my great grandfather was born around 1810. He would have been twenty years of age in 1830. At that time, a man named Steven Austin was founding the state of Texas. He made an agreement with Mexico to begin establishing immigrants from Europe. Imagine that my great grandfather was one of those first three hundred immigrants to come to Texas. Instead of slaving away in the docks of Bristol, he became one of the first immigrant families in Texas in the early 1830s. At that time, by simply volunteering to be an immigrant you were granted four thousand acres of land. This was immediately given to you when you signed an agreement to stay for at least several years. You had to agree to farm a certain percentage of the land within two or three years.

So, here is my great grandfather living in Texas farming a good portion of land. At that time, no one knew what was under the land or how valuable that land would become. Imagine that my grandfather, who inherited the land from his father, discovers that the land is rich in oil and gas. My grandfather begins digging oil wells. What would that make my grandfather? My grandfather would have become a multimillionaire rich Texan! What would that have made me? I would be a multimillionaire rich Texan!

But my great grandfather made the decision not to come to America. Instead, he decided to continue slaving away in the docks of Bristol. As a result, I received nothing out of that deal! Can you see that his decision powerfully affected my destiny? I am not a Texan. I can't even talk like one. I don't have millions and millions of dollars in the bank, which I would love. to have. Can you see how this works?

My grandmother was a little Welsh lady called Mary Jones. She was converted in the Welsh Revival in 1904. She was powerfully impacted by the Spirit of God. She came from a stuffy Baptist background, but she started to burn after an experience with the Holy Spirit.

Chapter 13 – The Power of the Cross

She began a new heredity and generation in our family, which has gone from generation to generation. I am part of the fruit of her prayers. Her eldest son, my uncle, when he was a young man already had a degree from Liverpool University. However, he left all of that to go to Canada in 1905 as a pioneer missionary. He wrote a wonderful autobiography that was never published.

Recently, I visited the area where he was a pioneer missionary one hundred years ago. He planted the first Baptist church in Winnipeg. In 1907, he planted that church, and then in 1989 I preached in the same pulpit. I was following the trail of my grandmother's prayers, which were worked out in the life of her eldest son. He later moved to America and became an American citizen while living in Newport, Vermont. I am now becoming acquainted with a whole generation of American Vincents. They are a great genealogy. This godly genealogy seemed to flow in the British stream and has come to full expression through our family. We now have three generations, and we are linking up and discovering the beauty of our family heritage.

Through all of this, I want you to see what kind of responsibility you have in living your life. You will influence the destiny of many generations after you. If you fool around with a little Christianity on the side, you will produce children like that. They will probably go off into sin and produce all kinds of problems. If you are passionately committed to Jesus and bring up a child in the way he should go, then when they are old they will not depart from it.

My daughter Rachel, with her husband Gordon and their two small children, became the international crusade directors for Reinhard Bonnke's ministry. They started traveling the world together. They did incredible things in the Philippines. They saw incredible things in Kuala Lumpur, which is a Muslim country.

Section 4 – Ephesians Chapter 2

My little granddaughter said to her mum, "I know we have to get the world saved first, but when the world is saved, could we go back to England and have a puppy." She had her priorities right. We need to get the world saved first!

You can tell that I am a very proud grandfather. It does not take much insight to see that, but this is what we can all do. *You are not simply deciding what you will do with your life, but you are deciding what generations after you will do with their lives.* We must see this generational transfer and the importance of our decisions now. I want to make sure that I walk right, because when I do I will produce an exemplary life that my children will want to follow.

When I was seventy years of age, we had a celebration with people we knew and worked with from all around the world. They were there to thank God for our lives and what we were able to put into them. The most precious remembrance came from my oldest son. He said, "Dad, you are my hero! I want to be just like you." I thought, "What an honor." I want you to have your children look to their father or mother as their hero.

The power in the cross can totally obliterate our old man, as is brought out here in Romans 5 and developed further in Romans 6. It is frequently referred to throughout the New Testament. There is a power in the cross to cut me off from my hereditary past. Because of the law of heredity and because God has foreordained us for salvation, we are in Christ just as we were naturally in Adam. Just as I was involved with Adam when he sinned and brought death upon the whole human race, allowing the satanic nature to invade the human scene, in the same way I was actually in Christ as the second man. Adam was a type of the great new man Jesus Christ. What is true of my heredity in Adam is now true of my heredity in Christ once I lay hold of it by faith.

I was actually in the loins of Jesus, participating with Him in what He did to deal with sin. That is what the Bible clearly teaches us. This is not a theological concept. In the mystery of the spirit, it is utterly and absolutely real. My sinfulness was a not theological concept, but it was horribly and tragically real. I could not stop sinning because of the nature I was given. In addition to this, I was shaped in iniquity by the sinful circumstances in which I was brought up. These are the two things that shaped me to be the kind of person I was. I do have an inheritance in Adam, but I cannot blame him for everything. My circumstances also shaped me.

Participating with Christ

This is the best way I can put it into words. Somehow Jesus fully became that terrible cursed Adam in His death. He took it down to where it had to be justly dealt with, taking it to the depths of hell. We are told in Isaiah 53 that it pleased God to bruise Him. God, because He is righteous, had to take out the full penalty for sin. God cannot ignore sin. He must respond to sin by wrath. Wrath is not anger. Instead, it is something much deeper than anger. Wrath is the inevitable response of perfect righteousness toward sin. Sin must be punished and fully paid for.

The Father poured out His wrath upon the son, and I was in Christ while that penalty was paid. Just as I was, in Adam, sinning against God, now by faith I was in Him while He was paying for my sin. Therefore, God was not playing a pretend game when He said, "Your sins are paid for." They are paid for! I know this is hard to grasp intellectually, but my spirit knows these things. They burn like fire in me. Your spirit can know these things. This is absolutely biblical. I was in Jesus when He died and paid for sin. I was in Jesus when He went down to hell. I was participating with Him in all these things. I was there.

Section 4 – Ephesians Chapter 2

Do you remember that old song, "Were you there when they crucified my Lord?" I say, "Yes, I was there!" I was right there in Him. I participated with Him in what was happening on the cross. Therefore, if Jesus was raised from the dead by the glory of the Father, then it is absolutely righteous that I should be raised with Him. The Jesus who rose from the dead was not the one who died.

All of Adam's sin was put upon Christ. It is important to note that Jesus is called the last Adam in 1 Corinthians 15:45. Jesus gathered up all that Adam is, all that Adam was, and all that Adam has done, including all the pollution and foulness of that nature. As the last Adam, He went down into death and died. However, something happened to Jesus while He was hanging on the cross. In 1 John 5:4–6, it says:

> For whatever is born of God overcomes the world. And this is the victory that has overcome the world–our faith. Who is he who overcomes the world, but he who believes that Jesus is the Son of God? *This is He who came by water and blood* – Jesus Christ; not only by water, *but by water and blood*. And *it is the Spirit who bears witness*, because the Spirit is truth.

John is saying something very important here, and the Spirit is bearing witness to this. In John 19:30, it says, "When Jesus had received the sour wine, He said, 'It is finished!' And bowing His head, He gave up His spirit." The centurion who was in charge of the execution looked straight at Jesus and, seeing the way He died, fell to his knees and said, "Truly, this is the Son of God." This man had seen many men die. He had put men to death in battle and had executed countless others. But he had never seen anyone like Jesus, who was in charge of His own execution. Jesus chose the moment when it was appropriate to dismiss His spirit and go be with His Father. He was totally in charge. As a result, the centurion said, "This is the Son of God."

Chapter 13 – The Power of the Cross

In the mystery of paying for sin, Jesus had accomplished everything He needed to do on the cross. It was time for that whole sin-cursed, Adamic-filled body and, presumably, soul to go down into hell and finish the payment. I believe His spirit ascended to the Father at that time. These are mysteries that are hard to understand.

At that point a soldier came, and Jesus cried out, "It is finished!" First of all, this is a loud cry. The cry was not a cry of pain or anguish, but the cry of victory a gladiator makes when he makes the killing thrust in a battle, "It is finished!" The Greek word is *teleos*. This word was also used in accounting when a bill was owed. When someone owed money, a record was kept by a money lender of what they owed; when someone came to the money lender to settle the debt, they would write over that debt, *teleos*, meaning, "Nothing to pay." It is finished.

This was when Jesus dismissed His spirit. He was totally in charge of His own execution. When they saw that He was already dead, they didn't break His legs. But in John 19:34, one of the soldiers pierced His side with a spear, and immediately *blood and water* flowed out. In the next verse, John 19:35, it says, "And he who has seen has testified, and *his testimony is true*; and he knows that he is telling the truth, *so that you may believe.*" In other words, the Spirit of God said to John, "As you watched that blood and water flow out, it was a powerful prophetic sign that you need to take note of." When he wrote his letter some sixty years later, he said, "This is the one who came by the water and the blood."

The way God created the woman was a great allegorical sign of what He was going to do when He gave birth to the church. God could have simply taken the dust of the ground and made a woman out of it. Instead, He put Adam into a sleep, and then opened His side. He took out a rib, and from that rib He built the woman.

Section 4 – Ephesians Chapter 2

When Adam came back out of his sleep, it is like a picture of Jesus going to death and being put in the grave lying in the tomb. When Adam opened his eyes and, figuratively speaking, came back to life in a manner of resurrection, the first thing he saw was this fantastic woman. In the Hebrew it literally says, "Adam opened his eyes," and the first thing he said was, "This is it: bone of my bone, and flesh of my flesh." She was part of him.

When Adam's eyes opened, he said, "This is it. This is bone of my bone and flesh of my flesh." The soldier who pierced the side of Jesus did not know what he was doing. He was actually serving God like a surgeon making a caesarian incision in the womb of God so that God could give birth to something new. What are the elements of birth? What happens to a woman just before she gives birth? What flows out? Blood and water flow out.

In John 16:20, it says:

> Most assuredly I say to you that you will weep and lament, but the world will rejoice; and you will be sorrowful, but your sorrow will be turned to joy. A woman, when she is in labor, has sorrow because her hour has come; but as soon as she has given birth to the child, she no longer remembers the anguish, for joy that a human being has been born into the world.

While Jesus was on the cross, He was not only the Lamb of God taking the sins of the world away, but He was also like a mother in travail, giving birth to something. What we see on the cross is not only the pain of bearing sin, but it was also the labor pains of giving birth to something new. The blood and water gushed out. They carried His body into the tomb. This is when the labor pains became intensified as He went to pay the price of hell. Only God knows what that was. However, at the end of the pain of that travail, God gave birth to something completely new.

Jesus: First Begotten from the Dead

On the third day, God gave birth to a new man who owed nothing to Adam or Adam's race. This man has a totally different genealogy. Jesus in His resurrection was the first fruit of His own womb. I like the King James Version, which describes Jesus as the first begotten (or born) from the dead (see Rev. 1:5; Col. 1:18; Rom. 8:29). Notice what it says in Colossians 1:13–15, 18:

> He has delivered us from the power of darkness and conveyed us into the kingdom of the Son of His love, in whom we have redemption through His blood, the forgiveness of sins. He is the image of the invisible God, the *firstborn over all creation*... And He is the head of the body, the church, who is the beginning, the *firstborn from the dead*, that in all things He may have the preeminence.

In Romans 8:29, it says, "For whom He foreknow, He also predestined to be conformed to the image of His Son, that He might be the *firstborn among many brethren.*" Jesus was the last Adam in His death. Never call Him the second Adam. He is not called the second Adam. In 1 Corinthians 15:45, it says that in His death He is the last Adam, but in His resurrection He is the second man, the Lord from heaven, "'The first man Adam became a living being.' The *last Adam* became a life-giving spirit.... The first man was of the earth, made of dust; the *second Man* is the Lord from heaven" (1 Cor. 15:45, 47).

This second man, the risen Christ Jesus, has nothing to do with the last Adam who died as the total, final, and complete payment for sin. What He became in His death never rose from the dead. Instead, a new creation came forth, a whole new beginning and genealogy of people. The devil never had his fingers on that genealogy. That genealogy has never sinned and never committed these things. Instead, it is a totally new generation. When you are born of that, the old has no claim over you.

Section 4 – Ephesians Chapter 2

This is what it means to be born again. You come out of the same womb. That is why it tells us in Hebrews 2:11 that He who sanctifies and those who are sanctified are of one origin. Literally, they are from the same womb. Therefore, Christ is not ashamed to call us brethren. When you get this, you realize that the cross has the power to completely close one genealogy and literally open a new genealogy, starting a completely new life. What you were and what Satan had claim over is dead forever in Christ Jesus. It is finished *in Him*. What you are in Him is now what He is when He was raised from the dead. It is not enough to be like Jesus on earth. Instead, we are like Jesus in His resurrection. This is totally a faith exercise. As you grab hold of one, while letting go of the other, it becomes reality in your life. When I realize my new heredity, then my life cannot stay the same.

In Romans 6:11, it says, "Likewise you also, reckon yourselves to be dead indeed to sin, but alive to God in Christ Jesus our Lord." The word *reckon* in the NKJV or *count* in the NIV is an accounting term. If accountants come and begin looking over the accounts of a company and discover the company is $857 short, they do not say, "Let's get on our knees and reckon them into existence." Accountants do not think that way. They live in total reality. If the money is not there, it is not there. If the money is there, it is there. They only deal with reality, because they can only reckon with what is there. The accounting term is used because these things are reality, although they do not actually manifest in the material world. They already exist in the realm of the spirit.

When Jesus talks about doing things in His name that is what He is talking about. You get into Him so that He becomes your new heredity. As a result, you draw your hereditary characteristics from your new family line, which is Father, Son, and Holy Spirit. This is so powerful, so practical, and so real. As a result, we are now living in the new genealogy of Jesus Christ. He is my brother, because we are from the same womb. He and I love the same Father.

Chapter 13 – The Power of the Cross

The same Father loves us equally. The glorious Holy Spirit is the mediator of all these incredible benefits. It is absolutely real. This becomes the most incredible reality you can live and enjoy.

14

SEATED TOGETHER WITH CHRIST

In his writings, Paul mentions the following phrases more than eighty times: *together with Him, in Him, in Christ, in His name*. When this becomes reality in us then everything He is and has becomes ours. All that the Father has becomes equally mine. This is not some pretending game, but it is utter reality. Jesus is not ashamed to call me brother, because that is exactly what I am. I am as much from above as He is. I am as much God's son as He is. I have the same access to the Father by the same Spirit that He has. John said, "As He is so are we in this world" (1 John 4:17). This truth is all over the Bible. It is so staggering and so gloriously true. If this really explodes in us, then it will change everything!

We needed to establish the law of heredity before digging deeper into Ephesians 2. Many things will start to click in your spirit when you understand the power of the cross and the law of heredity while reading this chapter. Let's start in Ephesians 2:1:

> And you, He made alive, who were dead in trespasses and sins, in which you once walked according to the course of this world,

Section 4 – Ephesians Chapter 2

> according to the prince of the power of the air, the spirit who now works in the sons of disobedience (Ephesians 2:1–2).

If you let the world push you into its mold, then it is really the devil that is manipulating your life. He still exercises authority in that system, which lives in defiance to God and His Kingdom. That is how I would identify the world. It is that system which defies the rule and government of God. We are to love the world in a redemptive way, but not its rewards, attitudes, and values. If you love the world, you love the devil. It is that simple. Paul continues:

> Among whom also we all once conducted ourselves in the lusts of our flesh, fulfilling the desires of the flesh and of the mind, and were by nature children of wrath, just as the others. *But God, who is rich in mercy, because of His great love with which He loved us, even when we were dead in trespasses, made us alive together with Christ (by grace you have been saved)* (Ephesians 2:3–4).

I want you to see the significance of verse 4 and the power of the word *but*. God's decision to show us the exceeding riches of His grace had nothing to do with how nice we were, because we were not. There was nothing we could do to earn it. God simply made a decision. He said, "I will love you to death, literally!" The result is that *you* (your old man) won't want to live anymore. Instead, you will want the full revelation of the risen Christ in you. God loved us to death.

In verse 5, these mysterious and important phrases begin to appear. God "made us alive together with Christ." This is where our understanding of the law of heredity becomes absolutely necessary. He continues in verse 6, "*And raised us up together, and made us sit together in the heavenly places in Christ Jesus.*" This verse takes us back to Ephesians 1:20, where we read that Christ was gloriously raised from the dead and was immediately seated at the right hand

Chapter 14 – Seated Together with Christ

of God in heavenly places far above all rule, authority, and dominion. Here is the great truth we must understand.

The pattern for the book of Ephesians is the same pattern as the book of Hebrews. When the letter to the Hebrews was written, the church was under severe persecution. They were in danger of turning back. The writer to the Hebrews wrote that letter to steady them in a time of great persecution under the Emperor Nero. The methodology was to set out in chapter 1 the glorious revelation of who Christ is. In chapter 2, he gave a glorious revelation of who we are in Him. We cannot see who we are in Him until we see who He is in us. We cannot see the full glory of what God has made you until you see the full glory of what God has made Him.

I still remember my revelation of Christ in Mumbai, India, back in 1965, just after my baptism in the Holy Spirit. Paul's prayer in Ephesians 1 became reality in me. I didn't receive a vision, but I had a revelation in my spirit, and I saw the glory, power, and majesty of our Lord Jesus Christ. It was suddenly offensive to me that these demons dared to defy Him and His Kingdom. That is when I got angry for the first time for the right reasons. I was indignant on behalf of Christ that He was being prevented from coming into His inheritance. I wanted to work with Him to see it happen. After seeing Him in all of His majesty, the next step was to see what I was made to be in Him.

This is why we must see the flow of this letter to the Ephesians. In Hebrews 2, we are shown all the things that Jesus has brought us into by being in Him. We have the same flow and intention here in Ephesians, The first thing we are told is that, having been raised together with Christ, we now sit with Him in heavenly places. Again, the Greek word *kathizo* is used. *Kathizo* means to sit down comfortably as if you feel and know you belong there. You must have a sense of knowing that you rightfully belong there.

Section 4 – Ephesians Chapter 2

If you sit there nervously, thinking, "I'm not supposed to be here," then you cannot exercise your proper authority, and you have not understood the revelation.

Remember that this is all "risen" revelation. This is greater than anything Jesus was during the days of His flesh. I know this might cause some to gasp, but this is completely biblical. We are greater in Him in His resurrection than He was in the limitations of His flesh during His thirty-three and a half years on the earth. That is why He said, "When you get this, the works I do, you will do, and even greater works than these you will do" (see John 14:12). It is not us, but we are the vehicle for the power of almighty God just as Jesus was. He never claimed that the works were His, but He said the Father was working through Him.

We must see that we are not like Him as He was on earth, but we are like Him as He is in heaven. We are not with Him on earth, but we are with Him in heaven. This is a rule, a throne, with incredible power and authority. We are seated with Him comfortably, sure of what we have been called to be. We are here to exercise rule, government, and authority. You must learn to sit with Christ first. Only then can you move into the right kind of powerful activity. You must be absolutely sure of your position in Christ. We have been made to *kathizo* with Him.

Paul continued:

> And raised us up together, and made us sit together in the heavenly places in Christ Jesus, that in the ages to come He might show the exceeding riches of His grace in His kindness to us in Christ Jesus. For by grace you have been saved through faith, and that not of yourselves; it is the gift of God, not by works, lest anyone should boast (Ephesians 2:6–9).

The purpose of my salvation is that I am delivered from the bondage of sin and the Adamic nature, over which Satan has always exercised power and control. But in the new risen Christ, Satan has no access to me whatsoever. He was never able to touch the risen Christ and never will. In Him we are as impregnable to the devil as the risen Christ is. The secret is to stay in Him. This is a process we must learn. I have a whole series on the book of Romans where I teach the process of learning to live by the Spirit in great detail. I am raised with Him. I am seated with Him. I am called to reign with Him.

The Law of Life in Christ Jesus

At the end of Romans 7 and into Romans 8, Paul began to talk about laws in the scientific sense. The Bible talks about *law* in three ways. First, it speaks about law as a principle. For example, you can say, "I believe in law and order" or "I believe in anarchy." *Law* is used here as a principle.

Second, the Bible uses *law* to describe the package of rules which were put together by Moses and added to extensively by the scribes and Pharisees. The scribes and Pharisees put a burden on people that almost killed them. This is what it means when the New Testament refers to the "the Law." The Jews decreed these rules and regulations were necessary to make you right with God.

Third, *law* was used in the sense of a scientific principle. We have already talked about the law of heredity in this sense. It is also like the law of gravity. It works for anyone, anywhere, anytime. You can jump off a building anywhere in the world, and you will accelerate to the ground at a predictable speed because the law of gravity is always working. It does not matter whether you are American, Chinese, German, or Indian. The law works the same regardless of your nationality, gender, intelligence, age, or size. You can even leap off a building screaming, "I don't believe in gravity!"

Section 4 – Ephesians Chapter 2

To your surprise, the law still works. There are laws in the spirit that work in the same way.

If you believe and see that you are saved by grace through faith, then you are brought into the throne life. The whole purpose of being saved is to bring you into the throne life. The purpose of being saved is not that you should escape an eternity in hell, but God wants to bring you into a total relationship with Him, exercising rule and government together with Him. But you must learn how to walk in the Spirit.

Romans 8 tells us that there is a law called the *law of the Spirit of life in Christ Jesus*. This law sets us free from the law of sin and death. Both of these laws are spiritual laws in the scientific sense. They work for anybody, anywhere, anytime. We are told in that passage that if we try and live in the flesh, even when our flesh has become religious and is trying to live a holy life by not trying to sin, then we will discover ourselves being pulled down by sin into defeat.

In Romans 7:15–24, Paul uses the pronoun I more than thirty times. He says:

> For what I am doing, I do not understand. For what I will to do, that I do not practice; but what I hate, that I do (Romans 7:15).

Paul found a principle working within him called the law of sin and death. When he tried to change his life by his own power, it did not lead to liberty but to death. You cannot change yourself by the power of independent self, because it was the power of independent self that put you into sin in the first place. This is a totally futile exercise. You cannot save yourself by yourself because it was being yourself, rather than being submitted to God, that brought you into the bondage of sin in the first place. The only thing you can do is stop trying to do it yourself and let a new power take hold of you.

In the history of aerodynamics, we find a perfect illustration of what we are talking about. The French in particular seemed determined to conquer gravity. They made all kinds of weird flying machines. They were so confident that it would work that one man stood on the Eiffel Tower. He jumped off, flapping furiously, and crashed to the ground. He was killed by the law of gravity. The weakness of such effort is found in the fact that people try to conquer gravity *in their own strength*. When they attempted to conquer the pull of gravity in their own effort, they always ended in defeat.

One day they discovered the first law of aerodynamics. The first law of aerodynamics says that a flow of air passing over a curved surface creates what is called lift. The curved surface will lift against gravity simply by the passing of the air. As air flows across the top of a curved surface, it creates a partial vacuum underneath called lift. This is how modern day jet aircraft fly. They have learned to exploit the power of the wind. When man discovered the first law of aerodynamics, he stopped trying to defeat gravity by his own effort and learned to exploit the wind. He learned he could fly with no effort of his own.

Today we can enter an incredible jumbo jet that weighs hundreds of tons and sit comfortably while we are flown from London to Cape Town. We can even guarantee the day and exact time of our arrival. There is no sudden moment when an announcement is made, "All flights are cancelled, because somehow things are not running as normal. The law of aerodynamics is not working." It is never like that. If you jump off a building anytime, anywhere, you will always crash to the ground. The law of gravity never has a day off. No one is insulated from it. But the secret to overcoming its power is to get in the plane and stay there.

Section 4 – Ephesians Chapter 2

The Secret Is *In Christ*

When a plane takes off, it is exploiting a superior law, the law of aerodynamics. It looks to us like the law of gravity ceases to work. But if you open the door of the plane, you will soon find out that the law of gravity is still working. It is only when you are in the plane that the law of gravity has no power over you. Get out of the plane, and it will pull you down just as relentlessly as it ever did. This is why it says, in Romans 8:1–3, that through Christ Jesus the law of the Spirit of life set me free from the law of sin and death. It is in Christ Jesus that the law of sin and death ceases to pull me down. If you step out of Jesus Christ, you are defeated by sin and death just as before. You will never ever make it on your own, not even for five seconds.

If you have been a Christian for fifty years and lived in victory over sin for fifty years, it is because you have stayed in the plane. If you get out of the plane in your fifty-first year, you will be as defeated by sin as you ever were. The key is to stay in Christ Jesus. *In Christ Jesus*, He bears you. You are in Him. You can fly above gravity's pull only when you are in Him. I hope you understand what it means to be in Him. This is a hereditary thing. The mystery, however, also includes our choice. You must choose. That is why it says, in Romans 8:1, that we must learn first not to walk in the flesh before we can walk in the Spirit.

We are so used to running our own lives, so accustomed to doing our own thing, so used to making our own decisions that we don't even realize we are doing it. We must learn to be passive in our lives so that Jesus can live His life in us. This is a learned quality. When you decide to do this, you experience longer and longer periods of not walking after the flesh, and as a result, you can walk in the Spirit. This is always in Christ Jesus. It is not in you or of you. Your humanity can never defeat sin or exist alone. You must be in Christ Jesus. Then He will give you victory.

Good Works Are *In Him*

In Ephesians 2:8–10, it says:

> For by grace you have been saved through faith, and that not of yourselves; it is the gift of God, not of works, lest anyone should boast. For we are His workmanship, created *in Christ Jesus* for good works, which God prepared beforehand that we should walk in them.

Almost every other phrase includes "in Christ Jesus." This is not just flowery language, but a fundamental principle of spiritual life. We were created in Christ Jesus to do good works, which God prepared in advance for us to do. Even good works are not our own, but they are His good works. There is no room for boasting in anything. It is all from Him, for Him, to Him, and through Him.

This is how we walk in victory. This is how we rule from the throne. We must know this as a reality. That is why it says in Galatians 3:27, "For as many of you as were *baptized into Christ* have *put on Christ*." The phrase *put on* is the Greek word *enduo*. This word is very hard to translate into English. It takes a whole phrase to explain it. The idea of *enduo* is that you sink down into something. What you sink down into comes all over you, becomes intrinsically part of you, so that what you sank down into becomes indivisibly one with you. You are no longer separable. That is what it means to put on Christ.

We are told later in the book of Ephesians to *put on* the whole armor of God. We are to *put on* righteousness. We are to *put on* the new man. Every time a *put on* is mentioned, the Greek word *enduo* is used. You sink down into Christ in such a way that He is intrinsically part of you. It becomes like your skin. You can't take it off because it is you. You don't know anymore where Christ begins and where you end or start. You don't even need to know! Your life has been swallowed up in His.

Section 4 – Ephesians Chapter 2

If possible, I believe in teaching these things for people when they are being baptized. I say, "When we go to the act of baptism, I believe something will happen in the spirit realm that will hit you like a ton of bricks. You will never be the same again." I don't believe baptism is just an outward sign of a change of heart. I believe a change often takes place in the very act of baptism. I believe there is a mystery about baptism that we have lost. We've made it a dead old routine when it should be a powerful experience when people leave behind the old man. They walk out of the water, and the old man is left behind forever. I have seen habitual smokers walk out of a pool totally released from that bondage because they were rightly prepared for the act of baptism. I have seen people physically healed and many other miracles. We need to restore this powerful truth to the church.

15

TWO BECOME ONE

While I may be a proud religious Jew after my Adamic nature, there is no such thing in the resurrection. In Christ, there is neither Jew nor gentile. Outside of Christ, these distinctions exist, but in Christ they are wiped away in the reality of the new man after which we are created. In Christ, there is neither slave nor free, neither male nor female. This is all in Christ.

In Ephesians 2:11–12, it says:

> Therefore remember that you, once Gentiles in the flesh–who are called Uncircumcision by what is called the Circumcision made in the flesh by hands–that at that time you were without Christ, being aliens from the commonwealth of Israel and strangers from the covenants of the promise, having no hope and without God in the world.

Imagine that a bus is driving along with fifteen gentiles and twelve Jews inside. These two groups were at war with one another. Imagine the bus has an accident, and they are all killed. They lay the bodies out in the morgue. These bodies are not at all fussy about who is next to them when they are dead. They don't even know or care about these things.

Section 4 – Ephesians Chapter 2

In Adam it is a big issue, but in Christ it cannot be. It is life from the other side of the grave.

The moment we begin to understand what it means to be in Christ, we must tackle the issue of true unity. True unity is much deeper than trying to do a few things together. As Paul says in Ephesians 3:1–6:

> For this reason I, Paul, the prisoner of Christ Jesus for you Gentiles–if indeed you have heard of the dispensation of the grace of God which was given to me for you, how that by revelation He made known to me the mystery (as I have briefly written already, by which, when you read, you may understand my knowledge in the mystery of Christ), which in other ages was not made known to the sons of men, as it has now been revealed by the Spirit to His holy apostles and prophets: that the Gentiles should be fellow heirs, of the same body, and partakers of His promise in Christ through the gospel.

When you see the phrase, *for this reason* or *therefore*, the apostle is referring to what has been said before. He was talking about the power of the cross to bring about perfect peace. Perfect peace is the complete reconciliation of those who were separated and at enmity with each other. There were walls and resentments, rules and regulations that separated two parties. All that has been broken down and the two have become one new man. The phrase *fellow heirs* joins two words for inheritance and fellowship. We are joined together in a common life for a common purpose in order to receive a common inheritance. This would be a good translation of *fellow heirs*.

We have a long way to go in learning to walk this out. I believe a time is coming when God will do a mighty work among Jewish people. They will be powerfully gathered in to the church. Currently, it is a tragedy when Jewish people come into the church. They should be rejoicing in their Jewish roots, including their founders like Abraham, Moses, and Jesus.

Yet, in the church there is nothing left for them to identify with. The church has become so gentile through the Jewish period of blindness that when they try to come back in, there is nothing there they would be attracted to.

I am not saying the church should become Jewish. But the emphasis in Ephesians 2:12 and 3:6 is that the gentiles have the privilege of coming in and being an equal member of the commonwealth of Israel, equally grafted into the same root of Abraham, equally having the same glorious heritage and access the Jews should have had if only they would have believed in Jesus. Those roots are not annihilated because of their unbelief. When I saw this, it really hit me. I thought, "How easy would it be for a Jew to come into a church I attend or one that I have planted?" I concluded that it would be very difficult for them. I believe I need to do something about this.

We now have separate Messianic fellowships around the world in order to give these people some sense of identity and belonging. I believe we have lost something in this dynamic. I am not saying we must get on the Jewish bandwagon and begin wearing Jewish clothing, singing Jewish songs, and learning Hebrew. That is not what I am saying. But I see Paul speaking to the gentiles an important message. Paul is saying to them, "When you were in Adam, you were all these things, but now you are in Christ. You have been brought in as equals, joyfully gathered to the commonwealth of Israel. You are now the beneficiaries of the covenant and the promises given to Abraham. When you were outside, you had no hope, and you were without God in the world. But now, in Christ Jesus, you who were once far away have been brought near by the blood of Christ."

Section 4 – Ephesians Chapter 2

Being One in Christ

Then, in Ephesians 2:14–15, it says:

> For He Himself is our peace, who has made both one, and has broken down the middle wall of separation, having abolished in His flesh the enmity, that is, the law of commandments contained in ordinances, so as to create in Himself one new man from the two, thereby putting to death the enmity.

Let's come back to this word *peace* for a moment. The word *peace*, in its deep meaning, is fulfilled when two groups that were at enmity with each other, hating each other, lay down their arms and bring the war to an end. That is not biblical peace, but simply the end of the war. For biblical peace to be fulfilled, they must fall into each other's arms, really love each other, really enjoy each other, really want to be with each other and come into an intimate relationship with one another. This is what God wants with us. He wants us to be intimate with Him. He does not want us to be so conscious of our past that we live like we are just saved sinners, not going to hell, but without a life with Him. We read in Colossians 1:20 that God made peace through the blood of His cross. God was the innocent party in this dispute. Humanity was the totally guilty party. Humanity was the rebel. Humanity went away from God. Humanity created their own false religion to make themselves feel a little better. Humanity lived in constant defiance and disobedience to God. Even when God gathered together His own nation, Israel, it was still the most rebellious and disobedient people. In the end, God had to divorce them.

In the person of our Lord Jesus Christ, God came to deal with that Adamic nature that caused the strife and separation. When sin entered into Adam and Satan put his fingers on him, Adam became incompatible with God. He ended up hating the very God who loved him and created him. Humanity became an enemy of the very one who loved them and wanted fellowship with them.

The thing that amazes me is that God took the entire initiative to make peace. God revealed His love toward us in that while we were enemies He died on a cross to reconcile us. He did not wait for any response from us. He did not wait for us to want to heal the breach. Instead, He came to bring that mighty healing of the breach. It was that costly love that finally woke people up to love Him back. This is how it works. This is a pattern to be followed.

Peacemaking, Reconciliation, and a City-Taking Church

In Matthew 5:9 it says, "Blessed are the peacemakers, for they shall be called sons of God." There is something mature about peacemaking. You can be a child of God and a trouble maker at the same time. But if you are a mature, grown-up son of God, you must be a peacemaker. You have no choice. I want us to learn this lesson here. When you are raised to new life in Christ, you are now the peacemaker in Him. You so want reconciliation and peace that you are prepared to take the initiative to mend a breech, even if from your perspective the cause of the breech was completely the other person's responsibility.

I find again and again that the initiative for reconciliation is often from the person who was the offended party. Once you are raised with Christ, you can't chose the bits of Christ you like and leave the bits you don't like, "I want His power, but I don't want all this forgiveness stuff." This is impossible! You are either in Him or you are not in Him. You are either entirely what He is, or you are not at all what He is. There is no picking and choosing the pieces you like or think you need most.

In Ephesians 2:6, the declaration that we sit on a throne is followed, in the rest of the chapter, by a discussion of moving out in this costly way to be a peacemaker. Jesus took to the cross and put to death what was in those arrogant unsaved religious Jews. They went from place to place killing people because they would not conform to their doctrine.

Section 4 – Ephesians Chapter 2

One perfect example of this was the apostle Paul. By the time Paul received Christ, he was a murderer. He was out to murder anyone who was deviant from this precious Jewish religion, which he held to be the only truth.

Then he received the revelation that the proud, arrogant, murdering Pharisee went down into the grave to never come up again. Instead, Paul became a new man who loved the lost and loved his own nation, even though they tried to kill him several times. The only response you get from Paul is found in Romans 9:2–4, where he says, "I have great sorrow and continual grief in my heart. For I wish that I myself were accursed from Christ for my brethren, my countrymen according to the flesh, who are Israelites...."

Paul was a peacemaker. He went to the gentiles, to the terrible, blaspheming, dark, demonic, and wicked Thessalonians who worshipped idols and danced before demons. He went into that hell hole and snatched them out of the darkness to turn them into the most marvelous jewels that the church had ever seen. This is the ministry of reconciliation. I want us to comprehend this, because if it is not in us, then we will not produce a city-taking church.

Come back to Ephesians 2:14–15:

> For He Himself is our peace, who has made both one and has broken down the middle wall of separation, having abolished in His flesh the enmity, that is, *the law of commandments contained in ordinances...*

This is what makes the difference. In many cases, if anyone wants to relate to you, then they must adjust to your standards. I lived in India for fourteen years. I did not live in a white missionary bungalow, but I lived right in the middle of the darkest heathen parts of Mumbai. I didn't see another white face for months at a time.

Chapter 15 – Two Become One

I came to the point where I didn't even notice or care. I became thoroughly transformed culturally. Things I found offensive previously–things that Indians do that is very different from Western cultures–didn't bother me anymore.

The Jews said that a person could become a Jew by learning all the Jewish customs and laws. They must be circumcised and keep the law of Moses. Only then would they be received, yet they would still be considered a second class citizen. But at least they could then eat with such a person and have fellowship with him. But if someone didn't keep all the rules and regulations and obey the standards of what was considered pleasing to God, no fellowship was allowed. Therefore, an enmity existed between them, a dividing wall.

In many of our attempts at reconciliation, we are not prepared to yield up one particle of our culture. I hope this makes sense to you. In Christ Jesus, all these things went to death. The wall of partition with its rules and regulations was put to death. Most of the rules were not biblical. The majority were doctrinal or cultural. Some would say, "I can't fellowship with you because you have a different view of end-time events." That is what some Christians say. Others jump to quick conclusions after hearing you teach once and label you as a certain kind of Christian. We set boundaries and requirements of conduct. There are certain doctrinal beliefs that are a prerequisite for having fellowship. If we have a prayer meeting, then you must do it our way.

You can go to all kinds of churches around the world, and within the perimeters of certain basic truths, there are differences of doctrine and culture, and yet you find Jesus perfectly happy in the midst of them. I've been to Venezuela, and the women will grab you and take you into a swirling dance with nothing improper about it. If you are a respectable Englishmen, that is quite a challenge. You are swept away by an enthusiastic Hispanic woman while she embraces and kisses you.

Section 4 – Ephesians Chapter 2

Once you get over the shock of it, you realize how fantastic it is. Is Jesus there? Absolutely!

I've been to rural Africa, and these people are amazing. They know things about God and His ways that we know nothing about. I said, "Please teach me. I am a stupid, intellectual white man. Something happened to my mind. Please pray for me. Instruct me!" The men and women in Nigeria, Uganda, and other African countries are so sensitive in the spirit realm. Many have a way with God that is totally beyond our realm of experience.

Years ago, we were crying out to God for a change in London. God sent many Africans who are mighty in prayer, dedicated and persistent. They knew how to deal with the demons and clear the atmosphere. I was told by these faithful praying people, "God spoke to us to come to England in order to pay our debts. One hundred and fifty years ago, young people from the evangelical awakening in Europe came to our shores and died. Their life expectancy was between one and two years. They died of every kind of sickness and disease. These young people risked their lives to bring the gospel in order to give us life. In our nation, we are reaping a mighty harvest as a result of what they sowed one hundred years ago. We have come back to England to say thank you and to pay our debts.

I have learned to hate the little boxes of our impenetrable ethnicity as much as God does. If the apostle Paul had not received this revelation, we would have had separate Jewish and gentile churches from day one. I don't think we would have taken any cities in the New Testament, because a house divided against itself cannot stand. God is not going to save a city through the white church or through the African American church, but He will save it through *the one church* of Jesus Christ.

It is one thing to have nice, polite reconciliation meetings where we wash the feet of our dear brother and then after that we don't see one another for another year until there is another event. This is not what we are talking about. We are talking about making two groups into one. I believe that when this thing cracks, it will be the major breakthrough that gives us the city. Until it cracks, we will not take the city. You can go to Argentina as often as you like. You can visit many of the hot spots around the world and see what works there. But you cannot bring it back to a divided church and expect it to work effectively.

Having said this, you must not fall off the log on the other side. Some would say that we cannot do anything until we have total unity. That is not true. In the hearts of those God will use for His purpose, there must be a heart that is as wide as the city. It must be willing to receive love and embrace anyone. But you cannot wait for everyone to get on board, because you will wait forever. This is the balance between these truths. If your heart is wide open and you are a peacemaker, doing what you can to bring reconciliation, then you will see this thing develop.

Jesus abolished the enmity in His flesh. In the flesh of Jesus, the enmity was taken in the Adamic nature down to hell, never to return. He took all this junk upon Himself, into His flesh, and put it to death. Then He created in Himself one new man from the two, thus making peace. If any ethnicity is raised in Christ, it must be of the Kingdom. What we are ethnically that causes division can no longer continue in the resurrection. There is only one new man in Christ. In Christ, there is neither Jew nor Greek. There is no ethnicity and no gender. There is no social status. All that stuff is dead in Christ!

In real peacemaking, the person who has been wounded and offended is often moved by Christ to take the initiative to mend the breech.

Section 4 – Ephesians Chapter 2

I believe our precious African American brothers need to hear this when I speak. If you go and forgive white people for all they have done to black people, without waiting for them to say sorry, God will release something so supernatural and amazing that it will break millions of hard hearts. It will melt them. If they say, "We want our rights…," something else will be released that will only thicken the walls of partition.

I understand the anger. It has been a learning experience for me to live in San Antonio, Texas. I have read the history, and I was shocked at some of the brutal and wicked events in this nation. I am absolutely ashamed to have the same color skin as those who perpetrated those injustices and cruelties. I can understand the offense and difficulty of those who were abused by land grabbing, greedy, money-making men. If you are Caucasian like me, then we have much to ask God for in forgiveness. We cannot stand on some proud pinnacle, because we are disgusting in Adam, but in Christ we are a new creation. We must also be received in the same way by the offended parties.

In so much peacemaking, when Christ gets hold of a man, and he is really raised with Christ and the old Adamic nature is put to death with all of its prejudices, resentments, and offenses, then that person becomes the tool in God's hand for transformation. When the person who had the most right to say, "I'll do something when they say they are sorry," instead humbles himself and goes to make the first move, it is so endorsed by God and so crushingly powerful that it removes all dividing walls. No one can resist the power of such an act.

When this great unity comes we will see something powerful come out of it. Ephesians 2:18–22 continues:

> For through Him we both have access by one Spirit to the Father. Now, therefore, you are no longer strangers and foreigners, but fellow citizens with the saints and members of the household of God, having been built on the foundation of the apostles and prophets, Jesus Christ Himself being the chief cornerstone, in whom the whole building, being fitted together, grows into a holy temple in the Lord, in whom you also are being built together for a dwelling place of God in the Spirit.

When the apostles and prophets are foundationally laying these truths, it causes the whole church to get on board. Many talk about the foundation of apostle and prophets and are very confused. We are talking about reconciliation. This is the first layer that is laid on this house that God is building, which will take our cities for God. The first layer of stones must be a layer that makes us one in Christ. A house divided against itself will not take a city.

I hope you can feel the pain in my heart, because I am apostolic. I can see these things. If you are prophetic, you can also see these things. You see this as a matter of first priority. You say, "We have to get to work on these matters." We cannot be a nice Caucasian or African American church that attends the annual reconciliation meeting and then returns to our setting to keep doing our own thing. We cannot live like that anymore. I believe apostolic and prophetic ministry must lead the way in these things if it is truly foundational.

Once again, we all end up with a deeper appreciation for our Jewish heritage. I want to be very sensitive and helpful for the Jewish people to come into the Israel of God. This is a multiracial people for God. We are one household made up of people from every tribe, tongue, and nation. Paul said the whole building is being fitted together and growing into a holy temple in the Lord. He concluded, "You also are being built together for a dwelling place of God in the Spirit."

Section 4 – Ephesians Chapter 2

When we build this kind of church, the Spirit of God can come and live powerfully within and among us. This is a church that will shake a city and fill it with the Kingdom of God.

SECTION 5
Ephesians Chapter 3

16

BIBLICAL MYSTERIES

I want to talk to you about Bible mysteries—what they are and how, why, and to whom they are revealed. We have seen already that apostles and prophets have a particular responsibility as foundation layers. Another reason we must have the apostolic and prophetic ministries flowing is that they are the ones God has chosen to give access to the mysteries of Christ. Therefore, I want us to look at what a Bible mystery is and how it works. I also want us to learn what some of those mysteries are.

In Ephesians, we saw that Paul concentrated on the mystery of how the Jews and gentiles fit together. That was a particular revelation that Paul had. Even Peter did not fully understand that mystery. This was especially true when the pressure was on, and he separated himself from the gentile brethren and went back to acting like a Jew. Paul confronted him, saying, "Yesterday you were eating pork chops, but today you have retreated to kosher food. What is this all about? What hypocrisy are you playing?" Jewish brethren had come from Jerusalem, and Peter was not prepared to be unashamedly the new creation in Christ, which is neither Jew nor gentile. It seems then that only the apostle Paul was living in the power of that revelation.

Section 5 – Ephesians Chapter 3

In Matthew 13 and Mark 4, we see how Jesus dealt with the matter of mysteries. In the first few verses of Matthew 13, which is the great chapter on parables of the Kingdom, Jesus teaches the parable of the sower. This parable appears in Mark 4 and Luke 8 as well. It is the only parable that appears in all three synoptic gospels. I want us to hear what this parable is saying. Having spoken the parable, Jesus said, "He who has ears to hear, let him hear" (Matt. 13:9). If you go through all three synoptic gospels, then you will find that Jesus said something like this no less than eighteen times: "He who has ears to hear, let him hear."

His disciples then came to Jesus and said, "Why do you speak to them [the people] in parables?" (Matt. 13:10). Jesus replied, "Because it has been given to you to know the mysteries of the kingdom of heaven, but to them it has not been given" (Matt. 13:11). Jesus divided all His hearers into two categories–the *you* category and the *them* category. We need to cry out that we do not end up in the *them* group, but in the *you* group.

Many people listened to the same preacher teach the same things – even the Son of God – and one group received nothing from it, and another group had fire burning inside them. The reason for this division is that God decided in one case to grant them understanding, but in the other case to not grant them understanding of the mysteries. You would agree with me that it is important that we end up on the right side of the line. He also said:

> For whoever has, to him more will be given, and he will have abundance; but whoever does not have, even what he has will be taken from him. Therefore I speak to them in parables...But blessed are your eyes for they see, and your ears for they hear. For assuredly, I say to you, many prophets and righteous men desired to see what you see, and did not see it, and to hear what you hear, and did not hear it (Matthew 13:12–13, 16–17).

We must see that the mysteries revealed are not only a matter of attitude, but also a matter of timing. There was nothing wrong with the prophet's hunger. In fact, even the angels longed to look into these things, but they were not permitted to see. We must have the right attitude at the right time in order to become someone to whom God reveals mysteries.

If we are considered worthy to have that revelation given to us, then we must respond correctly. How we handle the first revelation will determine how much more we will receive. If we handle it correctly, then we will receive much more, and we will have abundance. If we handle it incorrectly, then even what we have will be taken away from us. This ought to scare the pants off of us. Our attitude and timing will determine the depth of revelation we receive.

In Mark 4 we find a list of qualities that help determine which category we will belong to. The disciples had asked Jesus questions about the parable of the Kingdom. Then Jesus said to them, "Do you not understand this parable? How then will you understand all the parables?" (Mark 4:13). In other words, Jesus said that understanding this parable is the key to understanding all the other parables. We tend to put this parable into Sunday school class category, but this parable is one of the most profound things Jesus ever said. This is not a Sunday school kids exercise; there is something incredibly deep and important here. Understanding this parable will determine how much of the revelation of Jesus we are able to receive. He said, "If you do not understand this parable, then how will you understand any parable?"

Then, it says in Mark 4:33, "And with many such parables He spoke the word to them as they were able to hear it." Jesus spoke the parables because they were able to hear them. He spoke many parables to them, because they had a mindset or spiritual attitude such that the word was getting into them. He said, "OK, I will give you more...."

Section 5 – Ephesians Chapter 3

Then, in verse 34, it continues, "But without a parable He did not speak to them. And when they were alone, He explained all things to His disciples." It was the deliberate policy of the Lord Jesus Christ to teach everything He taught in parables. He deliberately intended to divide between those who were going to hear and those who would not hear.

What is a parable? A parable is a story with a deeper spiritual meaning. Every parable has a surface meaning, but underneath are much deeper spiritual meanings. The Lord frequently uses allegory, meaning that certain things in the parable represent clear spiritual truths or principles. Certain images and allegories are consistently used throughout scripture. Until the Lord reveals to you what these things mean, you will remain shut out from the mysteries of the Kingdom. No matter how intelligent you are or how much you learn the original languages or how much information you have about the Bible, you are absolutely stuck unless God decides to reveal the mysteries to you. But if He decides to reveal it to you, then He will give you keys. Then you must be teachable and open to what He wants you to see.

When I began to see these things, I found that being a teacher of the word is very different than teaching chemistry. I was a successful chemistry teacher for years. To be a good chemistry lecturer, you must know your subject. Unless you go into a temporary amnesia, you don't forget what you have taught. But when it comes to the revelation of God, I can teach something with tremendous revelation one month, but when I come to the same subject again, I am as dependent on God this time as before. It would be as if I never taught the subject before. You cannot carry these things in your intellect, because these things can only come to you by the Spirit.

I am totally dependent on God every time I teach. But even then, as the words come out of my mouth, however much they are the word of God, something is required to happen in the hearts of the hearer or the eyes of the seers. Both of these analogies are used in scripture. I do not believe there is any difference between seeing the scripture or hearing the scripture in that biblical sense. We are not talking about physical ears and eyes, but spiritual ears and eyes. Sometimes what you have heard or seen in the Spirit you cannot even put into words. You cannot even explain it, because your intellect has not yet caught up with what your spirit has received.

I struggled with a very serious physical condition from which I nearly died on several occasions. This condition occurred before I went to India. It was the reason we were turned down as missionary candidates by every missionary society. Nonetheless, God told us to go. Therefore, when I boarded the boat for India, I expected to be miraculously healed. But I was not healed until twelve years later. I struggled with this disability and nearly died several times. In the seventh year of my disability, something important happened to me. I had already been baptized in the Holy Spirit. I started to read works from men like Smith Wigglesworth. In the circles I was in at that time, that was like reading soft porn. I kept the books in a brown paper bag so that no one would know what I was reading.

I read the book called *Ever Increasing Faith*, which tells the story of a woman who had a goiter on her neck. Smith Wigglesworth conducted annual meetings for healing where this woman came for healing. Each time she praised God for her healing. She would stand up and testify how God had gloriously healed her. She did this one year, and then the next, and then the next. The only problem was that the goiter was still there as big as ever.

Section 5 – Ephesians Chapter 3

Finally at the annual conference she stood up again and said, "I want to thank God that He has completely healed me, and I am praising Him for this wonderful healing miracle." The goiter was as large as ever on her neck that everyone could see. Finally, the people couldn't stand it any longer, and they said, "Woman, you are living in a dreamland. You are crazy. The goiter is on your neck, and it is as big as ever!"

She didn't defend herself or fight back. Instead, she went to her room and said, "Lord, I don't need the physical miracle, because I know you have already healed me, but there are many people who need the physical sign. I know you healed me three years ago, but they can't believe it until they see the physical evidence. Would you please remove this goiter physically to help these people believe? I don't need it, but they do!" When the woman finished praying, the goiter instantly disappeared. She walked back to the meeting and said, "Listen, everyone! The goiter is gone. You needed this, but I didn't."

When I read this story, my scientific mind was trying to grapple with it. I came to the place, however, where I knew I had been healed. I was told by the Spirit to first testify to my wife and family and then to the church. The Lord told me that the symptoms will continue for some time, but I would be trained in the ways of a man of God. I was testifying like this crazy woman, and yet in my spirit it all made sense. My condition continued for five more years.

I had violent hemorrhages from an arterial capillary from the back of my nose. It didn't just bleed, but spurt blood everywhere. If I couldn't stop it, I could easily lose three or four pints of blood in one hour. At times I thought I would bleed to death. It was very difficult to get to the hemorrhage site in order to stop the bleeding. Several times I went unconscious on the bathroom floor while Eileen frantically stuffed my nose with gauze in order to stop the bleeding. My fight with death was very close on a few occasions.

I lived like that for twelve years. I learned things from God that are beyond the realm of reason and rationalism. I kept testifying to my healing even though nothing was visible.

Please do not lie about symptoms. You don't have to pretend that something has happened when it hasn't. My clothes were drenched with blood, but I knew I had been healed. I requested people to please not ask me to explain what I was saying. I couldn't explain it. I knew I was healed, although I was still waiting for the complete physical manifestation.

It reached the point when Hindu friends of mine who were very loving and fond of me couldn't bear to see me suffer in this way. They said, "We have tremendous power in Ayurvedic medicine." This is a form of homeopathy mixed with witchcraft and other occultic activity. They said to me, "If you come to see one of our healers, then I know you will be healed." Then they said, "Your Jesus doesn't seem to be doing very much for you."

My response was very forthright, "I deeply appreciate your loving concern for me. I understand what you are saying to me, and I really do appreciate your love and concern. But I just want to make something clear. I know that in the spirit realm I have already been healed. I would rather die believing in Jesus then have the physical manifestation come by the instrument of a demon. I would rather die believing in Jesus then be healed by the devil."

Somehow, when I said those words, something was settled in the spirit. As a result of that statement, my physical healing manifested. As you can now see, I am a fine physical specimen of a man. In those days, my weight went down to 130 pounds. I was skin and bone, because my blood was running out just as fast as I could put nourishment into me. I could hardly stand up to preach. I couldn't carry anything, and sometimes I had to be carried. Eileen bore the brunt of that burden all those years.

Section 5 – Ephesians Chapter 3

These were very difficult years, but we learned things we couldn't learn any other way. I have learned that my spirit can grab hold of things that my mind cannot comprehend. I had revelation which helped me enormously in great spiritual battles I was engaged in. I can grab hold of a city and know it is saved and transformed before anything visible begins to happen.

I came to faith for the city of Mumbai, and that city is being transformed. I came to faith for the city of London in 1980, and that city is being transformed. God moved us to San Antonio, and it took some time before coming to faith for that city, but it has happened. I know that something incredible will break forth in that city, and I believe it is soon to happen. I know God will do something fantastic in the United States of America. It is not just hoping, because I have grabbed something in the spirit that I cannot easily explain to you in words.

There is a revelation that comes which is beyond your rational mind and physical senses. When you see and hear the word, it allows you to come to faith for many things. The two are so connected that you cannot separate them. How does faith come? Faith comes by hearing and hearing the specific spoken word of God (see Rom. 10:17). We are not hearing with our physical ears, but with spiritual ears. When you have heard God say it, and you have the attitude that does not regard His speaking lightly, then it becomes faith to you.

Hearing with Certain Attitudes

If you will be the kind of person who hears, then you must possess certain attitudes. *First, you must have a child-like attitude toward the word of God.* This does not mean you abandon your intellect. Child-like simplicity is different than being intelligent. In fact, you can be quite unintelligent and stubbornly refuse to receive the word of God. You can be brilliant intellectually, like the apostle Paul, and yet maintain a child-like attitude that easily welcomes the word of truth.

Two of the greatest research workers that I am aware of in the field of leukemia are two great men of God in Cambridge, England. They are working at the Cambridge University research department, and they are Spirit-filled men of God who get on their knees and seek the face of God for revelation on how to beat this devilish disease that is killing so many children. They battle in the spirit realm. They travail in prayer on how to get revelation from God so as to beat this disease. Then they put their leads into medical practice. They are brilliant in the medical realm, yet they have maintained a child-like attitude toward God and His word.

This is not intellect verses childlikeness. You can be brilliant and still have this attitude, or you can be very unintelligent and have the wrong attitude. Childlikeness is the willingness to trust your Father. It means saying, "I will receive what He says, and then afterwards I will process it through my understanding. But I will not hinder Him speaking to me by making it first fit through my understanding." Of course we want to understand God's things intellectually, and we want to be able to teach it intelligibly, but that is not the way we receive the revelation. We receive revelation through childlike openness. Then the revelation is processed through other faculties of understanding and reason. Finally, you can put it into communication in order to pass it on to others.

The second quality important for hearing is hunger for the word of God. Up until the point I received Christ, my grandmother gave me a New Testament every Christmas. I used to take them and throw them away in the trash. I am so ashamed to say that now, but that is exactly what I did. I said, "I don't want to read that silly old Christian book."

When I received Christ, it was just before the long summer vacation for British university lecturers. I was saved on July 3, and I didn't return to work until October. Exams had just been completed, so it was a perfect time for God to save me.

My wife went off to work every day, and I opened her Bible to read. I read it from cover to cover during that vacation.

During my reading, I had another encounter with God where He rewired my mind to think in this childlike way I am trying to explain to you. I made a decision to have a childlike acceptance regarding whatever the scripture says. I became hungry for the word of God. It was a supernatural gift. I read it as soon as Eileen went out the door. I read it until she came back in the evening. I made notes of various things while reading. I have been like that ever since. I read the Bible right through several times a year, as well as when making preparation for ministry. I keep both quite separate. I have a regular reading program for me personally. What I have for ministry, I keep in a separate category. I believe that the word of God is absolutely incredible. I used to throw it away, but now I am totally changed.

Closely associated with this kind of hunger is another attitude called value. My question to you is: *What valuation do you place on the word of God?* In Mark 4:22, it says, "For there is hidden which will not be revealed, nor has anything been kept secret but that it should come to light." Before Jesus comes again, there will not be any unrevealed mysteries. This is how I understand the scriptures. There is nothing hidden that will not be revealed. Even though I have read through the Bible more than one hundred times, there are still many things that we do not understand. I put such things on the back burner, but one day God will show me. More and more of the locked things are becoming unlocked. But there will come a day when nothing will be hidden. Everything will be revealed, not because we are a special generation, but because we are in a generation when it has pleased God to reveal everything.

Then comes the statement we are familiar with:

> "If anyone has ears to hear, let him hear." Then He said to them, "Take heed what you hear. With the same measure you use, it will be measured to you; and to you who hear, more will be given. For whoever has, to him more will be given; but whoever does not have, even what he has will be taken away from him" (Mark 4:23–25).

If you put a one dollar valuation on a great truth of scripture, it will be measured back to you as a one dollar valuation. In other words, it will have that much of an effect in your life. If you put a one thousand dollar valuation on the truth, it will be measured back to you as a one thousand dollar word that will have a much larger transforming effect upon your life. You determine how powerfully and richly the word of God can work in you and how richly it can work through you. I decided to put a high valuation on the word of God and His truth spoken to me.

Your valuation of the word of God will determine the measure with which it will be measured to you. Two people sitting in the same room side by side, even a married couple in the same meeting, can have a totally different valuation of what the word of God does in their life. It is all decided by the valuation they put upon the word as it is given to them.

The final attitude is obedience. The purpose of having the word revealed to us is that we should obey. In John 15, Jesus said:

> If you keep My commandments, you will abide in My love, just as I have kept My Father's commandments and abide in His love.... You are My friends if you do whatever I command you" (John 15:10, 14).

Section 5 – Ephesians Chapter 3

He continued in John 15:15:

> No longer do I call you servants, for a servant does not know what his master is doing; but I have called you friends, for all things that I heard from My Father I have made known to you.

This is an incredible statement! The *you* category includes those who have this attitude. The *them* category includes those possessing the opposite of these values and attitudes. They are not hungry for the word of God. They do not value the word of God. They do not put a high price on it. They are not childlike and teachable. In fact, they will filter the word of God through their own minds.

You can find this attitude in a person or in a church. The Corinthian church had Paul resident with them for almost three years. But notice the way that church valued the word that came through the apostle when reading his two letters to them. Some said, "His letters are weighty and powerful, but his bodily presence is weak, and his speech contemptible" (2 Cor. 10:10). I give Paul's message on a scale from 1 to 10 a 6. Peter gets a 7, because he tells more funny stories." The Corinthian church marked every preacher and graded them by how much they received out of their preaching. As a result, that church was full of every kind of problem imaginable. The church was mean and not financially prosperous. The church had gross immoral problems. There were deep relational problems. That church was full of every kind of problem. It was a charismatic nightmare.

But in Thessalonica, who only had Paul for three weeks, we see the power of these attitudes at work. Thessalonica was one of the darkest, demonized cities in Europe at that time. The economy in that city was not very good either. But when they received the word from Paul, it says in 1 Thessalonians 2:13:

> For this reason we also thank God without ceasing, because when you received the word of God which you heard from us, you welcomed it, not as the word of men, but as it is in truth, the word of God, which also effectively works in you who believe.

As a result, this church followed the example of the apostles, and they became an example to the entire region of Macedonia and Achaia. Their faith went out everywhere. My paraphrase of what the apostle Paul said is, "We don't even need to come back to this region, because you are doing such a fantastic job of living out your faith in the power of the Spirit" (1 Thess. 1:8). The key was that they received the word of God for what it was. They put a high value on the word!

There is mystery in the Kingdom, and Jesus spells out the important attitudes necessary to receive and understand those mysteries. If we will have the right attitudes, then the mysteries will be made known to us. The apostle Paul in the Ephesian letter is basically saying the same thing. He says one extra thing: that the mystery will come to us through the agency of holy apostles and prophets. If you will receive it, then it will have a transforming affect upon your life.

17

MYSTERIES BEING REVEALED IN THIS SEASON

God uses the ministry of apostles and prophets for revealing mysteries. A few years ago, there was tremendous revelation on church government. There are many issues that are important to the church that are receiving fresh revelation from the scriptures. Here is a list of things that I feel are current and common issues.

1. The role of women in the church. We are not talking about women having to become man-like, but women in all their glorious distinctive femininity being allowed to have their full part in the church of Jesus Christ. God created humanity male and female. Something was taken out of Adam in order to make Eve. Without Eve, Adam was not complete. Together they expressed the full image of God. I am receiving more and more revelation on this mystery. I am continually updating and refining my theology all the time in order to keep up with the revelation. I don't think we are finished on this subject.

2. The role of Africa's nations and maybe African Americans. I told you earlier about the Nigerians coming to Britain and teaching the British church how to pray. It was critical for becoming a powerhouse where demonic principalities are attacked and pulled down.

Section 5 – Ephesians Chapter 3

The British Christians seemed to be too dull and deceived to realize that they were dealing with demonic principalities in their cities and regions. They had no idea how to deal with these things. The Nigerians came to introduce British Christians to the reality of the spirit world and the necessity of wrestling with it in the spirit. They also demonstrated the power and authority we have in that realm.

Many African nations have learned to fight for their nations. There is a spiritual boundary line in Africa between Islamic fundamentalist nations and Christian nations. There are five presidents of African nations who are born-again, Spirit-filled believers. The president of Zambia has re-written the constitution with the approval of parliament to declare Jesus Christ as the only Lord and Savior of the nation. All matters of government and political life will be conducted according to the principles of the word of God. That is right in the constitution. This transformation occurred in less than six years. Under the old president, Zambia was one of the most wicked and vicious systems in Africa. It will take a long time to get out of the hole the previous presidency dug, but they are on their way!

Five years ago, it seemed that Nigeria was irretrievably in the hands of the Islamic camp. It became part of the league of Arab nations. The Muslim leaders were in total control of the country. Something happened, however, in the sleeping giant of the church of Jesus Christ. People paid a price in prayer and some in martyrdom, but they have broken that country open for the Kingdom of God. Reinhard Bonnke sent me a recent email expressing his excitement on what is happening in Nigeria. He said that 3.6 million people gave their lives to Jesus Christ in six days. The majority of these converts were Muslim. There is still much ground to recover, but the battle is on.

Chapter 17 – Mysteries Being Revealed in this Season

There were certain men of God in these countries that most of us have never heard of. They are completely humble and unassuming, shunning the lime-light of Christian superheroes. When they are invited to America, they refuse to come. What a difference. They don't want to come to America, because they know about the publicity and prominence that often produces corruption in those who receive it. They want to stay in their places of ministry to do the will of God. Many of them have formed prayer and healing camps. They have insight into prayer, healing, and miracles that many of us do not have. I have a high priority to go there at the right time in the right way in order to learn from these men. I feel such a burden to see these things happen in the United States of America.

They have seen the most incredible healing miracles take place. Some people can get healed by the laying on of hands in a meeting, and that is wonderful. But nine tenths of people do not get healed in that way. We have no answer for that except to go on to the next crusade and the next and the next. I am not criticizing healing ministries or crusades. Please do not misunderstand me. But what about all the people who are not touched in an instantaneous way? These African ministers have found that in a week or two of soaking prayer, remaining in the presence of God, many of the things that resisted healing through the quick laying on of hands suddenly gave way and cracked under the bombardment of that persistent prayer. Again and again, they have seen impossible cases receive healing and miracles.

Quite often the spiritual condition of the person hinders the healing. It might take them a week to bring the person to a place of spiritual health that allows the healing to take place. For one week or two, they deal with attitudes that are sinful and behaviors that are sinful until it is all cleared out of the way so that there is no obstruction for God's power to flow into that person. I know these brothers have something to give us that we do not have.

Section 5 – Ephesians Chapter 3

I am convinced that Africa will be a forerunner for the gospel of Jesus Christ in the twenty-first century just as Europe was a forerunner in the nineteenth century and America in the twentieth century. I believe African nations will be changed in the whole of their morality, ethics, and principles of business and government, and it will cause them to rise up as leading nations in the world. I believe they will be the primary source of the spreading of the gospel of Jesus Christ in these last days. Look out, the Kenyans are coming. Look out, the Nigerians are coming. Look out, the Ugandans are coming. They will come not to raise money for their buildings. That is a thing of the past. Instead, they will give to America out of the riches and treasures that they have dug out, which we do not have. This is a mystery that is being revealed.

It requires us to be open and teachable. There are things we do not know that we must be ready to receive if we hope to be useful to God in these last days.

I said "maybe African Americans" because, even though they should have a distinct advantage in spiritual things, it seems they have been slightly paralyzed by hanging around Caucasians. If I was African American, I would get to the place where the raw power of God is being revealed in African nations. They could pick it up much faster than many Caucasians, who struggle with the supernatural. They have a natural ability to quickly absorb these things so that they can take it back to the needy parts of the world, primarily Europe and North America. These are the two most desperate parts of the world right now.

Some of you might consider visiting these nations. Just be ready for a few shocks culturally. Don't judge everything by American standards. Seven tenths of the world lives without ice in their drinks quite successfully. They don't have a shower every day, and they still survive.

When you all smell the same, it doesn't seem as noticeable. They definitely have hygiene, but it is simply different to what we are accustomed to. Simply say, "I will go with an open heart and an open mind to be taught."

Historically, we have traveled to Africa with such condescension, thinking we have the riches. That was nothing more than Laodicean Christianity. We were rich, increased with goods, having need of nothing, but when we got there, we realized that many of us spiritually were poor, blind, wretched, and naked. They can teach us so much. I don't prophesy, but I do say the time for Africa has come. I want us to be wide open to it. I pray that our precious African American brothers and sisters in the United States will get it. They are like Joseph. They were not willing to come here, but now that they are here, they might be the salvation for the whole nation. That is what I believe. The power of what God can release into America through African American brothers and sisters is so incredible, but we must be wide open to receive it and let it happen. This is a mystery.

3. The role of Hispanic nations. Here is a similar dynamic. In places where revival is breaking out in Central and South America, they are discovering things about the spiritual realm about which we know nothing. I was privileged to share a conference with a woman who had been used by God as one of the main battle axes by the Spirit to break through in the nation of Mexico. We were in Poland together. While ministering together, I had the chance to hear her story.

She sat with me for forty-five minutes and talked about the spirit of death, revealing things to me in that realm. I sat there like a little child trying to learn. When she prays and speaks, demonic mountains tremble. God will lift up many more of these kinds of people from Central and South America.

Section 5 – Ephesians Chapter 3

I believe they will come into the southern part of the United States with a power to so move the Hispanic community, resulting in massive a turnabout to Jesus Christ. I am convinced that the drug supply will be cut off by this action. When these nations turn to Jesus Christ, with no one wanting to grow or sell drugs anymore, the supply will dry up. Can you see this? I can see this as plain as day, and I am so excited.

We must see these mysteries. These are things that were hidden, but are now being revealed. Those who have the right heart attitude, hunger, and teachable spirit will see it and much more. There is a particular responsibility with anyone who has apostolic or prophetic gifting. We must bring these holy gifts to the feet of Jesus in order to be useful for what He wants. We must not see the prophetic ministry as a means of impressing the saints. The real purpose is for mysteries to be revealed so that we will have a strategy by which we can destroy the principalities and power opposing the establishment of God's Kingdom.

4. The role of the Jews at the end of time. I have said things about this before, but I still need more revelation on this subject before I feel qualified to teach you. I have shared what I know and understand. I know God has convicted me in that I am not in the position to fully lead the church into the fullness of this mystery. I am sure that the excessive obsession with the Jewish people as Jews being restored to their land in totally natural circumstances is not what God is saying to us right now. Although He may complete the shadow on the side, the shadow is not the reality.

What God is doing among the Jewish people is completing the shadow, while also completing the reality. The reality is the church, and the shadow is what He is doing with historic Israel. The true Jerusalem is heavenly. There is a true Jerusalem, a true Jew, and a true circumcision.

Chapter 17 – Mysteries Being Revealed in this Season

There is a true "everything" which Paul carefully explains as multiracial and spiritual. Obsession with the natural will cause us to loose our passion for the reality. You cannot have a shadow without a reality.

A few years ago, I was doing a conference in Florida, and Eileen was coming to join me. We had been apart for several days, and I was anticipating her coming. However, she arrived earlier than I had expected. I was sitting in a conference room with a group of leaders, and we were dialoguing together. There was strong sunlight behind me coming through the window. All of a sudden a familiar shadow was cast across the table in front of me. I recognized it instantly. It was my wife. She came one day ahead of schedule. I immediately jumped from my chair, but I did not embrace the shadow on the table. The shadow told me the reality was there, but I turned and grabbed the reality. I thank God for what the shadow told me concerning the reality. In that sense, even the shadow was precious to me, because it told me the reality was there. But I grabbed the reality and showed my love for it.

I believe God is calling all races, including the Jews, to come into the Kingdom. There is an appreciation we show the Jews, but we cannot deviate from this truth: We are all gathered up into the one new Israel, grafted into the one root; we all partake of the one Spirit in the one Body; we are all fellow heirs and fellow citizens of the one nation; we all have the same glorious one inheritance; we will all live forever in one heaven, so we better get used to it now. God will give us much revelation on this subject, and it will be the responsibility of apostles and prophets to lay a foundation once again in our age, as the apostle Paul did in his time, to stop the senseless division of Jew and gentile.

5. The mystery of iniquity. This phrase comes from 2 Thessalonians 2:7, "For the *mystery of lawlessness* [*iniquity* in the KJV] is already at work; only He who now restrains will do so until He is taken out of the way." I believe this mystery of iniquity is an understanding of the devil and how he works. I have already hinted that our African and Hispanic brothers and sisters will give us incredible insight and information on understanding the mystery of iniquity and how it works. We will not be ignorant of the enemy's devices. He won't be able to take advantage of us. We will understand not only the ways he works, but also how to always overwhelmingly defeat him and render him totally and utterly powerless. Furthermore, we won't be simply mopping up after his attacks, but we can prevent the attacks from even taking place.

There are so many places in Texas that I am aware of where pastors came together with serious intent to pray and establish the Kingdom and were subsequently hit by the devil, blown to pieces, or received a hard knock and were set back. While I know the war is real, we do not need to suffer these unnecessary attacks. In many cases, we were totally oblivious to the advancing the attack and took no measure to defend ourselves against it. We must become much wiser. The mystery of iniquity is an essential part of our preparation for effective city taking.

There are two great purposes for these mysteries being revealed. First, mysteries are revealed so that we might see the glory and see the harvest. By a special outpouring of grace upon Paul, he was able to make the unsearchable riches of Christ known to the gentiles, causing everyone to see. They could see the glory and power of this mystery hidden in God from the beginning of the ages. The result was a fantastic harvest. When we are able to communicate the mystery by God's grace, then we will reap a fantastic harvest.

The second reason for these mysteries being revealed is that they give us power to glorify God and defeat the enemy. Ephesians 3:8–11 says:

> To me, who am less than the least of all the saints, this grace was given, that I should preach among the Gentiles the unsearchable riches of Christ, and to make all see what is the fellowship of the mystery, which from the beginning of the ages has been hidden in God who created all things through Jesus Christ; *to the intent* that now the manifold wisdom of God might be made known by the church to the principalities and powers in the heavenly places, according to the eternal purpose which He accomplished in Christ Jesus our Lord.

The intent of these mysteries was to make the manifold wisdom of God known by the church to the principalities and powers in the heavenly places. The word *manifold* could be translated *multicolored* wisdom of God. This is the ultimate purpose of coming together in unity.

When we come together against principalities and powers as the multicolor one church of Jesus Christ, it has a power and authority so amazing that we could run every devil out of town without the slightest difficulty. God's plan is to make known His multicolored wisdom. If you think of all the different things different ethnicities could put into the pot to make us one hundred times wiser and better equipped than we could ever be on our own, then you can see how much more powerful that church would be. There is an incredible power in unity. One can chase one thousand, and two chase ten thousand, but what happens when it is one indivisible unity that is joined together to chase demons out of town. That is why it says, "A kingdom divided against itself cannot stand."

A second purpose of this mystery is to bring an amazing unity, which brings a fantastic authority so that when the unified body of Christ addresses the principalities and powers saying, "Get out of our town," they must flee. Then we can reap the most incredible harvest in Jesus' mighty name. These mysteries are not for intellectual satisfaction. They have glorious warring purposes once we can see it.

18

REVELATION OF THE FATHER

I want to look at one significant truth at the end of Ephesians 3. We have looked at some of the mysteries being revealed. There should be a multicolored church with the multicolored wisdom of God being expressed. Wisdom will come to us through various sources throughout the body of Christ. Through this multicolored wisdom, we will be equipped to declare to principalities and powers in the heavenly places the glory of our Lord Jesus Christ and His triumphant victory in every place.

We must realize that Paul is writing all of this after four years in prison. He is not saying, like John the Baptist, "Are You the one who should come, or do we look for someone else?" Can you see the difference between the Kingdom and the anointed individual? Paul was part of the Kingdom. The fact that he was in prison did not affect his ability to proclaim the Kingdom.

We know from history and the writings of the early church fathers that wherever God put Paul, he blossomed. Everyone who came in contact with Paul got saved and transformed. Half of Caesar's household was saved before they moved him on to the next place.

Section 5 – Ephesians Chapter 3

Wherever he went, he was always victorious. This is the attitude and reality of those who really see the Kingdom. Darkness does not overpower the light, but the light always overpowers the darkness.

Paul's concern was that these believers would not lose heart because of his circumstances. Paul was not asking, "Where is the Kingdom?" Instead, he was more convinced and utterly committed to the irresistible power of God's Kingdom. In Ephesians 3:14–21, it says:

> For this reason I bow my knees to the Father of our Lord Jesus Christ, from whom the whole family in heaven and earth is named, that He would grant you, according to the riches of His glory, to be strengthened with might through His Spirit in the inner man, that Christ may dwell in your hearts through faith; that you, being rooted and grounded in love, may be able to comprehend with all the saints what is the width and length and depth and height– to know the love of Christ, which passes knowledge; that you may be filled with all the fullness of God. Now to Him who is able to do exceedingly abundantly above all that we ask or think, according to the power that works in us, to Him be glory in the church by Christ Jesus to all generations, forever and ever. Amen.

This is the most incredible prison prayer! This is the most indomitable man of faith still battling a more powerful war in prison than at any time in his life. I want us to look at this prayer in detail.

The first thing I want you to note is that in the Greek language there is no separate word for family and fatherhood. It is the same word, *patria*. I would translate verse 15 in the following way, "I bow my knees to the Father...from whom the whole fatherhood, all fatherhood in heaven and earth derives its name." Paul is simply praying for the revelation of another mystery. We have touched on this before, but now we need to see it in depth. We need to see why this is so important as we prepare an army for an assault upon a city.

Chapter 18 – Revelation of the Father

The mystery we are talking about is the *revelation of fatherhood*. We will see later in John's gospel and letters that he has this same revelation. It was this revelation, more than anything else, that enabled him to be the mighty conqueror of Artemis. Therefore, we need to understand this precious mystery of fatherhood. In John's writings, references to the Father appear approximately two hundred times. By contrast, the gospel of Mark mentions the Father four times. In the gospel of Luke, the Father is mentioned fifteen times. In the gospel of Matthew, the Father is mentioned thirty-five times. I want you to see that the apostle John had a revelation of the Father far greater than the other writers of the New Testament. I want you to see why this is an essential preparation for war and what happens when we receive this revelation.

One of the purposes of meeting the Father is so that He can reveal to us the glory of our sonship. The revelation of the Father was so important that Jesus told His disciples in the upper room before His departure, "This is the most important thing that can happen to you when the Spirit comes: He will show you the Father! When you see the Father and know the Father, then you will come into a relationship with God as His son, which you did not know before."

The revelation of the Father concerns the revelation of His love and the security that love produces. Second, the revelation of the Father includes the revelation of His discipline in our lives. God brings us from Christian babyhood to warriorhood through discipline. We need to say, "Lord, I want that discipline!" The same thing is basically said in the book of Hebrews. The parallels between Ephesians and Hebrews are astounding. Both of these books were written to prepare churches for warfare. Therefore, you find similar things being repeated in both books.

Section 5 – Ephesians Chapter 3

All I know about Fatherhood I received from God. My natural father was a good man, but he was very remote and distant. He provided for the family, but he remained in his world of engineering. I can't even remember receiving any kind of display of affection or indication that he ever wanted any kind of intimacy with me. He was a good father who provided for the family, but we never knew each other. That was the way I was raised. I don't resent that fact. It really didn't impact me until I found out there are other ways of being fathered.

Unfortunately, I began repeating the same cycle in my own family. I was totally absorbed in my scientific work. Then I became totally absorbed in the preaching of the word. In my younger years, I neglected my children terribly, thinking that was women's work. I was a lousy father. I must admit that. My own children would confirm what I am saying.

When I took over the pastorate of the one and only Baptist church in Mumbai, I was powerfully filled with the Holy Spirit, along with ten to twelve other people. That was the little core that God used to shake a city. One of my experiences, after being filled with the Holy Spirit, was that He began showing me the Father. I went crazy! I was fortunately on my own in my study when this experience occurred. I ran around my study like a spring lamb crying out, "He loves me! He loves me! He loves me!" I had a revelation of the love of God which was much more than simply head knowledge. This occurred in 1965, and I have never lost it. It was a totally transforming experience. I came into this adoptive love of the Father. My response was exactly how the scriptures described I would respond, "Abba, Father!"

When you read the Thessalonian letter, you notice a progression in Paul's relationship with that church. He first came to them like a mother. He said, "I came to you like a nursing mother, and I gave you the milk of the word" (see 1 Thess. 2:7). It wasn't long, however, until that relationship progressed into something far more powerful and beneficial.

Chapter 18 – Revelation of the Father

He said, "I was able to exhort you, command you, and discipline you as a father" (see 1 Thess. 2:11).

The Thessalonian church received such treatment from Paul, but the Corinthian church never did. Paul said to that church, "I had to treat you like babes. I had to keep feeding you with milk. I could never grow you up, because whenever I tried to exercise any discipline you simply left the church" (see 1 Cor. 3:1–2). There are many people who live like that for decades. If anyone tries to loving work on them to bring them to maturity, they run off to the next church.

There are certain pastors who specialize on milk bottle churches. These leaders do not bring up issues in people's lives. Instead, they spew mother love on the people all the time. They say, "The Lord loves you...." This is true and certainly not a wrong message. But if you only live on the word of comfort and mother-cuddling, then you cannot grow up into maturity. Some pastors have said, "If I confronted my people, then they would all leave the church." There are Corinthian churches today. Some men have found it is the best way to keep a church growing, by simply giving people milk. They never deal with issues of growth and, therefore, rarely produce maturity. If we want to mature and become the powerful warring sons that God wants to produce, then we must receive him as Father.

The dimension first mentioned about this Fatherhood is His incredible love. When we have grasped the love of God, then something can begin to happen. God may ask, "Do you really know that I love you?"

You say, "Yes, Lord."

"Do you know that I love you enough to transform you into my son?"

You says, "Yes, Lord."

Section 5 – Ephesians Chapter 3

God says, "Therefore, I need to begin disciplining you until you have fully developed My nature. Will you receive this?"

The apostles John and Paul both realized it was essential to bring believers into the revelation of the Father. This is what will hold them in love as He transforms them into true warring power.

I started to learn fathering from God. We read here that all fatherhood in heaven and earth derives its name from God. God Himself is a great person to learn fathering from. It was unfortunately too late for my children. My youngest son was the most fortunate, but my two oldest children were already teenagers when I began to see it. All I could do for them was to apologize. They have been very forgiving and understanding. They know it was not a deliberate plan. Instead, I didn't know any better. I didn't read the books they read that have helped them to become great parents.

The irony of all this is that God has so taught me to be a father that I have become a father to men around the world. That is what God has called me to be at this stage in my life. I am known as a father to many men. This is a total grace gift from God. It does not matter how late in the day you get this revelation. It is not too late for God to transform everything. If you have messed up with your children, you can go back and make things right. If you messed up with one or two churches, because you didn't know how to be a father, then it is not too late to make things right and learn how to do it right.

Here is a word for single mothers as well. If you connect your children with the Father, then He can do a fantastic job of filling the hole the natural father left behind. If you get them into the Father, then they can learn from Him. I have listened to mothers I have taught this message to, and they said it completely transformed their ability to manage their children. You can be a vehicle for the fatherhood of God to flow through you.

Chapter 18 – Revelation of the Father

You can say to your children, "My heavenly father loves you. He is your Father as well. He wants us to do the following.... If you have any problems with this, then you will just have to talk with Him." You can bring your children into a relationship with the Father to even enjoy the Father and to be submitted to the Father. He can do the impossible job of filling that void in the life of your child.

There is a tremendous power in this revelation that I trust you will grasp. When this revelation comes, you become wide open to Him. There are certain consequences of this relationship that Paul begins to elaborate on starting in verse 16. Out of His glorious riches He strengthens you with power through His Spirit in your inner being. There is an empowering of the Spirit within you in far greater intensity. You become mighty through God.

Another consequence is highlighted in verse 17. Christ will dwell in your hearts through faith. You will be rooted and grounded in love. You will have power, together with all the saints, to grasp how wide and long and high and deep is the love of Christ, and to know this love that surpasses knowledge so that you may be filled to the measure of all the fullness of God.

The more you know of God, the more you want of Him. You get filled up more and more until you are completely filled up with all the fullness of God. This has the effect of giving you an intense security. It results in being grateful for other relationships, but you are not dependent on them. If necessary you can walk alone. No one would want to or chose to, but the deep rooting of your relationship with God can keep you in any and all situations. Talk with those who have spent years and years in solitary confinement suffering for Jesus. They could tell you much better than I can. They will tell you it was the relationship with the Father that was so real and deeper than anything else which kept them sane and actually growing spiritually.

Section 5 – Ephesians Chapter 3

This revelation of the Father has the effect of filling you up with all the fullness of God and filling you with the Spirit of His might. You become totally satisfied in life. When this Father love fills your life, then the agape love of God absolutely overwhelms you. It totally satiates you. Your dependency on other forms of love, although you deeply value them, is no longer necessary.

Many problems in marriage are the result of a woman or man looking for a God-sized love from their partner, which is totally impossible for them to fulfill. People become frustrated and hurt because they cannot receive all that they are looking for from their partner. This was the problem with the woman at the well in John 4. She had five disastrous relationships because she tried to fill the great craving in her heart for God with other men. She put such unreasonable demands on them, and they could not fulfill them. The relationship eventually blew up, and she went off to the next relationship. This was repeated again and again. The same can occur between parents and their children and children with their parents.

When you are totally satisfied with the love of God, which comes through the revelation of the Father, then it takes the pressure off from other relationships. Also, the power of His might enters you to such a degree that you now have the capacity to not only enjoy that love, but also to begin giving that love to other people. It says in 1 John 4:19, "We love Him because He first loved us."

When I had this experience of being filled up with the love of God in the Baptist church in 1965, I was far more loving to my wife and less demanding of her and the children. I deeply love my wife, but it is no longer the desperate necessity that it was before. I found the same in my relationship with other Christian workers.

At the time of my experience with the Father, we lived in the Muslim section of Mumbai. It was a dark and devilish place.

Chapter 18 – Revelation of the Father

I went out every morning to buy fresh bananas, because that was our breakfast every morning, bananas and tea. I went to the lady on the corner of the street where she sat cross-legged with her basket of bananas on her lap. She was an old lady, shriveled up, with two teeth sticking out of her mouth. She chewed a red betelnut, which is like a drug. Many Indians chew this stuff addictively. They could spit the red juice a surprising distance. Her mouth was stained with this red juice, and she was quite repulsive to look at. I used to shut my eyes when buying my bananas.

But on this morning I danced down to the woman, and when I saw her I could have kissed her. I was so transformed in my ability to love, because I had a revelation of the Father's love. I was filled up with all the fullness of God, and it has become richer and richer all the time. This revelation has a powerful effect on all our relationships.

I worked at a Christian printing press at the time. I was the technician in charge. I set the program up and trained the staff, but the pain in my neck was a New Zealand missionary who had come. He was a great artist, but he was an artist. You know what artists are like. They are even more difficult to get along with, especially if you are a scientist. He would draw these exquisite things which were totally non-reproducible. I would say, "We can't print that with the kind of colors and equipment we have here." He said, "You must." I said, "We can't." We tried our best, and he would be quite abusive in his response to our attempts. I could have cheerfully hit this man many times.

What amazed me about this revelation of the Father is that I even found love for this man that totally transformed our relationship. This love is so powerful and so supernatural. It heals and makes relationships possible that would otherwise be impossible. This is the most essential revelation for our lives.

Section 5 – Ephesians Chapter 3

When we are filled up with all the fullness of God, then He is powerful. It is interesting to note in Luke's gospel that the miracles that Jesus did were attributed to the Holy Spirit. However, when you come to John's gospel, the same miracles and a number of other miracles were all attributed to the Father. Have you noticed this? Jesus said, "I do not do anything by my own initiative. But the Father who dwells in Me, He does the works" (see John 14:10). He said, "Whatever I see the Father doing I go and do it with Him."

In John's gospel there is an incredible intimacy of relationship where the Father and Son are moving together. The Father, through the Son, does His fantastic works. Jesus attributed everything to the Father. Incredibly, He calls His disciples into the same relationship. *It is one thing to work for God, but it is another thing altogether to be workers together with God.* We simply go and do things together with the Father. I have learned in some degree what this means. There is no sweat and striving effort. Instead, you are along with this incredible almighty God.

Many Christians have had a revelation of Jesus that has saved them. Many have had a revelation of the Spirit who has filled them. They enjoy the gifts of the Spirit. But when you receive the revelation of the Father then you are complete. This is what brings power. Notice how Ephesians 3 concludes:

> Now to Him who is able to do exceedingly abundantly above all that we ask or think, according to the power that works in us, to Him be glory in the church by Christ Jesus to all generations, forever and ever. Amen (Ephesians 3:20–21).

The power flow comes out of relationship with the Father, just as it did in the life of Jesus. When the Father has come to live in you and has been revealed to you, then you understand like Jesus how to work in partnership with the Father. God will be just as capable of doing His

Chapter 18 – Revelation of the Father

works through you as He was through Jesus. You simply go and do it together with the Father. Therefore, He is able to do immeasurably more than you can ask or imagine according to the power that works in you.

Therefore, Paul bows his knees to this great Father. This is the second great apostolic prayer. The first prayer concerned our eyes and the necessity of being opened to see the power of His risen glory and authority. Now we are being asked to see the wonder of His Father love, including the intimacy this creates. We are then filled up with all the fullness of God so that Father God can do His mighty works through us. The result is that you can go to prison and not be moved by it at all. Paul was in prison, but God was mightier in him as a result.

When this Father revelation comes over you and you cry out in the revelation of a true son, then your prayer life is totally transformed. You can ask the Father for anything, and He will do it for you. This was the key and power of Jesus' prayer life. It was the relationship with the Father that enabled Him to pray and act as He did.

Through relationship with the Father, the power of His might comes upon you. The power of God begins to work through you toward the working of miracles, just as it did in Jesus. This is how He worked His miracles. The same Father will work the same miracles through us when we come into the same kind of relationship Jesus had with the Father. All we do is love the Father and give all glory to Him.

The final thing I want to show you comes from 1 John 4:16–17:

> And we have known and believed the love that God has for us. God is love, and he who abides in love abides in God, and God in him. Love has been perfected among us in this: that we may have boldness in the day of judgment; *because as He is, so are we in this world.*

Section 5 – Ephesians Chapter 3

Notice what it says at the end of this verse. We are just as much the darling son of the Father, God's treasured possession, as Jesus Himself. Therefore, the thought of dying and being with Him is immensely attractive. You just can't wait to get there! I have been with several Christians when they died, and I have seen in one case where the Lord actually appeared to them. When I watched the person die and pass through to glory, I simply wanted to go. I have talked with two persons from India who were raised from the dead. They spoke to me about this heavenly realm in such terms that made me hungry for that place.

When this revelation comes to us, we are told that it casts out all fear. We are told in Hebrews 2:14 that the devil has been able to hold many people in bondage all their life through fear of death. There are certain ways of dying that do not particularly thrill me, but I am not afraid to die. I know the day when God took that fear away. It is simply not in me. I love my wife and precious family, but the thought of going to be with Him is simply wonderful. At my age, many of the men and women I worked with and loved for years are rapidly leaving the playing field. It gets more and more desirable to join them.

I believe in keeping my body in good shape. I believe I have a responsibility to look after this vessel and complete the work God has given me to do. But I cannot wait to get there in many respects. I was praying this morning, and the Father and I were having a great time. I said, "Lord, I know I have to stay here. I am happy to do that, but it must be fantastic to pass through that veil."

When I come home from one of my trips, I anticipate meeting my wife. I do not think, "I wonder whether she will remember when I am coming home. Will she be in the house, or will she be off somewhere having forgotten my coming? Will she be in a bad mood or angry? I did my best to keep communication, but there were two days when I didn't call her.

Chapter 18 – Revelation of the Father

Will she forgive me for this? Should I throw my hat through the door first to see what happens?" I don't think this way. Whether I let her down or not by being as considerate as I should be doesn't matter. I know the love she has for me. When I appear, I know the welcome. I can't wait to be restored to her again.

I feel the same way about my Father. There is no fear. He won't say, "Look, we have a few things to work out before I can show you how much I love you." God does not have a list! As He is, so are we in this world! The love and acceptance of the Father are tangible and real. It tells us that we can have confidence in the day of judgment, because as He is, so are we in this world. Jesus in heaven is the darling of heaven. There is no fear in love, but perfect love casts out fear, because fear involves punishment or torment. But he who fears has not been made perfect in love. Perfect love casts out all fear. We love because He first loved us.

Once God gave me the capacity to love by giving me His love, then I could love back. There is no sense of fear or any other negative emotion. It is simply not there. When we go and take a city by upsetting violent and vicious demonic powers, I cannot say we will do it without some people laying their lives down for it. When you think of the mafia in America and its control on many U.S. cities, imagine the battle when the Kingdom comes to displace that manipulative and violent control. When the Kingdom deprives them of all their revenue and they lose their customers, causing the drug scene to fall apart, do you think they will sit there saying, "Isn't this terrible?" Instead, they will try to eliminate those who are upsetting their business. This has already happened in Columbia.

This revelation of the Father's love and the subsequent deliverance from fear makes you invincible to the devil. I remember a Romanian pastor leading a large church in Budapest, Hungry. They said to him,

Section 5 – Ephesians Chapter 3

"You can carry on leading your church, but we will make a few changes in your operations. We need you to give us information on all those who are in your church deviating from our communist position. We will also write your sermons on what you are to preach." Of course, he told them he would not cooperate.

They intimidated him by informing him what they were prepared to do to him if he did not cooperate. He did not cooperate with their demands, and as a result they beat him up and threw him into jail. They asked him again, "Are you ready to comply now?"

He said, "Absolutely not."

Their intimidation grew deeper, "Don't you realize we can kill you?"

Then he said the following statement, "Your ultimate weapon is to kill, but my ultimate weapon is to die in faith. If you chose to use your weapon, you will force me to use mine. The weapon I have is thousands of times more powerful than yours."

When they realized they could not intimidate him with death, they became completely paralyzed, and they let him go. His statement was the fruit of a man who had been delivered of fear by the love of the Father, "If you chose to use your ultimate weapon, to kill me, you will force me to use mine, to lay down my life in faith, which is a thousand times more powerful!" Remember this verse, "They overcame him by the blood of the Lamb and by the word of their testimony, and they did not love their lives to the death" (Rev. 12:11).

I am quite sure that for us to see significant city breakthrough, to really change the spiritual map of America, some of us will glorify the Lord by dying in faith. I am convinced of this. If I am one of them, as far as I am concerned, it is a settled issue. In India, Indonesia, and many other countries, the devil does not win by intimidating Christians with death, because they already have this kind of love in their hearts. This love casts out all fear.

Paul had to write similar exhortations to Timothy. When looking at Timothy's life, you have to wonder where all the men were. Timothy had a powerful grandmother and mother, and the same faith was in him, but where are the fathers? We know that fathering produces worth, value, and confidence, things mothers cannot give in the same way a father can. I conclude that Timothy was suffering from an absent father syndrome. As a result, he had troubles with security, worth, and value, and like so many, he was paralyzed by fear.

The apostle Paul took Timothy on as a son. As a father, Paul had to deal with his timidity. He said to him, "Timothy, don't be afraid. God has not given us a spirit of fear, but a spirit of power, love, and a sound mind." Then in 2 Timothy 1:8, he said something important. Paul was writing from prison. He knew Timothy had the tough job of leading the church at Ephesus with all the threatening and intimidation of Artemis, not to mention the persecution of Rome. Timothy not only had pressures from outside the community trying to destroy it, but he also had pressures from within the community trying to destroy it. His future looked a little insecure, but Paul said, "Don't be afraid of taking your share of the suffering which accompanies the gospel of power."

We don't know what happened to Timothy, but church historians believe he was finally martyred under the tyranny that broke out under Domitian. Timothy simply disappeared off the scene of church history, but it is almost certain that he paid the price. I am sure he found the grace of God's love making him unafraid to pay the price that many others had paid at that time.

19

FATHERING AND WARRING MATURITY

Let's look now at another purpose of fathering, which is warring maturity. This is another reason Paul prayed for this revelation to be revealed. In Hebrews 12 we see this reality. We are told first of all to look to Jesus, who is the pioneer and trailblazer of our faith, who for the joy set before Him endured the cross, despising the shame, and sat down at the right hand of the throne of God (see Heb. 12:2). We are told further on that He is expecting all of His enemies to be made a footstool for His feet. We are to look to Him as our example. Although He was a son, he learned obedience through the things He suffered (see Heb. 5). Having become perfect in suffering, He became the author of eternal salvation to all those who will obey Him.

Now look at Hebrews 12:5–11, which says:

> And you have forgotten the exhortation which speaks to you as sons: "My son, do not despise the chastening of the Lord, nor be discouraged when you are rebuked by Him; for whom the Lord loves He chastens, and scourges every son whom He receives." If you endure chastening, God deals with you as with sons; for what son is there whom a father does not chasten?

Section 5 – Ephesians Chapter 3

> But if you are without chastening, of which all have become partakers, then you are illegitimate and not sons. Furthermore, we have had human fathers who corrected us, and we paid them respect. Should we not much more readily be in subjection to the Father of spirits and live? For they indeed for a few days chastened us as seemed best to them, but He for our profit, that we may be partakers of His holiness. Now no chastening seems to be joyful for the present, but painful; Nevertheless, afterward it yields the peaceable fruit of righteousness to those who have been trained by it.

Can you see how often the word *chastening*, or *discipline*, is used? The word for *discipline* is the Greek word *paiduo*. The noun is *paidion*. We receive our English words *pediatrician* and *pediatrics* from this word. The verb has a very specific meaning used for a child three to eight years of age. A child of that age must accomplish a process of discipline important for his nurturing. The verb means to strike once with the hand or with a blunt instrument for the purposes of discipline or correction. In other words, the only way God brings babies to sonship is to smack them when they are naughty. If you do not receive the smacks as disciplinary action, then God will move on to another stage of discipline. God does not beat people to release some resentment in His own heart. Instead, the purpose is to bring you to the peaceable fruit of righteousness so that you can become a partaker of His holiness.

If the smacks do not work and they have a negative affect on you, then He stops smacking you and leaves you in your immaturity. That is why many Christians in churches get away with murder and never go anywhere spiritually; they are the kind of Christian who will not receive the fatherhood of God. They only want to live in the milk of His motherhood. After forty years, they are still living on milk. After all that time, they still have the same besetting sins.

They still have the same character flaws. After forty years, they have accomplished nothing except suck the life out of the church. I have seen this over and over again.

If you cross the line, then you must know that God will discipline you. He will smack you in some way and inform you, "Don't do that!" If you respond correctly, then the matter is completed. He has corrected you in this area, and you won't go there anymore. What God is looking for is simple and joyful obedience. If this stage of discipline does not work, He has other means. God is not in a game of just beating people for no purpose. Instead, after two or three attempts with no response, He moves to the next stage of discipline. In our passage, the word *rebuke* is used to describe this stage. The Greek word used for rebuke is *elegcheo*. The noun is *elegchos*. This word was used in the legal profession, especially in criminal courts to describe the person and activity of a prosecuting attorney.

Imagine that the person sitting in the dock is accused of a crime and obviously guilty. The only problem is that as the prosecuting attorney I must prove to you that he is guilty. I turn to the jury, and I reason with them by presenting all the evidence I have on this individual's crime. I reason with you in such a way that it convinces you that this man committed the crime in exactly the way I have described it. As you listen to the reasoning of this prosecuting attorney, it carries you to the place where you have actually seen the crime with your own eyes. You are totally convinced of the reality of the crime that he has committed. The result is that you have no doubt at all about bringing a guilty verdict against him.

We are told that faith does the same thing for us in Hebrews 11 concerning the word of God. Faith has the powerful effect upon us of so persuading us that we feel we have seen things when we actually have not. We act like someone who has seen something when we have not.

Section 5 – Ephesians Chapter 3

Faith is the convincing proof of things not seen. When the *elegcheo* activity of God is finished with me, I think, "Wow. I can see this now with absolutely certainty. I feel like I have been there. I have seen it with my own eyes. I am as convinced as anyone who might have been an eyewitness to the event."

Here, the word is used in the sense of rebuking and correcting. When God smacks someone a few times and they do not respond, then His next stage is to say, "We need to talk." You can imagine God sitting down with you, reasoning with you like a prosecuting attorney presenting evidence to convince you that your actions or attitudes need to change. God is not convincing a jury somewhere, but He is convincing you about the reality of your sin. When He is finished with you, then you see that sin the way God sees it. You even hate it the way God hates it. When you have the same attitude that God has toward your sin, then it is not difficult for Him to remove that sin from your life. However, until you see the action or attitude in the way He does, you will continue to excuse yourself, refusing to comply with the smacks that are telling you to change.

When you are rebuked by Him, you should end up with seeing things the way He does. You agree with God that the action is terrible and must not continue anymore. John said the same thing in his first letter when he said, "If we confess our sins, He is faithful and just to forgive us our sins and to cleanse us from all unrighteousness" (1 John 1:9). The Greek word for *confess* is *homologeo*, and it means "to say the same thing." In other words, once you see it the way God sees it, then it is not difficult to remove things from your life. When you hate it the way God does, there is no reason or power that will cause it to continue in your life. But if you continue secretly loving it, then you will continue in that besetting sin. When you hate it like God does, a power from God comes and deals with it, and that will be the end of it.

Chapter 19 – Fathering and Warring Maturity

This same word was used in the Greek version of the Old Testament called the Septuagint. In Isaiah 1:18, God said:

> "Come now, and let us reason together," says the Lord. "Though your sins are like scarlet, they shall be as white as snow; though they are red like crimson, they shall be like wool."

God was saying, "Listen to me nation of Israel. I want you to see your sin the way I see it. Then you will hate it the way I hate it. It will be washed out of your life by the power of the blood, and you will be as white as snow. I want you to see it!"

If this does not happen, then God moves on to stage three, which is called scourging. The Greek word is *mastigoo*. We received our English word *masticate* from this word. You already have an idea of how this stage of discipline might feel when you understand the definition of *masticate*, "to chew and reduce to a pulp by crushing or kneading." When you masticate something, you literally chew it to pieces. You reduce something to a pulp.

This word describes a process of discipline accomplished through a Roman wipe called a flagellum. This whip had bits of bone and stone in it so that when you flogged someone's back, it literally tore the person's flesh to pieces. If you do not respond to God's smacks and stubbornly refuse or ignore His reasoning, then He will take you to the woodshed and knock the hell out of you. This is painful.

Peter was a precious and wonderful apostle-to-be, but he had to be processed in order to come to maturity. One of the things you find in scripture is that he carried a rather high opinion about himself. Please tell me who were the main apostles among the twelve that stand out to you? The usual answer is Peter, James, and John. These guys were the largest trouble makers in the team. They fought and competed with each other quite fiercely.

Section 5 – Ephesians Chapter 3

The Zebedee and Bar-Jona families were jostling for the top position in the Kingdom. James and John even solicited the help of their mother. They wanted to be big in the Kingdom.

No less than seven times, Jesus sits them down and says, "Look, this is how it is in the Kingdom. If you want to be great, then you must become the servant of everyone. If you want to be someone, then you become the least, you become like the younger." In Asian and African cultures, they can understand these things better. In these two cultures, they are very conscience of age. They greatly respect age. If a group of men were to sit down in a village, they would automatically note the age of each other mentally. The person who was the youngest would never presume to speak first. He would speak last, if at all. He thinks, "How could I speak first when these men who are older and have greater wisdom are here? How dare I dishonor them in this way?" These younger men keep their mouths shut and behave like the younger.

We don't do this in America or most Western cultures. We have lost something very valuable here. Peter was arrogant, pushy, and always speaking first. James and John were not much better. Here is a principle for building leadership teams: The strongest horses are the hardest to break in, but they end up doing the greatest work. Take the time and trouble to bridle them and break them in. You cannot leave them as unbridled, rebellious horses, because they will not accomplish much good for the Kingdom.

Seven times Jesus sat down with His disciples and reasoned with them. He put a little child before them and said, "You need to become like this little child." Seven times they listened, and seven times they decided to ignore His instruction. In the upper room, in Luke 22:24, Jesus was in travail, anticipating the cross. He was sorrowful within Himself. Judas had just gone out to betray Him.

But what were the disciples doing? The disciples were arguing among themselves about which of them would be the greatest.

In the context of this event, Jesus said, "Simon, Simon, Satan has asked to sift you as wheat. But I have prayed for you, Simon, that your faith may not fail" (Luke 22:31–32). I want you to see something that is happening to apostolic men and apostolic ministries around the world, and it has rightly put the fear of God in me. Like Jesus did here, He removes the protective shield around people to allow them to be exposed to the flagellum of Satan. It is Satan who does the whipping. Satan beats him to a pulp until Peter is quite sure he is worth nothing and cannot do anything.

The good thing about Peter is that when he was finished with the beating in the woodshed, he was a different person. Before, Peter said arrogantly, "I will never deny you! The others might, but I won't deny you. I am Peter. I'm out in front. I am not like these others. I will do the most adventurous things…." But following this woodshed experience, Peter developed another opinion about himself, "I am not even fit to live anymore. I am finished." God said, "Finally! Now I can start with My life in you." This event was the beginning of Peter's usefulness.

Are you familiar with Alexander the Coppersmith? This man was the brother of Rufus, the two sons of Simon of Cyrene who carried the cross. Alexander the coppersmith first appears in Ephesus in Acts 19. He is the man who made a defense with Paul against the fury that broke out from the riots instigated by Demetrius, the silversmith. I see Alexander as a fiery, able evangelist who had a tremendous gift and high opinion of himself. However, he would not submit to anyone.

Paul said later on in his letter to Timothy, "Alexander the coppersmith did me much harm…" (2 Tim. 4:14). He might have said, "I tried to bring correction to this young horse, but he would not listen to me."

Section 5 – Ephesians Chapter 3

He made shipwreck of his faith along with another man named Hymenaeus. They went off into error. Then Paul said these tragic words, "…I delivered [them] to Satan that he may learn not to blaspheme" (1 Tim. 1:20). In other words, Paul released Alexander to the scourging of God through the beating that Satan would be allowed to give him. If God ever takes His protective shield away from us, we are done. There is not one ounce of strength, courage, vigor, or ability in us to withstand the beating of Satan. We better recognize that all we have is a gift from the Lord!

There are really only two possible responses to the scourging described here. In Alexander's case, it did not bring him to brokenness. If you ever go through this process, then I cry to you, please respond with brokenness and not with hardness. What happened to Alexander made him harder and bitter. The last words about him in the New Testament are, "Alexander the coppersmith did me much harm. May the Lord repay him according to his works" (2 Tim. 4:14). When Alexander was smacked, he did not respond correctly. When he was reasoned with, he resisted. And now the woodshed completely hardened him in his anger and rebellion. In the end, he was totally useless in spite of being a very gifted man.

When God called me to go India, I was battling with the physical condition I explained to you. I came to the place where every missionary agency turned us down. God said to me, "Kodak will send you." I was working for that company having achieved a very good place of service with many benefits. I loved my work. However, this call to India was becoming dull when I received the new job of leading a research team for specific advancements. It was the most wonderful job you can imagine. I was being paid a fantastic salary for doing what I love to do. It was easy to say, "There are obstacles in the way. No missionary agency will send me. I have this health problem. Let's just forget the whole deal."

Chapter 19 – Fathering and Warring Maturity

I was walking on the beach at a holiday resort in England, and Jesus came and walked with me. He said, "If Kodak was sending you to India to do consultant work putting you in a nice flat with a good salary, would you go?"

I said, "Yes, I would go. Kodak is a very reliable company. They have been in business for a long time."

Then God said to me, "I've been in business for much longer. Can't you trust Me?"

Something happened to me just before this event. One February morning, I was bending over. I had decided to bury the missionary call and just forget about it. I decided to be a good church-going Christian. I wanted to rekindle my passion for the research work that I was doing. I bent down to tie my shoelaces one morning and had what is medically called a spontaneous pneumatharax. Suddenly, my lung burst and immediately collapsed. I didn't hear anything, but I had intense pain almost immediately. Added to this trouble was that I was already suffering from an asthma attack. I could hardly breathe. I fell to the ground, gasping for breath. My wife ran out, stuck me in the car, and drove me frantically to the doctor. He gave me emergency injections of adrenaline and rushed me to the hospital. They brought me to the emergency department and put me under oxygen. I was just being held alive.

In this particular hospital they had an interesting arrangement. They had a long ward, but each room was divided from the next. There were only three beds in each room. These rooms went right down the corridor. At one end was the recreation area, and at the other end was the morgue. They moved you along up and down the corridor according to your physical condition. Therefore, you knew how you were doing based on your position on the floor. I happened to be in the room next to the morgue. I had tubes coming in and out of me.

265

Section 5 – Ephesians Chapter 3

In the area where I was located, there were two other men. One of them died in the night cursing and blaspheming his way into hell.

For the next months, everything went wrong in my body. I went from one emergency to the next. I was in hospital somewhat recovering. My lung was just beginning to reinflate. I happened to be in the room with two other men who were top executives of large international companies. The story was the same for each of us. Our careers and lives were coming to an end because we had lost our health.

Here is what I learned from this experience. Every breath I take and every day I live comes from the permissive will of God. Although I didn't realize it, I thought Kodak was paying me a salary. As long as Kodak remained a powerful company, I was secure. My security all the time was in God. He was giving me life. Suddenly I saw that to go to India and trust God was not a different situation at all. Every day I was dependent on God. He might use Kodak or a black bird to come and feed me. The foundation of security is God Himself. Until that point I had not seen this.

Because I was rebelling and not listening, God had to take me to the woodshed. He knocked the hell out of me. He totally broke me. When I saw this, I could say, "Lord, I see what you are getting at." Everything in me was going wrong at the time. My whole body was falling apart. I was a total mess. My health was disappearing. I was finished. Then I realized it was just God saying, "I want you to know that I am the only security there is. To go to India with only Me is the best place to be."

The moment I received that message was the first day I got out of bed. I asked the Lord when I would get out of that hospital. He said, "You are leaving today." I went out that very day. But I had an impediment that remained with me for the next twelve years. God had more things to teach me. Apparently, this was the only way God could get faith into me by putting me in these difficult situations.

I have learned that this is the way God trains sons. How many of you want to be a son now? If you receive this the right way, it will put the warrior spirit in you.

In 1 John 2:12–14, it says:

> I write to you, little children, because your sins are forgiven you for His name's sake. I write to you, fathers, because you have known Him who is from the beginning. I write to you, young men, because you have overcome the wicked one. I write to you, little children, because you have known the Father. I have written to you, fathers, because you have known Him who is from the beginning. I have written to you, young men, because you are strong, and the word of God abides in you, and you have overcome the wicked one.

A person came into functional sonship, according to the law, at the age of thirty. When did Joseph come out of prison and enter into his inheritance? When did the vision that he saw as a young man become fulfilled? It happened when he was thirty. When did David come to the throne in Israel? He came to the throne at thirty. If you go through scripture, you will find that thirty is the birthday of coming into your inheritance. God is speaking something prophetically to us here.

In the New Testament, coming to sonship and receiving your inheritance is not a matter of time, but of faith. For God to get you from babyhood to sonship, He must take you through a process of maturing. The process includes experiences that you pass through. Sometimes, maybe frequently, He must smack you and reason with you. In some extreme cases, He may have to take someone to the woodshed. This is not absolutely necessary, but it seems to be the common lot of everyone.

Section 5 – Ephesians Chapter 3

Once you have come to sonship, there is another stage mentioned here. The Greek word used for young men in the passage we read is the word *neaniskos*. This word describes a young warrior between the ages of thirty and forty. The Father's plan is to bring you to sonship, and then as a son, you learn to be a young warrior. You know the word of God. It is abiding in you, and you overcome the evil one. The word *overcome* appears many times in the book of Revelation. The noun in Greek is the word *nikao*. The verb form means "to tread down your enemies, to conquer, and to overcome." It carries the idea of "subduing, to prevail over, and to get the victory." An overcomer is someone who treads down his enemies and conquers them. The process we go through brings us to the place where we put on our Nike shoes and we crush our enemies under our feet.

This is what fatherhood does to us. If we are satiated with His love, then He can do this to us. Whatever God takes us through has purpose. If we handle the situations well, letting God do His work in us, then we will end up being nearer to mature sonship than we were before. If we respond quickly to God's work in our lives, then we can get to maturity and warrior-like sonship much more quickly.

SECTION 6
Ephesians Chapter 4

20

CRUCIFYING THE FLESH AND WALKING IN THE SPIRIT

Starting in Ephesians 4, we begin moving from our sitting position to walking in the Spirit. The things we learn to sit in come from crisis moments. You sit when you suddenly see the truth of something hitting you like a ton of bricks. You say, "Now I know what Paul meant when he wrote that." "Now I get what Jesus said when He taught that." "Now I know what brother Jim meant when he said that. It is aflame in my spirit!" These mysteries and truths become a grasped reality in our lives, and they transform us. They cause us to sit.

There is a moment when you sit on the throne. There is a moment when you are first baptized in the Spirit. There is a moment when you can say with absolute assurance that your old man has been crucified with Christ. You are no longer a prisoner to the old way of life. There is a moment when besetting sins no longer beset you.

I had several experiences in this area. There was one besetting sin that dogged me for years. It suddenly became a past event, and this is absolutely biblical. It's like unwisely allowing a very pushy salesman inside your house. He chases you around the house trying to get you to buy something. He plagues you to death and is almost irresistible when he is inside the house.

Section 6 – Ephesians Chapter 4

There comes a crisis when, through faith by the power of the word, the salesman is thrown outside the house. This may include deliverance from a demon. In any case, the pushy salesman is outside the house and not inside.

For a while, he will still knock on your door. When that does not prove effective, he will knock on your windows. He will ring the bell and do his best to persuade you to let him come in again. But this is a different level of temptation than having him inside the house. He can be easily resisted when he is outside the house.

I remember going through this process with uncontrollable lust and habits I don't even want to talk about. I developed these habits during my teen years and early twenties. However, there came a day long after I was saved, while actually leading the church in Mumbai, when I was baptized in the Holy Spirit. Shortly thereafter, God revealed to me that I became the possessor of the mind of Christ. I actually have a new mind. There was a moment when I put it on. That was a crisis moment.

From that day, the overwhelming temptation that I previously could not resist became resistible. The war was no longer inside me, but it was persistently trying to regain entrance to my life. Now it was much easier to resist. However, this lifestyle did require a persistent, disciplined life, not allowing the devil to regain the territory he had lost.

There is a crisis that is best described in these two phrases: sitting (in terms of power and authority) and putting off and putting on. Once the crisis is over, there is a process in which we walk. We must learn to make a distinction between these two things. If you do not walk in what you sat in, or if you do not walk in what you put off and put on, then there is no continuation of growth as it should be. This comes again and again in Ephesians 4 and 5. We must walk out the process that was started by the crisis.

Chapter 20 – Crucifying the Flesh and Walking in the Spirit

Imagine having a piece of ground where you have dug out deeply rooted weeds which have polluted the ground. Maybe there are strong trees occupying the ground, and there comes a day when you dig those things out to make room for more beneficial planting. You have cleansed the soil, but the problem is your next door neighbor is growing weeds, and the seeds are blowing into your garden continually. You must be vigilant to keep the ground clean, because things are blowing in all the time.

We live in a filthy, demonized world. The pressures continue on a consistent basis, and seeds are being regularly dropped in on our lives. James says that if we pluck them out as a seedling, then it is not hard work, but if we are not attentive to our garden, then these new seedlings will take root and prevent new life from growing within us. This is what we are going to look at in these next sections. We will look at this new walk in the Spirit. First we will look at the principle of walking; then we will look at the practice of walking. Once you have the principle, it is easier to walk in practice.

In Romans 7:24–25, Paul said:

> O wretched man I am! Who will deliver me from this body of death? I thank God–through Jesus Christ our Lord! So then, with the mind I myself serve the law of God, but with the flesh the law of sin.

The flesh is sin's happy hunting ground. Anything of the flesh is irresistibly possessed by sin. We read again and again that sin finds opportunity through the flesh, and it kills us. If there is any flesh operating in your life, then there will be a permanent door for sin to come into your life. If you will not deal with the flesh, then you will never know victory over sin. If you do not close the door to that invasion of sin, then you will not be able to walk in the realities we will talk about now.

Section 6 – Ephesians Chapter 4

Let me define the flesh. *The flesh is the union of body and soul to act independently of God.* The issue is independence. Perhaps the most subtle and dangerous form of flesh is religious flesh where a person genuinely tries to do the will of God by its own effort rather than letting the Spirit of God do it for him. Many people sincerely try to do God's will, but it is like trying to pull yourself up from the ground by your own boot straps. It is impossible. How can the flesh triumph over the flesh? If the devil cannot get you into obvious sinful living, he will try to get you into sincere religious activity where you are striving to reform yourself. Even striving to get hold of God's promises is nothing but fleshly activity. Even praying for a city and asking God to come in revival can be a work of the flesh. Subtly we think we can buy revival by our activity: "If we pray for so many hours then God must answer us." This is fleshly thinking that produces fleshly activity.

We must recognize that the flesh is very subtle. In the Old Testament, the Amalekites were a picture of the flesh, and king Agag was the epitome of the flesh. Saul was totally deceived by king Agag when sparing his life. Saul came to the prophet Samuel, saying, "We have obeyed the commandment of the Lord." Saul obeyed 97 percent.

Samuel asked, "What is this bleating of sheep that I hear?"

Saul reasoned, "We kept the best of the flock to offer as a sacrifice to the Lord."

King Agag is smiling, knowing that Saul will let him live. Saul would have let him live, but Samuel was more spiritually discerning. Samuel took a sword; it was the only time Samuel was furious with murderous intent. The prophet killed Agag and slaughtered all the remaining sheep (see 1 Sam. 15:8–27). The subtleties of the flesh are very deceiving, and only the spiritually discerning can recognize flesh from Spirit.

Chapter 20 – Crucifying the Flesh and Walking in the Spirit

For example, I may have a beautiful natural gift from God called administration, teaching, or music. I used to be a lecturer in chemistry long before I ever taught the word of God. It is so easy for me to slip into natural ability. *Your areas of greatest competence are your areas of greatest danger.* This is where you can easily manage without God. To manage without God is simply flesh. It is very easy to have a genuine vision from God of what He wants you to do, and once having the vision, you fill in the detail yourself. This was one of my mistakes again and again. I would get a genuine vision from God and say, "Thanks, God. I've got it now. You can go on now. Alan Vincent can handle it from here." It took me twenty years to discover how sincerely I was trying to serve God in the flesh. I have come to hate the flesh the way God hates the flesh.

This misery that Paul speaks of in Romans 7 is all in the present tense. It does not matter how many years you have walked with God, it is always a present possibility that you stop walking in the Spirit and start walking in the flesh. Anyone of us can do it at any place and at any time. We must be aware of this. While the old man is dead, the battle with the flesh is a daily battle we will have until we leave this life.

In the Bible, there are three crosses. The first cross is the one upon which Jesus died for me, taking away all the penalty of my sins. Jesus died for me in a once-and-for-all event, never to be repeated again. The second cross is the one upon which I am crucified with Him, dealing with my old man. This is a once-and-for-all event, never to be repeated. But the third cross is not His cross, but my cross. This cross is one we must take up daily, walking in a constant state of having crucified the flesh. You say to the flesh, "Flesh, you will not have any opportunity today to have your way in my life." You recognize that this is a daily, minute-by-minute, hour-by-hour commitment that never comes to an end.

Section 6 – Ephesians Chapter 4

The apostle Paul rebuked the Galatian church for having begun in the Spirit and then continuing in the flesh. This can happen easily in the exercise of spiritual gifts. A person starts in the Spirit and then at some point they move from Spirit to flesh. Very often, in the prophetic gift, you feel sympathy for someone. You say, "That poor brother…that poor sister…I want to give them a word of comfort." With a perfectly sincere intention, we manufacture with the best ability of our flesh a word from God to help them. The only problem is that it was not a word from God at all. It was just our best in trying to help them. In any area, we can move from Spirit to flesh very easily. As a musician, you can play and perform very acceptably in your natural ability, but when you move from flesh to Spirit, there is a different tone and quality in the music you play. The same is true with administration.

Paul concluded his discussion on this misery in Romans 7 by saying at the beginning of Romans 8, "There is therefore now no condemnation to those who are in Christ Jesus, who do not walk according to the flesh, but according to the Spirit." Notice the order in which this is described. We must learn how to not walk after the flesh and only then is it possible to learn how to walk after the Spirit. Many of us are already into flesh activity before we even realize we have done it. We are so used to running our own lives, so used to managing ourselves, that we are full of self-confident competence. We don't honestly feel a need for God in many areas of our lives. Learning to not walk after the flesh is a very important lesson to learn.

Let me say that it takes time to learn walking in the Spirit perfectly. We tend to move in and out of the flesh and Spirit life. If we make progress, then the periods when we unwittingly or deliberately step into the flesh become fewer and fewer. The periods of walking in the Spirit become greater and greater. In this way we progress until we come to the place where most of the time we walk in the Spirit. But first we must learn how to not walk in the flesh before we can learn how to walk in the Spirit.

Chapter 20 – Crucifying the Flesh and Walking in the Spirit

This is the underlying principle of all the things we will look at in the remainder of Ephesians. Nothing will work until we learn this foundational principle. Paul continued this thought in Romans 8:3–6:

> …He condemned sin in the flesh, that the righteous requirement of the law might be fulfilled in us who do not walk according to the flesh but according to the Spirit. For those who live according to the flesh set their minds on the things of the flesh, but those who live according to the Spirit, the things of the Spirit. For to be carnally minded is death, but to be spiritually minded is life and peace.

In Galatians 5, we have a list of the horrible works of the flesh. Here is a danger. In Great Britain, we have a very evil weed that I have never seen in America. The weed is called bindweed. This stuff is really sinister. It operates three or four feet under the ground. It travels a long way underground until finally popping up through the ground. It is no good plucking it out at ground level, because the root structure is still there. If you get bindweed in your land, then you have an almighty job to get rid of this stuff. You can pluck up the weed in one place, but because the root structure is still there, the weed will pop up somewhere else.

Living in any facet of the flesh is like bindweed. You may be struggling with a particular irritability. You say, "I must deal with this." If you simply deal with the manifestation of the flesh instead of dealing with the root, the flesh, then that manifestation will pop up somewhere else. When you read this list of the works of the flesh, you realize that any one of these manifestations is possible when the flesh is active. In other words, if you allow irritability in your life, you could end up in immorality, because it is simply another manifestation of the same flesh. We must not mess around with the flesh, because it is deadly. It will choke the life out of anything in the Spirit.

If you tolerate the flesh in one area, then that deep root system can spread over to other areas and pop up in other places. You may not want it, but because you tolerated the flesh in other areas, now you have a harvest of the flesh in places you didn't think possible.

How can we ensure the fruit of the Spirit as opposed to the works of the flesh working in our lives? The answer is in Galatians 5:24, "Those who are Christ's have crucified the flesh with its passions and desires." A. W. Tozer made a statement in one of his books that I know is absolutely true in my own life. He said, "There comes a point in your life when you take sides with God against yourself." This is a tremendous phrase. You say, "God, I agree with you. We will be at war together against the flesh." When you come to hate your own flesh and not excuse it, then you and God can be allies together in dealing with this wretched flesh that works in all of our lives.

The flesh is not the same as the old man. Many Christians confuse the two. They say, "The old man is troubling me." No, the old man was crucified with Christ. What you are dealing with is the flesh. The remedy is very different for both of these problems. My series called *The Power of the Cross* deals with this in much greater detail. I feel these are distinctions Christians must learn in order to be successful. One pastor received those messages and preached thirty-five weeks on that series. He said, "Our people are transformed!" There is a power in the cross that we have lost. We do not understand many of the things the cross has made possible for us.

When Paul came to Corinth, he said, "For I determined not to know anything among you except Jesus Christ and Him crucified" (1 Cor. 2:2). Remember that Paul preached and taught there for almost three years. I thought, "How did Paul preach on one subject for so long?" Now I understand. I could easily preach on the power of the cross for years. It is that incredible.

Chapter 20 – Crucifying the Flesh and Walking in the Spirit

Those who are Christ's have crucified the flesh. This is something you must do. There are certain things God cannot do for you. He can work with you when you are in agreement about it. But you cannot say, "God, please deliver me from the flesh." He won't do that. Instead, He says, "This is where we must work together on these things." The scripture always talks about us humbling ourselves. "Oh, Lord! Humble me!" The only thing God will do is give you a situation where you can choose to humble yourself or choose to remain in your pride. He will give you the situation, but the decision of how you handle it is yours. The humbling can never be done for you. God cannot crucify the flesh for you. You must do it together with Him. Those who are Christ's have crucified the flesh with all its lusts and desires. Paul then continued in verse 25, "If we live in the Spirit, let us also walk in the Spirit" (Gal. 5:25).

Here is a very important truth about walking in the Spirit. Right now we are in San Antonio, Texas. This is now my home. But for many of you, San Antonio is not your home. I spend most of my time on the road, so I know what it feels like to be in another town. If I am in Pittsburgh, Pennsylvania, I can imagine San Antonio and wish I was there, but because I am not living there, I cannot walk there. While in Pittsburgh, I can mentally imagine walking through the town of San Antonio. I can imagine walking through the store to pick up things we need for our home, but because I am not living there, I cannot actually walk there. You can only walk where you live.

If you live in the Spirit, only then are you able to walk in the Spirit. If you desire to be holy and desire all these great things to come into your life, then you must live there before you can walk there. If you live in the flesh and try to walk in the Spirit, you are living in as foolish a contradiction as the idea of me walking in my home town while being in Pittsburgh. You can only walk where you live. We must learn how to live in the Spirit in order to walk in the Spirit. The primary activity for living in the Spirit is communion with God.

21

WALK IN HIS PURPOSE

With this background, we can now examine the seven ways Paul enjoins us to walk in Ephesians 4 and 5.

1. Ephesians 4:10–Walk in His Purpose
2. Ephesians 4:1–6–Walk in Unity
3. Ephesians 4:31–5:2–Walk in Love
4. Ephesians 5:3–7–Walk in Moral Purity
5. Ephesians 5:8–14–Walk in the Light
6. Ephesians 5:15–21–Walk in Wisdom
7. Ephesians 5:22–6:9–Walk in Submission

The first way we are to walk is in His purpose for our lives. We are told in Ephesians 2:10, "For we are His workmanship, created in Christ Jesus for good works, which God prepared beforehand that we should walk in them." This says the same thing as Psalm 139:16, where David said, "…In Your book they all were written, the days fashioned for me, when as yet there were none of them." This is the amazing thing: We are so planned by God that before He created the world, in His great eternal design, He had already created you in the sense of spirit.

Section 6 – Ephesians Chapter 4

You were already designed by Him and put together in His creative spirit with all your unique attributes. Then, at a certain time and certain place, He called you forth to come into physical manifestation. The plan for your life was there before the foundation of the world. This is absolutely staggering and beyond comprehension.

Success is for you to get into God's plan. You cannot be more successful than doing what God planned for you to do before the world was created. However prominent you might make yourself, or however busy you might be, or however much people might admire what you are doing, if you are out of the will of God then you are wasting your life. At the start of my Christian life, it was important for me to be located geographically where God wanted me to be. I've not had difficulty hearing God, because I discovered on the day I was born again that I had good spiritual hearing. I do not believe anyone is born again spiritually with congenital deafness. No one is born again with a hearing impediment in the Spirit. But if you do not obey what you hear then you soon become dull of hearing. Spiritual hearing is a very sensitive faculty, which you must cultivate, causing you to hear more and more clearly until you can literally hear the Father the way Jesus heard Him.

Jesus said in John 5:30, "…As I hear, I judge; and My judgment is righteous, because I do not seek My own will but the will of the Father who sent Me." Here lies the key to perfect spiritual hearing. Jesus basically said that although there was a cacophony of impressions, sounds, and voices, including demons trying to deceive Him, He never once missed what His Father wanted Him to do. He always heard perfectly. He judged everything. He did not allow everything in with unselective credibility.

This is a mistake many make. Everything you hear that is purported to be of the Spirit is not. When you get into the spirit realm, you must learn to be discerning, picking out that unerring voice of God and obeying it to the letter. As you do this, your hearing gets better and better. It is like someone possessing a tremendous musical ear. It must be trained by a master musician in order to come to its full potential. The gift is there, but it must be developed. On the other hand, if you neglect this gift, it falls into waste and you lose this ability.

I discovered, within two hours of being born again, that God spoke to me for the first time. My wife and I gave our lives to Jesus in a person's living room. We came home from that experience, and both she and I were smokers at that time. I didn't smoke during the day very often, because I worked in a research laboratory where there were many fumes. Smoking was not permitted. However, during lunch I smoked, and during the evenings, my form of relaxation was smoking cigarettes.

On this evening when we came home, I sat down with Eileen and said, "Wow! That was some experience." I pulled out our cigarettes and gave one to Eileen. For the first time, I heard what I now know to be the voice of God. He said to me, "You don't need those cigarettes anymore. Throw them away." I took my cigarette and put it back in the pack. I didn't even ask Eileen, but put hers back in the pack and threw it into the trash. That was the end of it. I have never smoked since.

There is a moment when God speaks to us in our lives, and if we do what He says when He speaks to us, then there is power to make what He says happen. When the children of Israel were told by God after a short period in the wilderness to go into the promised land, they said no. They thought the giants were too big and the cities were too fortified. God said, "If you don't obey me now, then you will learn things through a long period in the wilderness."

Section 6 – Ephesians Chapter 4

After two months, the Israelites repented and said, "We are ready to go now." Moses said, "It is too late. You have missed your opportunity. You missed your *kairos* moment." They went in under their own strength, and it was a horrible failure. That is why many people struggle with besetting sins, because they don't deal with them at God's moment. If we learn to hear God and do what He says in that *kairos* moment, then it is a done deal. I have learned to hear God.

After four or five days of being converted, I was on my way to my first Christian meeting. On the way, I heard this voice again saying, "Buy some coffee and sugar." I thought, "I better obey this." I had no idea why. I stopped at the store and bought coffee and sugar. I put the goods in the bag connected to my motorcycle, and off we went to the meeting. After we parked and walked in, the ladies organizing the event came running out complaining, "We have run out of coffee and sugar." I said, "Don't worry." I walked out to my motorcycle and brought in the goods!

My daughter Rachel was almost killed in Zimbabwe through a devilish attack against her life. We moved her back to England. She was miraculously revived from a coma after doctors told us there was no hope for her. However, she still had totally crushed bones in her legs and was in plaster for five months. They did their best in one of the most renowned orthopedic centers in Britain, but some bones would not heal. They said, "We will have to operate." We couldn't face this, and neither could Rachel.

In those days, every Sunday night we had a warring praise night. This was a fantastic time with incredible power. We worshipped and praised God, and we would hit things in the spirit realm with prayer as He led us. It was not the time we prayed for Mary's back ache, but we went after the affairs of the Kingdom in a greater context.

Chapter 21 – Walk in His Purpose

Rachel was in the meeting with us. She had been in plaster for five months. Her legs would simply not heal. She pleaded with the doctors, "Please give me one more month to see what God will do." They reluctantly agreed.

God spoke to me during the prayer meeting and said, "The spirit of death that tried to kill Rachel is in her bones, resisting the healing." I come from a rational, scientific background. I was struggling with the information, because I didn't even know who or what the spirit of death was. The word didn't make any sense to me. But He said to me, "Cast it out!" I decided to obey what I heard, like a little child. I stood over her and said, "You spirit of death that tried to kill my daughter, now in her bones resisting the healing, in Jesus' mighty name I cast you out. Get out of her now in Jesus' name." All I know is that three weeks later when they x-rayed her the legs were perfectly healed. I didn't know what I did, but something worked. You can do things you do not understand, providing you obey what you hear.

My daughter is walking around gloriously healed because she had a father who was simple enough to do what he was told. What would have happened if I said, "This is irrational; I can't do that." I don't know what would have happened. I don't even want to think that way. I heard. I obeyed. She was healed! We need much more of this kind of simple, child-like obedience.

I want your ambition to be that you will obey the Lord in whatever He tells you. If your hearing has been impaired by disobedience, then repent. Ask God to restore your hearing, saying, "Lord, I want You to develop my hearing. The most important gift I can have is the ability to hear You. I want You to train me. Whatever I believe You have said to me, I will obey it." If you make a few mistakes along the way, God will not condemn you. *It is better to step out in misheard obedience than to live in reserved disobedience,* "I better not make a mistake.

Section 6 – Ephesians Chapter 4

Therefore, I better not do anything." If you read the scripture, God never deals with the entrepreneurial people in a condemning way. Instead, He says, "Go for it."

In many cases, you won't know the validity of what you have heard until you step out and do what you have been told. After stepping out in faith, you realize many times that you were right. You heard correctly. You discover that you are being used by God for wonderful works. These are good works that have been foreordained for us to walk in.

In Ephesians 4:10, we have a summary of what God is all about in this letter. The apostle Paul said, "He who descended is also the one who ascended far above all the heavens, that He might fill all things." I believe we must refocus our understanding of what God's purpose really is. Hear me when I say this: God's purpose is not to get people saved. This is a powerful and important byproduct of something else. *God's purpose is to bring the rule and government of God over the face of the whole earth with Jesus Christ as the undisputed Lord and King of that government.* This is where we are going.

In the process of this becoming reality, God is passionate for people to come to salvation, which means they must stop living in disobedience to the King. They must come in and be obedient to the King. The issue of the Kingdom is more about the willingness to obey Him than it is the issue of forgiving their sins. The willingness to obey Him is more important than the issue of their sins. Once this basic principle of being available for God, to live in obedience to Him, is appropriated, the forgiveness of sins is a joyful consequence of that decision to obey God.

God cannot forgive the sins of a rebel. Some believe that a person can receive Jesus yet not have Him as their Lord. As far as the Bible is concerned, no such position exists. I don't want to delude people into thinking that you can be a saved Christian without being a Jesus-as-Lord Christian. This person does not exist in the Bible.

Chapter 21 – Walk in His Purpose

We must walk in His purpose. There are many scriptures we could turn to, but Ephesians 4:10 says that Jesus' purpose was to fill all things, that He might be all in all. The majesty of scripture is incredible. I know the day I was filled with the Holy Spirit, the day my eyes were opened, the day I sat down with Him on my throne, I saw that my passion was to see Jesus' rule and government, along with His undisputed glory, be accepted and received in the city of Mumbai, where I was living at the time.

Obviously, as it says in Acts 26:18, when people's eyes are opened and they see there is evil and darkness, there is a Satan and a King Jesus, they repent from disobedience and turn to obedience. Then forgiveness of sins is a joyful, important byproduct of that decision. But the heart of the matter is that Jesus might fill all in all!

The apostle Paul walked in the purpose of God. That is why he continually preached Jesus and the Kingdom. Quite often, he just preached the Kingdom. Of course, he never lost sight of who was the king of the Kingdom, who was the glorious one who had the complete oversight of that Kingdom. That is why I feel so compelled to preach and teach on the Kingdom of God. We must comprehend it. We need to see how it works and what it will finally become.

Heaven is nothing more than the fruit of a relationship where God's will is perfectly done. Wherever God's will is perfectly done, the consequence of that obedience produces the environment we call heaven. Everything is beautiful and lovely. In this environment there is no sickness and disease. There is no death and no sorrow and suffering. These are the fruits of the obedience which brought the Kingdom. This is why it is called the Kingdom of heaven as well as being called the Kingdom of God. Heaven is the environment produced by obedience.

Section 6 – Ephesians Chapter 4

Conversely, hell is the environment produced by disobedience. This is always the root issue. I believe that when we see this clearly, coming fully into our lives and fully into the lives we lead, it begins to permeate our society. We will have heaven on earth to the degree we have obedience on earth.

This is what Jesus said, "Pray for My Kingdom to come." What is the next phrase? He said, "Your will be done on earth the way it is done in heaven" (see Matt. 6:10). Heaven is not so much a location as it is a relationship. When God's will is done perfectly, heaven is the consequence of the obedience. When I saw this, it absolutely exploded in my spirit. I thought, "Now I know what I am going for. I know what I am aiming for. I am focused on what my purpose is."

22

WALK IN UNITY

This unity must be walked out, not just believed in. The great peacemaker Jesus went to the cross while we were still hostile and enemies. There was no sign of a breakthrough in advance to encourage Him. In fact, the last week of the life that Jesus had on earth was the most rebellious and hateful He ever experienced. He might have thought, "Father, this is hopeless. Let Me come back to You in heaven. Why even bother with humankind?" But Jesus was a man of faith.

I believe His high priestly prayer is amazing. In John 17, He said, "I do not pray for these alone, but also for those who will believe in Me through their word." These disciples ran like scared rabbits at the time of His greatest need. There was a total collapse of everything He appeared to have built on earth. But Jesus had faith for them. He had faith in the power of the cross.

We must walk in unity. There are basic attitudes and activities necessary to walk in unity, as described in Ephesians 4:1–6:

> I, therefore, prisoner for the Lord, beseech you to walk worthy of the calling with which you were called, with all lowliness and gentleness, with longsuffering, bearing with one another in love,

Section 6 – Ephesians Chapter 4

> endeavoring to keep the unity of the Spirit in the bond of peace. There is one body and one Spirit, just as you were called in one hope of your calling; one Lord, one faith, one baptism; one God and Father of all, who is above all, and through all, and in all.

There are some important words here for us to grasp. One in particular is *hupomone*, translated as patient or longsuffering. These words mean "a longstanding perseverance with cheerfulness." In other words, I will continue in this day-in and day-out every minute of every day, regardless of what comes against me. This is what agape love is like, as described in Isaiah 50. When the Spirit of Christ spoke through the prophet Isaiah, He said:

> The Lord God has opened My ear, and I was not rebellious, nor did I turn away. I gave My back to those who struck Me, and My cheeks to those who plucked out the beard; I did not hide My face from shame and spitting. For the Lord God will help Me; therefore I will not be disgraced; therefore I have set My face like a flint, and I know that I will not be ashamed" (Isaiah 50:5–7).

Often, when you go out to make peace, you get slapped in the face for it. You get kicked in the teeth for it. That is what happened to God when He came to make peace. But He said, "I will love you to death! I will love you until that ruling hostile enmity in you dies, and you fall into My arms in reconciled love. Then we can become absolutely one!" There is a relentless perseverance in the Lord Jesus Christ to this end.

We will not solve the divisions in our cities by one attempt at unity. We must break through the demonic wall that separates us until there is a melting together. We must hit it again and again until it all comes down in Jesus' name! It will take perseverance and the same love God has for us. We will forgive and forbear. All these tremendous words will not be nice theological thoughts; they will become our experience.

Chapter 22 – Walk in Unity

I want to touch one more thing in verse 3. It says, "endeavoring…" or, "make every effort…" (NIV). There is tremendous strength involved here. There is an energy expended for a particular purpose: "to keep the unity of the Spirit through the bond of peace."

The word *bond* in Greek is *sundesmos*. This word was used to describe the chains used to bind prisoners or slaves together in what was known as a chain gang. If you were a slave and put into a chain gang to work, you didn't have a choice about who was chained next to you, "Oh, no! Not him! Not her!" You didn't have a choice. Furthermore, you couldn't get away. You were chained there. Do you have the picture?

We must maintain the unity of the Spirit in the chain gang of peace. You say, "God has put me into this church along with this particular group of leaders with this particular pastor as my spiritual authority. There is no place where I can go until God comes and legitimately unlocks the chain and takes me to re-chain me in another situation." You never escape the chains. He may change the chains, but you never escape them.

Paul used this vivid illustration that he could literally see every day. The Roman Empire was full of chain gangs of slaves working together. They didn't have a choice regarding who they were connected to. The chain decided it, not them. The master set them there, and that was it. So Paul wrote, "Maintain the unity of the Spirit in the chain gang of peace."

Sometimes you come under tremendous temptation to run out of a situation. However, quite often God put you next to someone because the two of you rubbing together can do marvelous work in each other. That person is a tool that shapes you to be like Christ, and you are probably doing the same thing to him or her. Although you cannot see it, you need each other until the work is complete.

Section 6 – Ephesians Chapter 4

I was reminded about the first time I came to San Antonio. I was on my way back to England from New Zealand. On the way I agreed to stop to minister at the Eagles Nest. Honestly, I was not thinking about the ministry engagement very much, but I had agreed to come. I was in transition at that time in our ministry. I had been told two years earlier by God to disengage myself from the day-to-day responsibilities of the five churches we had planted in England. I was to prepare for a move without knowing exactly where.

However, in my heart was a great passion to see the Kingdom breakthrough in London, England. I reasoned where our next move would be. I thought, "Now I am free to move from the outskirts of London into the center in order to plant something that would break the devil's stranglehold on that city." But all I heard from God was, "Get ready to move." All the other details were my circumstantial deductions.

On my way back from New Zealand, I stopped in San Antonio. It was a Thursday. At that time the church had a corporate meeting on Thursdays. I was scheduled to talk to leaders on Friday and Saturday, preach on Sunday, and then go home. When I landed in San Antonio from Los Angles, I went to my room to pray. During that prayer time, I had one of the most incredible visitations from God of my entire life. The roomed filled with His presence and glory. I heard God speak to me. I believe it is the only time I have heard the audible voice of God. I actually heard a voice say to me, "This will become your home." This is all He said, which threw me into a whirl. I didn't have any idea what this meant.

I came to the Eagles Nest that night, and Dennis Davis stood up. We had very little contact with each other. He was already living in San Antonio. God had spoken things to me, to Eileen, and to Eileen's sister who is a prophetic dreamer. The things spoken to us caused us to act in the way we were acting. I had normally refused invitations to the United States.

Chapter 22 – Walk in Unity

It wasn't that I didn't like America, but I reasoned that America was filled with teachers. They certainly didn't need another one. I went to Eastern Europe in those days. I went to India and Africa where the need was much greater. I concentrated on those areas while building churches in Britain. There was no need for me to go to America.

It was surprising that I had even agreed to come to San Antonio for this visit. So Dennis Davis stood up and prophesied to me, "You have been thinking about moving across town, but God is going to move you across continents. You said in your heart, 'What does America need another teacher for?' It is true that America has many teachers, but she does not have many fathers." Then he said to me, "I am calling you to come to this city and be a father." He went on to say many other things which absolutely blew me away. I knew it was the word of God for me. Coupled with what happened in that room that afternoon, it was absolutely clear what I was to do.

I shared the news with Eileen when I came to the London airport. We didn't even go home. I said, "Let's go and have a cup of coffee. Let me play this tape for you and explain what happened in my hotel room." Eileen went away to pray, and two or three days later God spoke to her as well, and she said, "I know this is God. I am as excited about this as I am when God first called us to India." We made steps to come to San Antonio.

When Dennis brought this earthshaking prophecy, I was in a state of shock. I am in America as a result of that prophecy as much as anything else. When I stood up to speak on that Thursday night, you can imagine the state of my spirit. I don't know how I made it through that first Thursday night meeting. God gave grace, and it was apparently OK. I was seriously thinking, "Is it time for me to close the door on India? Do I leave it to sons to go there now?"

Section 6 – Ephesians Chapter 4

I just cancelled a visit there because God showed me that I must give my priority to what is happening in Texas. I can see there are certain strategic places in the United States where I must give myself to the apostolic and prophetic men God is raising up in those areas. I will be obedient to that and serve these men as best as I know how. I believe God will give grace to make it fruitful.

I am like a great-great granddad. When I look at this sea of great leaders in India that are the sons of the sons of the sons of the men I lead to Christ forty years ago, out of the most incredible demonic darkness, I am amazed. They are now mighty apostles and mighty prophets and evangelists. I think, "If I hadn't obeyed God, then I would probably have just retired as the Director of the Kodak Film Company smoking cigars." I'm not quite sure I would still be alive or in what condition my marriage would be. Some people have said, "You made a great sacrifice to go to India!" I say, "That is absolute baloney!" I have become so rich with the true riches. I can't thank God enough that He saved me from a successful career to become an apostle of the Lord. What a calling! What a privilege!

Just as God is one yet three distinct persons, we are to replicate the Godhead in unity. This was a statement God spoke to me while I was preparing for this School of the Word. I never thought of unity in these terms. He said to me, "I am indivisibly one, yet I am three distinct persons, Father, Son, and Holy Spirit. We are indivisible, yet distinct." What God is looking for in unity is what Jesus prayed in His high priestly prayer, "Father, I pray that they may be one even as we are one." The kind of unity God is looking for is the unity that rejoices in diversity. It doesn't just tolerate diversity, but actually rejoices in diversity. Therefore, this unity is not looking for uniformity.

This is much harder to accomplish, but it is infinitely more powerful in its effect. It says in Ephesians 4:4–6:

Chapter 22 – Walk in Unity

> There is one body and one Spirit, just as you were called in one hope of your calling; one Lord, one faith, one baptism; one God and Father of all, who is above all, and through all, and in you all.

I believe the one baptism emphasized here is the one baptism by which we are all baptized into the one Spirit. The emphasis of unity is right there throughout this whole chapter. God delights in flowing in unashamed Asian cultures, in unashamed African cultures, and in unashamed Caucasian cultures. We don't have to merge into a uniformed blob. Imagine the palate of colors that God has made with all of their brightness and different shades. A painting becomes beautiful when the colors are put together while their distinctives are retained. If you blend them together into one, then you get a brown, dirty, dull mess.

We need to learn the fullness of diversity, including male and female diversity, ethnic diversity, rational and emotional diversity, intellectual and non-intellectual diversity. When all the dimensions come together, yet maintain their distinctiveness, then we are powerful.

I've had very few visions, but there is one I can remember very vividly. I saw something like a temple, a great and glorious building. It was built with a crystal kind of glass. It was a large dome made up of different shapes and pieces fitted together with no cracks between them. There were all kinds of shapes, none the same size or shape. Each one of those pieces in this glowing crystal cathedral was a different color. Inside the temple was the glory of God. When the glory of God shown through this fantastic building, it passed through each piece of crystal and came out the other side in a unique color all its own. It was still the glory of God, but it had taken on the color of the crystal it had passed through. God said to me, "This is the multicolored wisdom, the multicolored glory of God. This is a picture of the church."

Section 6 – Ephesians Chapter 4

I have never forgotten that vision. It definitely applies to what we are talking about here. It even speaks to the individual. The Spirit of God can pass through Alan Vincent so that what he says and does has an Alan Vincent color to it which God is not ashamed of. God does not mind being heard or seen with an Alan Vincent tint to what He says and does. God will speak to another and pass through Eileen. God comes through Gilbert, Dennis, Franz, and all of us in a unique way, and God delights in it. This expresses God's fullness more completely. It is His design.

In many of our attempts toward unity, we have prevented this truth rather than promoted it. Some of the discipleship movements have erroneously taught that everyone must reflect the heart and behavior of the apostle. In many cases, you were not allowed to be you, but only a copy of him. This is a denial of self and the unique way God wants to express His glory through each person. This is an abusive perversion of authority. I am not saying there should not be submission. We will talk about that later. But the fullness of the church is expressing itself in the varied colors of God's glory passing through each life. Some of the diversity is ethnic. Some of it is personality. Some of it is gender. Some of it is vocation and education. There are many things that tinge the color of God as His glory shines through us. As long as it is pure, that is OK. This is what we are heading for.

Paul said in Ephesians 4:7–10:

> But to each one of us grace was given according to the measure of Christ's gift. Therefore He says: "When He ascended on high, He led captivity captive, and gave gifts to men." (Now this, "He ascended"–what does it mean but that He also first descended into the lower parts of the earth? He who descended is also the One who ascended far above all the heavens, that He might fill all things.)

As long as the glory is the glory of God, then it pleases God to have a variety of ethnicity and personality. God delights in this. God showed me many years ago in Psalm 139 how beautifully He made me. Apart from the aberration of sin, I am absolutely fantastic. I really am! God made me. God does not want me to change. Instead, He wants to untangle the aberration of sin, which is not really me. Paul said, "When I do the things I don't want to do and don't do the things I want to do, it is not me, but sin dwelling in me" (see Rom. 7:19–20). Paul made a clear distinction between who he essentially was and the things which sin compelled him to do.

You must never hate yourself because you are insulting your Creator God. To hate yourself is the worst form of rebellion! You are saying to God, "You didn't know what You were doing when You made me. You made a mess of it. I hate me. I hate what You made me." That is a very wicked rebellion. But to rejoice in the wonder and beauty of what He has made is the only correct response to His creation. You work together with God to get rid of the sin, but what is left is absolutely and incredibly beautiful!

Having now seen this in yourself, the next thing for you to do is to appreciate it in others! This particularly applies to husbands and wives. I think God deliberately puts opposites together. If you squeeze the toothpaste at the end and like the cap to be put on afterward, then you will be married to someone who squeezes the bottom and never puts the cap back on! All the irritating differences after living together for years can serve to help you appreciate the differences in other people. It is amazing how one likes the air conditioning at 68 degrees and the other likes it at 75 degrees. In some cases, it has brought some couples to divorce. They are so rigid and inflexible, having little appreciation for the unique ways God has put other people together.

Section 6 – Ephesians Chapter 4

The worst scenario is when one partner says, "If only I can change my partner, they will be more palatable to live with." A campaign begins to change their partner to make him or her more acceptable. In reality, God likes them the way they are. It took me many years to get there, but I have learned to love all that God has made Eileen to be. Apart from the aberration of sin, she is absolutely beautiful. I love her being different from me. I didn't always appreciate the difference, but I do now. I had to learn it.

When you get on a leadership team or become part of a church, it is amazing how this understanding helps you to function, allowing the diversity that delights God to pass through each part of the body. That same diversity will delight you as well. These are very powerful truths, because they allow us to accomplish what we were created for. Honestly, when we get these things in place, it will make us an invincible city-taking team. We will see later that when these things are not in place we are vulnerable and easier to defeat. God loves diversity!

Knowing Your Place in the Body

In Ephesians 4:11, it says, "He Himself gave some to be..." This phrase is much stronger in the Greek. It literally says, "And He of Himself gave *some* to be apostles, *some* prophets, *some* evangelists, *some* pastors and teachers." There are some things Jesus does not delegate to anyone else. Jesus chooses as He wills, and no one else has any say in the matter. In other words, Jesus does not consult with anyone. Nor does He need help from anyone. Instead, it is a totally internal decision from within Himself. Jesus decides, and He has no need to consult with anyone else. What He has decided is totally non-negotiable.

The same construction is used concerning building His church in Matthew 16:18. Jesus said, in effect, "I, of Myself, will build My church."

Chapter 22 – Walk in Unity

He does not delegate church building to anyone else. He takes suitable building material, and He puts it into the building the way He chooses. He was talking about Peter, in this case. His name was *Petros*, which was a suitable stone for building. Once Peter had revelation, he could be put into the building that Jesus was building by Himself. Against that church, the gates of hell cannot stand. Jesus will design and build a devil-destroying church.

There is no church in any city that Jesus builds that does not have the fire power to destroy the gates of hell in that city. Jesus knows how to build devil's gate–destroying churches. We must be very careful to let Him do it. If we let Him do it, the church is invincible and impregnable. The devil cannot destroy us, but we can destroy him.

This is so unfair in a way. The devil has no chance. His only hope is for us to hinder Jesus' building of the church, which He Himself is building. In the same way, his only hope is to stop the church from recognizing those Jesus has appointed to be apostles, prophets, evangelists, pastors, and teachers. Even worse, the devil convinces the church that she can manage without those Jesus has appointed. We must see the sin of these things. To think we can soldier on with our idea of how the church in the city should look, while ignoring the One who has the only right and authority to do these things, is complete arrogance.

This is why we see Jesus, in Revelation 3:20, standing outside of the church He is supposed to be head of and building. He stood there asking, "How about letting Me in…?" He stood at the door and knocked. This is not a message of salvation for sinners primarily. Instead, it was a cry to a deaf church that would not let the builder of the church have the right to build. If anyone hears His voice and opens the door, He will come in and eat with that person, and that person will eat with Him. They will have fellowship together.

Section 6 – Ephesians Chapter 4

This is not something Jesus negotiates, but He appoints as He wills. Some say, "According to our standards, God is not fair." We are not here to decide whether God is right or not. Who are we to judge God? Paul said, "Can the clay say to the potter, 'Why have you made me this way?'" We must receive the fact that God knows wisely what He is doing. Whatever we have in terms of talent or ability is entirely a matter of grace. All of our abilities are what He has wonderfully given us.

There are not only varieties of gifts, but also a variety of measures. There are also varieties of spheres. This comes from 2 Corinthians 10:13. Paul talked about not building on another person's sphere. For example, I have certain spheres of responsibility. South America, for example, is not part of my responsibility. I have people twisting my arm to come to Peru. Eileen had a strong plea to come to a large ladies' conference in Peru. She declined in order to stay home for a prayer meeting in San Antonio. It's not that we are not concerned about Peru, but it is not our responsibility to go and work in that field.

Many of us must realize the sphere of influence God has given and work within it. I want to make sure I hear God and do the things He tells me to do. In the past, I have never pushed myself into places or invited myself to churches. But now, if I feel I need to come to your church in the will of God, I will call and express what I sense to be God's concern. This is something I have never done before, but I heard God tell me to do this. He told me, "Stop being so modest. If your modesty leads to disobedience, then that modesty is sin." I will obey Him. I don't need a preaching engagement, and I don't need the honorarium. Those things are not my motivation.

There are also varieties of measures. When Dennis Davis arises to speak, there is a quality in his prophetic ministry that I rarely hear. Chuck Pierce is a prophet with an unusual and great anointing;

I have never heard him miss the mark. Such people carry a governmental authority in the church. There are many who prophesy in the spirit at different levels. We must recognize the measure of the gift as well as the gift itself. If we are faithful in what we are given, then God may well increase the measure. If He does not increase it, then you have no right to grumble or complain.

We must use our gifts in the right measure and in the right place. There is a difference between the local church setting and an international conference. The prophetic word that sister so-and-so has might be out of place in the international conference. It might be appropriate in the meeting of the local congregation. The leader might say, "Sister, this is not your place now." If she gets offended and hurt, then she does not understand the ways of God. This does not mean that I, as a leader of that conference, should let her have her way so as not to hurt her. We must be more realistic with each other in some of these things, yet deeply love each other.

God does not assess or evaluate what we accomplish in gross terms, but in how faithful we are in what we have been given to do. To whom much has been given, much will be required (see Luke 12:48). God measures everyone by a different measure according to how much they have done His will. God is not stupid. If we use the Jethro principle, then we see how God measures each individual part. Remember that Jethro encouraged Moses to make captains of thousands, hundreds, fifties, and tens. These took the load off of his soldiers so that he was free to lead the nation where it was suppose to go.

I have been teaching on this principle, because it is very important to understand. I even identify in the church something parallel to captains of thousands. I believe this equates to the Ephesians 4:11 ministry. An Ephesians 4:11 pastor can pastor thousands of people without personally seeing everyone. Instead, this ministry puts many people to work in the ministry of shepherding. They train pastoral people. When it comes to people with lots and lots of problems in the church, the Ephesians 4:11 minister will rarely see them personally, because they could not fulfill their calling by giving so much attention to these needy people.

If you use your pastoral gift at a measure that is greater than other people, it becomes your job to sit down with individuals, spending an hour or two to get to the root of their problem and show them a godly answer. Each one of us is created by God for different functions. A captain of ten could represent the equivalent of a home group leader or a deacon in charge of a task. A captain of fifty or one hundred is an elder of a congregation.

If you think in terms of the numbers in the Bible, the numbers included the men, without the women and children. A captain of fifty includes about fifty families and a few singles. Altogether, the numbers include one hundred to three hundred people. This is a normal congregation. A captain of one hundred could have twice as much in a slightly larger local congregation. However, he does not have the Ephesians 4 gifting which allows him to lead and develop a much larger community of God's people.

If God creates one captain of one thousand, it is obvious that He will need one hundred captains of tens to serve him. This is simple mathematics. If you are created by God to be a leader, then you must face the fact that it is not so that you will be one of the "big guys." We sometimes look at numbers in earthly terms, but God does not see it that way. If God has created you to be a captain of ten and you do it with all your might and never get your name on the back page of Charisma, but faithfully did what God gave you to do, then you will get a 100 percent reward on His Day, because you did exactly what He created you to do.

Chapter 22 – Walk in Unity

If you are called to be a captain of one thousand, and you are a well-known apostolic figure with your name frequently in the front pages of Charisma, and you are totally faithful in what God has called you to do, then you get exactly the same reward. No more, no less. You have been faithful.

But if you are a person with an ability to lead one thousand, and you are half-hearted and indifferent about your gift, and you end up leading only two hundred people because of your slackness, you will be on the mat before God for wasting your gift. You will not be promoted like the person who was faithful as a captain of ten. God's way of judging people is quite different. God judges us by the progress we make, not by the numbers we lead.

I have responsibility to speak in a fathering way into men's lives around the world. Some are great men with vast works under God. One of the men I was responsible for came out of the most amazingly dark and demonic background. He was a walking miracle to be who he was and doing what he was doing. However, he carried with him the scars and maiming of his former life. He never really allowed the full work of grace to do its work in his life, although he was so gifted and so charismatic in the natural sense. He simply drew a crowd wherever he went. I received responsibility to father this man. To be honest, I was on my knees complaining about the ugly side of this man and the enigma he represented. I was not praying lovingly, but complainingly. He was embarrassing me by some of the things he said and did. When you are a father, the things your son does bounce back on you.

I was having my little grumble with God, and He spoke to me, "I do not judge a man by what he is. I judge him by what he refuses to become. Look at this man. Where was he three years ago?"

I said, "He was an unbelievable mess."

God said, "How about last year?"

I said, "He's made great progress this last year."

God said, "Right! But there certain things you don't like, and I don't like, but we will deal with them in due time."

Then God gave me the name of another man and said to me, "Look at this man." I viewed this person with great respect. This person was born in a godly family with godly parents and godly grandparents. The whole atmosphere for generations was godly Christianity. He said, "You've known this man for twenty years. How much has he moved?"

I said, "Not very far."

God said, "Which one of these men am I more pleased with?"

I said, "Lord, I see your point."

We must learn not to evaluate people in natural terms, because God's evaluation is very different from ours. I don't judge people by what they are, but I judge them by what they refuse to become. I will father, as God directs me, some very ugly ducklings. I will love them for what they will become, not for what they are! And if you think I am talking about you, I probably am!

The Ascension Gift Ministries

Let's look now at the ascension gift ministries. This phrase comes from Ephesians 4:8, where it says, "When he ascended on high, he led captivity captive, and gave gifts to men." Some people call these gifts the five-fold ministry, and others call them the Ephesians 4:11 ministries. It really does not matter what title you use, but let's be clear that these are not the same as elders. If the person is deeply involved in a local church, they may be an elder at the same time as fulfilling their Ephesians 4:11 function.

One example is Peter. Peter was an apostle to the Jews, yet at the same time, he told us in 1 Peter 5 that he was an elder. While I was located in a particular local church, involved in the day-to-day life of that church, I carried the title of elder as well as being apostolic in many other situations. I have not been an elder in a church for twelve years now, because I have no day-to-day, hands-on responsibility in any church. Therefore, I cannot be an elder. However, I am apostolic with a prophetic teaching thrust to my apostolic ministry.

The purpose of these ascension gifts is not to perform to an admiring audience. One of the weaknesses of the American church is that we have become spectator Christians. The American sporting world is much the same. Britain is much different to America in this regard. If you like rugby, for example, until you are somewhat impaired physically, you would rather go and play rugby than watch it. You find hundreds of little teams playing little games with twenty people watching. There is an adoring wife that must put up with the cold, rain, and snow, pretending she is enjoying these stupid men rolling around in the mud. But because she loves her man, she endures it. Very rarely do you find these vast stadiums of people with highly professional players performing. Every one in the stands is an expert, but they never play the game.

In America, we have highly professional players who perform to large crowds of spectators. I want to suggest to you that the American church has caught this disease. We have become a church that is largely spectators who want the professional performers to do the job on our behalf. But here, the purpose of the Ephesians 4 ministry is not to perform to an admiring audience, but to motivate the body to become the expression of their Ephesians 4 gift.

In other words, the prophetic Ephesians 4 person will produce prophetic people. They will all be moving in prophecy, and they will be instructed and taught to do so. An Ephesians 4 evangelist will

Section 6 – Ephesians Chapter 4

produce an evangelizing people. An Ephesians 4 pastor will produce a shepherding people. When an Ephesians 4 ministry sees a need, his first response is to ask, "Where can I get someone or train someone to do this job?" His first instinct is not to jump in and do it himself. Instead, he is wired by God to think and act differently. At other levels of the same gift, equally from God and just as beautiful, the instinct is to go and do it. Both are necessary; otherwise, the job does not get done.

If you insist on shepherding people in a hands-on way, then you guarantee that your church will not grow beyond one hundred people, because that is the limit of your ability. This is a captain of fifty or one hundred. He is called this because he is limited by the way he handles the people. He produces a people who depend on him, and this gives him fulfillment and satisfaction. He is passionately given to the job of seeing them come to maturity. This is a wonderful ministry and calling. However, numerically it is limited.

We must know at what measure the gift is in us. These Ephesians 4 ministries are the people called by God to motivate the body, getting them to function in the work of the ministry. If this kind of input into your church is not resident, then you are consigned to smallness. The Ephesians 4 ministry stretches and develops people, putting them to work and causing the faith and expertise of the ministry to be imparted to the people so that they can do the job.

The joy of an Ephesians 4 ministry is seeing many people functioning effectively because of the input he has put into them. This is where real satisfaction comes—when other people are doing the work. The Ephesians 4 person has had some part in bringing others to this function. He does not have to be some great performer in large public meetings. Instead, he is down there getting among the people, equipping them to work.

The Unity of the Faith

Paul said in Ephesians 4:12–16 what this kind of functioning will do for the body:

> For the equipping of the saints for work of ministry, for the edifying of the body of Christ, till we all come to the unity of the faith and of the knowledge of the Son of God, to a perfect man, to the measure of the stature of the fullness of Christ; that we should no longer be children, tossed to and fro and carried about with every wind of doctrine, by the trickery of men, in the cunning craftiness of deceitful plotting, but, speaking the truth in love, may grow up in all things into Him who is the Head–Christ–from whom the whole body, joined and knit together by what every joint supplies, according to the effective working by which every part does its share, causes growth of the body for the edifying of itself in love.

What does this unity of faith mean? This does not mean we all come to some common doctrine of belief. We are not looking for a statement of faith, but we are coming to that level of faith which is the faith Jesus said to Peter, "Peter, have the faith that belongs to God!" (see 2 Pet. 1:1; Mark 11:22). Peter caught this faith and received the supernatural power of God to believe. As a result, he became a faith-filled believer who could do things. The unity of faith basically means we have the same level of faith for the vision which the pastor or leader has set before us. This is not just a leadership thing, but pertains to all of us.

This unity is not a statement about our beliefs, "This is our statement of faith…" No, your statement of faith is that you believe God can do anything. It is not the faith of the pastor or one person, but there is a body of people who have come to unity about this. You cannot have a few individuals with vision and fire and a slow lethargic body that will not move. This is most frustrating.

Section 6 – Ephesians Chapter 4

The church growth experts say something I believe has much truth. I do believe the following is quite accurate. They say in any given church you will basically have 15 percent initiators. You will have 35 percent early responders. You will have 35 percent late responders, and finally 15 percent non-responders. This is the average church mix. In other words, 15 percent of your people want to go, 35 percent are quickly persuaded to go, 35 percent are slowly persuaded, and 15 percent are never persuaded. It is not hard to motivate the 15 percent. They will go crazy and move quickly ahead while tearing the church apart if you are not careful. You must have the kind of impartation of vision and gift for ministry to bring along the others.

I've had to teach this to many leaders. They will get a vision and then run off on their own with a few enthusiastic supporters. They will try and make something happen while grumbling and complaining, castigating the rest of the church because, "They are not with me!" The reason they are not with the leader is because the leader did not take the time to bring them along. At least you should have the knowledge that the early responders are with you. Then it should be percolating through to the slow responders. Once the early responders are on board, you can begin to move in that vision.

For example, let's say a pastor wants to turn the church around and begin moving with an evangelistic home group structure. He is convinced from God that is the way to reach his city or town. If you simply share this information with one or two enthusiasts, trying to push the rest of the church into it, you are destined for failure. However, if you carry all the early responders and enthusiasts and they begin to percolate through to the slow responders, then that is the time to move to forward. If you wait for the non-responders, you will never move. I know some pastors who are so scared of upsetting a few people that they never go anywhere. These are keys for leadership. When you understand these principles, you can take the church somewhere.

Chapter 22 – Walk in Unity

We all come to the unity of the faith and to the knowledge of the Son of God, to a perfect man, to the measure of the stature and fullness of Christ that we should no longer be children tossed to and fro and carried about by every wind of doctrine. What we are working on is a great growing and maturing of the body in its knowledge of Jesus until she comes to that full stature. Summarized, we are coming to mature sonship. Therefore, we are no longer little children tossed about by every wind of doctrine and the trickery of men.

When some ministry comes to your church and misleads the people or some false prosperity teacher comes to your church trying to rip off the people, the people are so well taught that it does not make any difference. The people have the sense to reject him. You don't have to clean up a mess afterwards. Obviously, the ideal thing is not to let such a person in the church in the first place. Speaking the truth in love, we will in all things grow up into him who is the Head, that is, Christ. From Him, the whole body, joined and held together by every supporting ligament, grows and builds itself up in love, as each part does its work. I believe you can see this at local church level. I believe we must begin to see this at city level. You can see that every part is supplying something. Every part must be working. This is the glory of diversity within unity. In other words, the great preparation for city-taking means we must put ourselves to work to get a body that will walk in unity in Jesus' mighty name.

23

THE MIND OF CHRIST

In Ephesians 4:17, we find another way we are to walk. Paul said, "This I say, therefore, and testify in the Lord, that you should no longer walk as the rest of the Gentiles walk, in the futility of their mind." We must abandon a certain way of walking mentally in order to have a mind that is renewed in spirit. Our mind can be rewired to think like God thinks. That is what a renewed mind is like. This mind does not think worldly anymore. You find this all over the Bible. You will find this in Romans, after Paul gave his great treatise of God's cosmic purposes, which comes to a conclusion at the end of Romans 11. It finally tells us how the Jews will fit into God's end time purposes. Paul said, "Oh, the depth of the riches both of the wisdom and knowledge of God" (Rom. 11:33).

Immediately following, in chapter 12, Paul began the practical application of everything he taught. He said, "I beseech you therefore, brethren, by the mercies of God, that you present your bodies a living sacrifice..." (Rom. 12:1). Then it says in verse 2, in the Phillips translation, "Don't let the world around you squeeze you into its own mold...." There is a tremendous pressure upon Christians to think in a worldly manner.

Section 6 – Ephesians Chapter 4

I don't mean sinful thinking, but a mind that has been shaped by the world. Your priorities, sense of values, and success are shaped more by the world than they are by the Spirit of God. I want to say lovingly that the American church is very much shaped by the world. For example, the way the church promotes itself is very worldly. There is a worldly thinking that is so accepted in Christian circles that it is not seen for what it really is. This is a great hindrance for God to accomplish what He wants to accomplish. We must be open to this.

Paul addressed this worldly thinking in Ephesians and described it as a vital element to put off. When this worldly thinking is transformed it allows us to move with God in the Spirit in a way we have never been able to do before. A British brother recently told me about his house in England, which is several centuries old. He said sometimes there is a funny feeling in the house which you cannot quite put your finger on. Somehow, the house feels cold. He was not sure whether it was a physical or spiritual sensation.

Later, two things happened. A brother from Rwanda came on a visit and stayed in this brother's house. He walked into the house and said, "Innocent blood has been shed in this house." He went straight to the room where it happened and drove the demons out. The house was instantly cleansed. From that day on, the house has experienced a totally different atmosphere. The brother later found out that his house was known as the haunted house in that region. Later, an American brother was passing through and stayed in the same house with this brother. He had a vision or dream where he saw a soldier in very old clothing, possibly two or three hundred years ago, killing a woman and child. It all happened in that bedroom.

Notice, one man walked into the house and smelled it immediately and dealt with it. All the Brit could do was walk around the house saying, "Something is not right here," but no one had any idea what the problem was.

Chapter 23 – The Mind of Christ

The man from Rwanda had a mind that was not westernized and was far more open to the Spirit in certain respects. There is a great need for us to be renewed in the spirit of our minds. We attribute many things to natural circumstances when they are not. I am not suggesting we run off into some strange extreme looking for demons under every bed or rock. We want to be spiritually practical.

We are told in Ephesians 4:17–20 what has happened to the world and what has happened because of Adam's disobedience resulting in our state of disobedience. It says:

> Having their understanding darkened, being alienated from the life of God, because of the ignorance that is in them, because of the blindness of their heart; who, being past feeling, have given themselves over to lewdness, to work all uncleanness with greediness (Ephesians 4:18–19).

The word *alienated* in verse 18 means to be cut off. It is a severe word. The day Adam and Eve stepped out into independence, the life flow in them was no longer the eternal life of God. This cutting off deeply affected the way they thought. It affected their ability to have their mind in right relationship to the Spirit so as to think, see, hear, and understand spiritual things. While the mind was a perfectly effective tool of intellectualism, it was no longer an effective instrument or tool to communicate with the Spirit of God. We must walk away from worldly thinking.

As a result of this kind of thinking, people have become lewd to work all kinds of uncleanness and greediness. I used to live this way. According to Ephesians 2, we all lived this way. For years I was a convinced evolutionist. This is a stupid way to think. I remember being troubled when I bought my first house on virgin soil and planted out a garden for the first time. I put all the shrubs and flowers in the ground. They flowered and were absolutely beautiful. I remembered battling with the thought, "How can this be just an evolutionary process?"

Section 6 – Ephesians Chapter 4

There was design with everything I planted. I was grappling with these things in my mind. However, my mind was possessed at the time, and I was incapable of thinking spiritually.

I thank God that very early in my Christian life I was challenged by God on my first read through the Bible to let Him renew my mind. This happened within three months of conversion. In one moment, I became a convinced creationist, not because I was reasoned into it, but because I was transformed into it by a spiritual renewal of my mind. The change was so complete that from that morning on I was able to think like God.

When I talk to students in universities I find a massive population of people who think just like I thought. It is not a matter of intellect or lack of it, but a matter of whether your mind has been renewed. Once your mind has been renewed you need all your intellect and much more besides in order to comprehend the mysteries that God is now able to show you.

We must make a decision not to walk in our former ways. This is an act which you deliberately chose to take. Then it says in verse 20, "But you have not so learned Christ." Jesus, in His humanity, had the perfect human mind. We are invited, in several places in scripture, to let this mind be in us which was also in Christ Jesus. We are to be renewed in the spirit of our mind. We have the mind of Christ. This comes again and again in scripture. This is not just poetic language, but a very practical reality. We will never get there until we begin to think straight.

A New Mind in Christ

Now, in verse 21, it says: "If indeed you heard Him and have been taught by Him, as the truth is in Jesus." Starting with the next verse, we are given a whole list of things we are to put on and put off. The putting off and the putting on is a crisis moment.

Chapter 23 – The Mind of Christ

Let me repeat what I said earlier. There is a time when you hear God speak to you about an issue. The time to do something about it is when you hear Him speaking to you. If you obey Him when He speaks to you with a hunger to obey whatever He says, then that is the time when the transformation will take place. You cannot do it by saying, "I need to think about this for two or three weeks." If you do that, then you will lose your opportunity. When you decide to come back later and want it then, you won't necessarily be able to have it, because you have missed your moment of opportunity. I cannot say this strongly enough. When God speaks to you, that is the time when you should do something about it.

On a particular morning in my life, when I was reading through the Bible, I came to Hebrews 11:3 where it says, "By faith we understand that the worlds were framed by the word of God, so that the things which are seen were not made of things which are visible." God spoke to me and said, "You will not go anywhere until you change your attitude to My word." He said, "Take all your doubts about the Bible, including Joshua making the sun stand still, and perform a prophetic act."

I could calculate mathematically what would happen if the sun did stand still and the earth stopped rotating. The results would be disastrous in all kinds of incredible ways. My intellectual, scientific mind could not literally believe that story, so I put it aside as mythology. I went through all the stories of the Bible, including Jonah and the whale and Israel and the Red Sea, and I concluded that many of these stories were myths.

But God said to me, "You will never get anywhere until you change your attitude toward My word." He said, "Take all your doubts about the Bible. Symbolically, put them into a box, including all your doubts and reservations about the creation story, Tower of Babel, the flood, and so forth.

313

Section 6 – Ephesians Chapter 4

When you have them all together, take them to the window and throw them out by faith. Make a decision that from now on you will trust every word of scripture like a little child."

He continued to convince me, "When you received Jesus as Savior and that man talked to you about believing in the cross, that it would take away your sins, did it make any sense to you?"

I said, "No."

He said, "What happened then?"

I said, "I decided to believe it."

He asked, "Did it work?"

I said, "Absolutely."

He said, "That is the way you must deal with these issues as well. Take all your doubts and throw them out the window and decide like a little child to trust My word."

I made this decision immediately. This stuffy intellectual professor was instantly delivered from intellectualism, and I became a childlike thinker who could think like God from a moment of obedience. That was my window of opportunity. I have never been troubled since with intellectualism. I thank God for my mind, because it is much better now than what it was before. My mind is totally submitted to His revealed truth.

In verse 21, it says, "If indeed you have heard Him and have been taught by Him, as the truth is in Jesus." There are crisis moments when the truth of God's word is appropriated to our lives. It suddenly becomes practical and experiential. Do not miss these moments. These great riches of our inheritance are in Him. We cannot receive the faith to appropriate them until we have heard Him and have been taught by Him as the truth is in Jesus.

Chapter 23 – The Mind of Christ

Too many Christians live on leaning faith or proxy faith. In John 4, the woman who was powerfully converted after encountering Jesus at the well came to her town and said, "Come, see a Man who told me all things that I ever did" (John 4:29). The whole town came out to meet Jesus, and then it says in verse 39–42:

> Many of the Samaritans of that city believed in Him because of the word of the woman who testified, "He told me all that I ever did." So when the Samaritans had come to Him, they urged Him to stay with them; and He stayed there two days. And many more believed because of His own word. Then they said to the woman, "Now we believe, not because of what you said, for we ourselves have heard Him and we know that this is indeed the Christ, the Savior of the world."

These Samaritans first had a faith because they believed what was said to them. This is what is called leaning faith or proxy faith. These Samaritans came and listened to Jesus and said, "Now we believe, not because of what you have said, for *we ourselves have heard* Him and we know that this is the Savior of the world." These believers went from being convinced by what the woman said to belief based on what they had heard for themselves.

This is a particular problem when teenagers or children grow up in a Christian home. They grow up believing all the things they believe because their parents have taught it to them. When I saw my children like this, I prayed for the day that they would have their own encounters with Jesus so that they would not only live the faith of their parents, but they would be living in their own experience of God. Before they went off to university, they needed to know where their feet were grounded and to whom they belonged. If they went off to university with proxy faith, then that faith would have been destroyed.

Section 6 – Ephesians Chapter 4

There comes a point when we must see Him and hear Him for ourselves. Only then does that word have the power to bring us to real faith. My wife Eileen sat in a conference and heard a wonderful preacher talking about the old man being crucified with Christ and living in holy victory over sin. She tried and tried to believe it, but she couldn't do it. Then on a motorcycle on the way home she heard Christ for herself. Suddenly, the old man was thrown over the hedge into the next ditch, and it was a done deal. It had come to her from the Lord Himself.

We must bring our people to this place in the Spirit where they have heard God for themselves. I remember the day when my children, one by one, had their own encounters with God. Then I knew rightly that they were hooked for life. I never had any more anxieties about them.

There must be a renewing of the spirit of the mind, which causes us to think differently. Paul then said:

> That you put off, concerning your former conduct, the old man which grows corrupt according to the deceitful lusts, and be renewed in the spirit of your mind, and that you put on the new man which was created according to God, in true righteousness and holiness (Ephesians 4:22–24).

These are the things we do. This must become practical. I have done my best to explain how this happens. On a Wednesday morning in 1965, I put on the mind of Christ and stopped thinking lustful thoughts, which I struggled with in my first seven years as a believer. It happened on one Wednesday morning, and I have never been troubled with it since. That was 1965. I have the mind of Christ.

I have been very careful to guard this new mind. I am very careful what I watch. I hardly ever watch television. I hardly watch any movies, not because I am some stuffy old prude, but because frankly they are contaminating. Even the advertisements are seductive and contaminating.

I have my hand on the switch for the television, because I do not want this lovely new thing God has given me to be polluted by the junk that comes through our various television programs. I would rather have my new mind than anything else I can think of.

Put Off and Put On

Then we come to a list of things that we could spend much time on. Paul said in Ephesians 4:25, "Therefore, putting away lying, 'Let each one of you speak truth with his neighbor,' for we are members of one another." Putting on truth is not as easy as one might think. I remember when I was going through this process a few years ago. I said, "Lord, I am a truthful person. Why do you write these things to believers all the time? These are elementary." I said to the Lord, "If I ever tell a lie during the day, just ring a bell in my heart." By the end of the day, I was deaf with this clanging bell!

Did you know that exaggeration is lying? Politicians have a wonderful way of wiggling around the truth. One of the British ministers said recently, "We have not lied, but we were simply economical with the truth." Put on truth! This is a great thing to put on. Always speak truth with your neighbor, because we are members one with another.

We are then told to put off unrighteous anger. We are specifically told not to let it continue past sunset. You might kid yourself, "There is righteous anger." Yes, there is, but you are not to let the sun go down on your anger. The times when that verse has convicted my wife and me saved our lives when we had our backs to each other in bed! We had a small altercation of words. My wife was always at fault of course! But I was willing to forgive her if only she would admit it. There we were on our king-size bed, as far to the edges as we could get with our backs to each other. Suddenly, this wretched verse pops up. We turned to each other and said, "We cannot go to sleep until we settle this. We must get right with each other by the end of this day."

Section 6 – Ephesians Chapter 4

Never let the sun go down on your anger. This saved us again and again.

This principle is also true between brothers. If there is any issue, then we must deal with it. Jesus talked about this. If your brother offends you, then you forgive him and forget it. If you cannot, then you must go and put things right with him. You cannot leave issues unresolved. This is totally unbiblical. You definitely do not go and talk to someone else about it first. You go to the individual first. The whole purpose of the exercise is not to repeat all your critical judgments, but the purpose of the exercise is to gain your brother. That is what my Bible says (see Matt. 18:15). If your brother sins, go and reprove him in private. The same Greek word *elegcheo* is used here. You go and persuade him to see it your way, but you must be open to possibly seeing it his way. There is a reasonable nature to your approach and speech. Things must be resolved.

These are the practicalities that keep us in the power to overcome any demonic assault upon our lives, church, or city. It says here in verse 27, "Nor give place to the devil." Failing to do these things gives place to the devil. Think of all the unresolved issues between brothers and sisters in a city, and you can imagine why the devil can keep his feet well established in the town. If these things are not resolved, then all our praying and casting him out means nothing. He will only laugh at us. These things are written for our help.

The apostle continues in verse 28 by putting on financial integrity. He says, "Let him who stole steal no longer...." Most Christians have been stealing from God. Pastors are some of the worst thieves I have known. If you don't give to God the full tithe, then you are a thief. You don't receive divine pardon because you are a pastor. In fact, we must be exemplary in these things. I can't teach things I am not practicing. I don't steal from the tax man even if I feel the taxes are unjust.

Chapter 23 – The Mind of Christ

I do my best to righteously minimize what I am liable to pay, but I do not go beyond that.

I drive at the speed limit even if I think it is stupid, because I am to obey every ordinance of law. Even if I think, "This is the most ridiculous place to put a 35 mile speed limit," I must still obey the law. These are the ways our practical integrity will be tested. Our finances must be impeccable.

I will not take other people's software programs and download them illegally onto our computers. I will buy a copy of my own, although it still annoys me to do it. But that is the law, and I am obliged to live by the law. I don't want to give the devil an opportunity to wreck my whole computer network because there is sin right there in the computer. I don't want one finger of wrongdoing being pointed against me. We had a good clean up on all our computers. I called an expert in and said, "I don't want anything, software or computer, that we have not righteously paid for. Wipe everything off, and we will buy what we need so that we are squeaky clean before God and before man." As far as I am concerned, this is true right through our entire organization. I don't really agree with the copyright laws, and I think it is very unfair, but that is where the law is, and I must obey it the way it is.

Then in verse 29, it says, "Let no corrupt word proceed out of your mouth, but what is good for necessary edification, that it may impart grace to the hearers." What you hear someone tell you about someone else is often corrupt. I am very careful how I pass on information. These days, there are many stories on the internet, and half of the time you learn that someone has invented them. If we don't know things are factual or something has no substance, then don't forward such information onto others. I keep many things to myself these days, because I am not quite sure.

Section 6 – Ephesians Chapter 4

Until I know for sure, I will be careful. I don't want to add to the miscommunication business currently active in Christian circles.

Let no corrupt communication come out of your mouth, especially in the area of judgment or criticism of another person, "He is a lovely brother, but…." Even if the news you heard is distressing, that is all the more reason not to repeat it unless you absolutely have to. However, if a person you know is a wolf in sheep's clothing, a charlatan gone to join another church that you know, then I do believe you must tell the pastor of that church. That is a matter of responsibility. You don't want that church to be messed up because of this person. That is not what we are talking about here.

The purpose of our speech is very clear:

Let no corrupt word proceed out of your mouth, but what is good for necessary edification, that it may impart grace to the hearers. And do not grieve the Holy Spirit of God, by whom you were sealed for the day of redemption (Ephesians 4:29–30).

The Spirit of God is grieved by many conversations that occur between Christians. We must also put away the following things in verse 31, "Let all bitterness, wrath, anger, clamor, and evil speaking be put away from you, with all malice." Then it says what we are to put on in verse 32: "Be kind to one another, tenderhearted, forgiving one another, even as God in Christ forgave you."

The church can be one of the cruelest places I know when a person is caught in sin. When a pastor fails and is kicked out of his home at a moment's notice, and nothing is done by the fellowship of pastors that prayed together with him every week, then something is wrong. The cruelty of the body of Christ to its own fallen ones is appalling. We may need to discipline someone, but we must also show a way of redemption in what we do. There must be a way back. A whole new kindness must come in. I could talk for one hour on this.

Chapter 23 – The Mind of Christ

I just want to drop seeds here and say the whole of our activity must be impacted by the Spirit of God. He must have the right and opportunity to go over everything we think and do, until what we think and do, does not grieve Him. I grieved Him for years. When you get more and more sensitive to God and closer to Him, then things you passed over two years ago are no longer acceptable. God caught me lying and really took me to the woodshed over that issue. I prayed to God to help me put away all exaggeration and false testimony.

SECTION 7
Ephesians Chapters 5 and 6

24

WALK IN LOVE, PURITY, LIGHT, AND WISDOM

Now we move into Ephesians 5, where Paul said:

> Therefore be imitators of God as dear children. And walk in love, as Christ also has loved us and given Himself for us, an offering and a sacrifice to God for a sweet-smelling aroma (Ephesians 5:1–2).

This is obvious in what it is saying. However, I want to underline these things three times in red until these principles become our practical way of living. Put away how much bitterness? How much wrath? How much anger? How much evil speaking and malice? All! We must put away attitudes that are contrary to love and put on attitudes that demonstrate love. It is not enough to tell your wife you love her. You must show her it is true. It is so easy to say, "I love you, brother. I love you, sister." Well, let's see it. We are to walk in love, imitating God and loving to the same standard as Jesus. This is a tall order and hard, but not impossible!

The word *forgiving* or *forbearance* has the idea of covering over. When Ham, Seth, and Japeth found Noah drunk, Ham exposed his sin, but the other two covered his sin. There is a right way to cover things up so that you don't let things out.

For example, say you, as a church member, come to the pastor's house, and you hear a first-class conflict going on inside. You could do one of two things at that moment. You could decide that you never heard it, or you could go and gossip it around to the rest of the church. There is a right place to deal with sin, but there is also a right place to cover sin. The Spirit of God must show us when these options are appropriate.

There are things you chose not to register, even though you can hear and see they are going on. Sometimes I visit homes, and being quite prophetic, I can pick things up very quickly. This is part of the equipment God has given me to do my job well. If I allow this gift to become judgmental or a source of gossip, then I am absolutely grieving the Holy Spirit, and I participate in an abuse of the gift God has given me.

Walk in Moral Purity

Now the scriptures move on into the issue of walking in moral purity. Paul said in Ephesians 5:3–4:

> But fornication and all uncleanness or covetousness, let it not even be named among you, as is fitting for saints; neither filthiness, nor foolish talking nor coarse jesting, which are not fitting, but rather giving of thanks.

It is very interesting that greed, or covetousness, is put in there along with fornication and other impurities. If you have ambition for things, and you are coveting things, God puts it in the same category as being immoral and fornicating. That staggered me and took me a long time to understand why. Basically, both immorality and greed satisfy lust. But you must not allow yourself to be that kind of person. Avoid covetousness, which is another kind of lust that comes from the same root. If we don't deal with it, we will be disqualified and become another spiritual casualty.

If you are covetous and greedy in one area, then it can pop up in another area. It is amazing how God connects covetous living with sexual immorality. This comes again and again. If you are uncontrolled in your eating habits, you will likely be uncontrolled in your sexual habits. If you are uncontrolled in your desire for things, then you will be uncontrolled in many other areas as well. They are all branches of the same root. That is why I am very careful regarding the way I eat. I am on the road very often, traveling from place to place, and everyone wants to take me out to eat great dinners. It would be very easy to overeat. God has taught me a certain routine that helps me.

One of the things that has been very valuable to me is not long fasts, but maintaining a life of daily self-discipline. I conduct a daily fast very regularly. I go without food for a day. I have a day when I can be alone with God so that my body learns to survive without food for a day. It has this kind of training. It is like an athlete who will keep his muscles in shape so that when he must run a race he is ready. This keeps the body in constant submission. Paul said the following, "I discipline my body and bring it into subjection, lest, when I have preached to others, I myself should become disqualified" (1 Cor. 9:27). Keeping my body under authority, where my spirit can rule my body, is a vital part of my personal discipline.

It is almost impossible for me to think about a forty-day fast, because it means you must shut down on everything. Personally, I think it is very impractical to ask churches to commit themselves to forty-day fasts in this strict sense. A real fast means not eating food and only consuming water. This means building up to the fast gradually and slowly breaking the fast. This is a great time commitment and severely affects your normal living capacity. Personally, I think this kind of fast is often done with an ill-thought extravagance.

Section 7 – Ephesians Chapters 5 and 6

Many churches say, "We are going on a forty-day fast." This means as a body each person will give up something during that forty-day period. Jill will give up watching soap operas on a Thursday afternoon. This is a discipline and needed. Jack will give up sweets during the forty day period. But this is not a fast in the biblical sense. It is a good discipline, highly advised, which will bring certain benefits. Biblical fasting, however, means abstaining from food and drinking water.

Three days is appropriate for anyone. I have found in the churches that I have led in various countries of the world, including Great Britain, that when people start a one-day fast and understand that they can survive without dying, and then extend that period to three days, that this is compatible with maintaining ordinary, everyday life. The churches that I have had leadership over conducted periodic three-days fasts. I found these to be far more powerful in destroying demonic principalities and powers than one special event of forty days. This is not reality, because most people do not really participate.

When the whole church does three days, there is a power, because the whole church can handle it. Most people with a minimum of training can handle three days, and they discover they are much stronger at the end in every way than when they started. You can also meet for two or three nights in special meetings for prayer to target something. Even if you have to go to work during the day, you can still gather at night and hit those demonic principalities. Once every three months for two days is possible. It is practical and incredibly powerful. Think and pray how God can build these things into your life.

I am determined that food will never rule over my body. The cravings of the flesh will be dealt with by my grace-filled spirit ruling over them! I am serious about the Kingdom and being in proper condition for God both physically and spiritually. Any modern army is serious about getting you physically fit in order to be an effective soldier.

We must be just as serious in every respect. We must be fit for war. Part of our fitness is a proper regulation of our physical habits and needs. I don't think you can be effective in spiritual warfare when your body is an uncontrolled heap of flab. Excuse me for being blunt, but I feel I must say these things. Eating right is just as important as having the right kind of prayer life. They all work together toward the same end.

Notice what Paul says in Ephesians 5:4, "Neither filthiness, nor foolish talking, nor coarse jesting, which are not fitting, but rather giving of thanks." This is particularly true when a group of men come together. It is unfortunately true even when a group of godly Christian men come together. There is a certain kind of joking, coarse joking, which I find offends my spirit and the Spirit of God. If you have to change the conversation because a lady comes in, then there is something wrong with your conversation. There is a certain way of joking that is inappropriate and unfitting for us. Paul says it should not even be named among us, as is fitting for saints. I believe this includes jokes that poke fun at a particular ethnic group. We don't need these things in our midst. They must be stopped and put out!

Paul continues in verse 5, "For this you know, that no fornicator, unclean person, nor covetous man, who is an idolater, has any inheritance in the kingdom of Christ and of God." If you want an inheritance in the Kingdom of God, then put immoral things away and walk in moral purity. I don't believe this verse is arguing whether someone is saved or not, but whether a person comes into their inheritance in the Kingdom of God. By conducting ourselves in these sinful ways, we forfeit any inheritance in God's Kingdom. We cannot advance the Kingdom. Rather than being a help to the Kingdom, we are a hindrance.

Verses 6–7 conclude, "Let no one deceive you with empty words, for because of such things the wrath of God comes upon the sons of disobedience. Therefore do not be partakers with them."

Section 7 – Ephesians Chapters 5 and 6

Walk in the Light

Then Paul described another way in which we are to walk. He said quite emphatically: Walk in the light!

> For you were once darkness, but now you are light in the Lord. Walk as children of light (for the fruit of the Spirit is in all goodness, righteousness, and truth), finding out what is acceptable to the Lord (Ephesians 5:8–10).

Much is said about this in 1 John as well. Light and darkness are mutually exclusive and cannot coexist. If you walk into a dark room and turn the light on, the darkness ceases to be there. This is obvious. It is also a basic scientific fact that light is now recognized as the ultimate source of power and energy. Light in laser form is one of the most precise means of destruction that man has yet invented. There is a laser beam that now exists that can take out human cells one at a time. They can actually begin to destroy a cancerous area with such precision by using the laser beam. God's light is the ultimate source of power and energy.

Light has three important dimensions. First, light exposes. If we walk in the light as He is in the light, then we have fellowship one with another. Jesus said that there are those who refuse to come to the light because their deeds are evil. Some people love darkness rather than light, because their deeds are wicked (see John 3:20–21). The first work of light is to expose and show things the way they really are.

If we are serious with God, then we are not afraid of that light. Instead, we welcome the light! We ought to walk in that light. God has an answer for everything He exposes. It is the blood of Jesus Christ His Son. When something is hidden, God cannot remove it. When something is exposed, it is not hard for Him to deal with it.

Second, when light has exposed something, it has the power to destroy what has been exposed. These are all scriptural concepts expounded in 1 John and here in Ephesians 5.

The third dimension is that light has the power to create. Photosynthesis is a means by which God uses light to manufacture things. Light is a form that God uses to create things. Things are manufactured by the activity of light. Certain plants have a gift from God; no man could create what God has put in plants. A little leaf in the simplest of plants conducts an incredibly complex photosynthesis. As a scientist, this is absolutely amazing to me. I spent much of my life investigating the activity of light.

My job in research was to chart any light reaction and try to produce products from this research. This is a highly specialized sphere. I literally became a student of light. I discovered various dynamics of light reactions in various physical and chemical substances. I had just been converted at the time, and I could see God as the creator of all these wonderful and complex things. For example, the way textiles are manufactured, the way aircraft parts are made, the way microchips are manufactured, all rely on products that I was involved with for the Kodak research department so many years ago. I became absorbed and obsessed with photosynthesis.

In God, spiritually, the light of God can come and create what was not there. The area of shame, which you don't even want God to see, can become your greatest area of beauty. When you let Him see it and are open and frank to let God get at it, a transformation will take place. You say, "I lay myself bare. Please deal with this!" First, the light exposes. Then, light destroys what is darkness. Then, light creates that which is beautiful. The area of shame becomes the area of greatest beauty in your life. This is what happens when you walk in the light. This is a quick summary of it.

Walk in Wisdom

Then, in Ephesians 5:15–21, we are told to walk in wisdom:

> See then that you walk circumspectly, not as fools but as wise, redeeming the time, because the days are evil. Therefore do not be unwise, but understand what the will of the Lord is. And do not be drunk with wine, in which is dissipation; but be filled with the Spirit, speaking to one another in psalms and hymns and spiritual songs, singing and making melody in your heart to the Lord, giving thanks always for all things to God the Father in the name of our Lord Jesus Christ, submitting to one another in the fear of God.

When it says, "Be filled with Spirit," the verb is in the present continuous tense. It is not commanding you to be filled with the Spirit. Instead, it is commanding you to go on continuously being filled with the Spirit. In other words, you have learned to drink consistently from the fountain of life in the Spirit. Again and again, you will find this expression which exhorts us to give thanks.

25

WALK IN SUBMISSION

We come now to the final way in which we are to walk in submission. Ephesians 5:21 says, "Submitting to one another in the fear of God." I want to say a few words about biblical submission. Submission has several elements to it. It is certainly having true humility, which is denying self for the purposes of the Kingdom of God. It means denying anything of the flesh, including self-seeking, self-exaltation, and self-promotion. Humility is esteeming others as higher than self. The word *submission* means "to put self under." This was a military term, which means you now recognize that the body of Christ has God-ordained ranking. We are not all equal. The church is not an egalitarian system. We are not all the same. We are certainly all equally valuable, but we are not all the same.

God has put order in His Kingdom. We don't kick against, resent, or try to buck in opposition. The difference between submission in the Kingdom of God and in the world is that we joyfully recognize it as our God-given blessing and God-given security. God is very careful to teach those in His Kingdom how we exercise authority and how we practice submission. This is far too large a subject to cover here, but I believe this is a vital part of understanding the Kingdom of God.

Section 7 – Ephesians Chapters 5 and 6

There have been some terrible perversions of this, but this does not give us the right to throw it all out and say, "From now on I don't submit to anyone but Jesus." This attitude is not permitted in the Kingdom. There are certain relationships where submission is very clearly taught in scripture. Biblical submission is a passion to put yourself under those in the Kingdom that God clearly indicates have been given a responsibility of leadership and authority, in the best biblical sense of the word, over you and your life. Certain relationships automatically indicate this. In a family, the wife in the Kingdom cannot marry a husband without recognizing her need to submit to him. That does not mean he stomps around having his own way.

We will see that the apostle Paul immediately addressed marriage to make sure there is no misunderstanding about the kind of submission he is talking about. What God requires of the man is a thousand times more, better, or harder than what he has given to the woman. All a man has to do is be like Jesus, and he will be the perfect husband. You have to love your wife like He loved the church and gave Himself for her. What a calling! He is to wash her with the water of the word until she is without spot, blemish, wrinkle, or any such thing.

The man has tremendous loving responsibilities. He is to nourish and cherish his wife. These are two wonderful old English words. There is no good equivalent. He is to be a source of fatness of supply to feed and develop her spirituality. He is to provide for her in every way. He must give her the security so that she is not carrying any of those providing burdens. That is his domain. Most women do not have a problem with a husband who behaves like Jesus. The only problem is that there are too few of them around.

Submission is not blind obedience! There is a difference between submission and obedience, although they are connected. There is an order of authority that must be grasped. I have developed the different kinds of authority in the Kingdom of God and their counterfeit, and I put them in their proper order. It says in Romans 13 to obey the highest authority. Sometimes there is a conflict of authority. Here is the order of authority:

1. God–He has complete authority.

2. His Word

3. A Word-quickened Conscience–Imagine a magnet that is lubricated in a clean pure bath of oil under a strong magnetic field. That magnet will swing in the right direction. If there is no strong magnetic field, then the magnet will wander around not knowing which way to point. If the magnet is on rusty bearings, not properly lubricated, it can be stuck because of the lack of oil and lubrication. It will give you a false reading.

Imagine a compass in perfect working order beautifully oiled floating in a wonderful bath of oil with sympathetic bearings under a strong magnetic field. This compass will always point in the right direction. This is the picture of what I have called a word-soaked conscience. The word is like the magnetic field. The oil is the lubricating power of the Holy Spirit.

The Bible talks about different kinds of consciences. There is a weak conscience. There is a seared conscience. There is a false and true conscience. Apart from hearing God, one of the most important faculties we need is a word-soaked conscience that unerringly points to truth. Whatever you hear and whatever impressions come, your dial always swings in the right direction, "I know that is true. That is not true!"

The anointing you have received will teach you all things so that there is no need for people to teach you. That does not mean you need no one to teach you, but there is in you an unerring truth detector. Even if you have not heard something before, that anointing says, "That was a word from God." It tells you that. When you have this kind of conscience, it is number three in the order of authority.

4. Delegated Authority–This is where problems often arise. Delegated authority might be a pastor in a church. It might be the apostolic ministry that God has shown you to have authority. It is delegated from God. Other relationships of delegated authority include husbands to wives, parents to children, employers to employees. What a delegated authority tells you cannot contradict what your conscience is telling you, providing it is a genuine word-soaked conscience.

In scripture you will find that the apostle Paul would never override another person's conscience. This is our safeguard. If I have a young child, then I know he does not have a conscience that works properly. As a parent, I must direct the child and build his conscience to work properly. However, the relationship with the child changes when he grows up to maturity. The relationship with my son, for example, is a constantly changing dynamic.

Notice how the apostle Paul dealt with the apostle Apollos. Even though Apollos was under Paul in authority, Paul said, "I wanted Apollos to go to so and so, but he didn't think it was right, so he didn't go." This is how it reads in 1 Corinthians 16:12, "Now concerning our brother Apollos, *I strongly urged* him to come to you with the brethren, but *he was quite unwilling to come at this time*; however, he will come when he has a convenient time." That was not rebellion or defiance. Paul recognized that Apollos was mature enough to hear God for himself.

Chapter 25 – Walk in Submission

If Apollos did not feel good about it, then Paul would not force him to do what he did not feel good about. This is the way authority and submission work. We could spend much time on this.

We need to see how this works in the church and the Kingdom. There have been many abuses of this, but we must get it right. For some, the abuses have given them the excuse to live in total independent rebellion against all authority. Both extremes are wrong. The act of submission and the attitude of submission are two different things. I can act in submission without having a submissive attitude, and I can choose not to submit while maintaining a submissive attitude. If a leader has an attitude of submission, then he fearfully recognizes he has been given a responsibility from God, to whom he is responsible. He will not abuse or misuse the authority God has given him. He knows he must give an account to someone who will deal with him. Submission runs right through the Kingdom.

Obedience is conditional upon conscience. For example, one day a boss told his accountant employee to falsify figures in order to save tax expenses. But the accountant said, "I will obey you in all things, but I will not do that!" That was the right response. He had to disobey his employer in order to obey God. There comes a point even in civil law where a higher authority must be obeyed over a lower authority. Peter stood before the Sanhedrin saying, "We must obey God rather than man. We cannot accept your order to speak no more in the name of Jesus" (see Acts 5:29). Yet it was Peter who said, "Submit yourselves to every ordinance of man for the Lord's sake, whether to the king as supreme, or to governors, as to those who are sent by him for the punishment of evildoers and for the praise of those who do good" (1 Pet. 2:13–14). There was a line drawn that Peter could not cross; he could not disobey God in order to obey civil authorities.

Section 7 – Ephesians Chapters 5 and 6

I've had the unfortunate experience of dealing with Christian marriages with husbands who are perverted. Hear this carefully: Marriage is not a legalizing of lust. You cannot do what you like when you want and how you want just because you are married. The Bible says, "Let the marriage bed be undefiled." There is a godly way of enjoying this great gift from God, and there is a foul, perverted, worldly way that should never be known or exercised among Christians.

I have been called in on several occasions to counsel a marriage relationship where the husband wanted to get into all kinds of perverted things, and the wife cannot participate with him because of conscience sake. I have to say, "She has a right to say no." She can say, "I will obey you as my husband, but not to the point of violating my conscience and obedience to God in order to satisfy your wrong, sinful lusts, even when they are within marriage." These are lines that must be drawn. In a very submissive way, you can say no. Walking in submission is very powerful in overcoming all the powers of Satan, because it establishes an obedient and pure church.

Three Major Bomb-Proof Relationships

I want us to look at three major relationships that must be bomb-proof through proper submission. If these relationships are not impregnable to satanic attacks, then what begins as a great city-taking movement ends up in disaster. If you study the whole strategy of city-taking under Nehemiah, then you will find that when it came to the city, the first thing Nehemiah did was put a wall around the city. When I was doing research on this subject, something staggered me. Since the year 516 BC, they had completed the temple. It took time, but the temple was finally built. Later, they completed their own comfortable homes, creating a nice environment in which to live. However, they had to travel back and forth from their comfortable homes to the temple, where they were having fantastic meetings with God's presence falling on them. But in between their homes and the temple was a ruined city.

Chapter 25 – Walk in Submission

This is such a picture of where many of us are in our cities and towns.

We have much teaching in the church. We have our own Christian schools running. We have homeschooling functioning very well. Apart from some men and women going to work, we can live fairly well with minimal contact with the world. In our homes, we have godly order. Every time I step into a house, I can almost always tell if the children are homeschooled or not. There is a glory about them you do not find elsewhere. I have observed this again and again. There is something special about this dynamic. It is possible to have a wonderful home while traveling to a wonderful worship and praise center having fantastic meetings. Then you zip back to your comfortable home, and all the time a ruined city cries out for redemption. This is where we are in many places. We have a fine and wonderful church, which we deeply love. Our kids like it as much as we do. We have fantastic things happening. It is pretty easy to live this kind of isolated life where you hardly need to touch this dying world at all.

It staggered me that this situation in Nehemiah's day went from 516 BC to 445 BC. This is approximately seventy-one years. The city of Jerusalem lay in ruins, yet the temple was built and their nice homes were functioning normally. It seems to me that is where we have been throughout this last century in the United States of America.

Nehemiah had a high job in the capital of the Median-Persian Empire. He was the king's cup-bearer, a high place of responsibility. It is like being the top security person for the President of the United States of America. This person made sure that nothing came through to the emperor that could possibility harm him. This was a very trusted position which was very well paid. Someone came to Nehemiah with a report about Jerusalem, and he was totally undone. Nehemiah's journey and the restoration of the city all began with a heartbreak for the city. This is where it must begin for us.

Section 7 – Ephesians Chapters 5 and 6

When you cry out to God with the heartbreak for the city or nation, God will bring you through to faith for its transformation. When Nehemiah went to talk with the king, he was asked, "What do you want to do?" "Please let me go, give me funding from the government, and I will rebuild it." Nehemiah had utter confidence in this task. Then he began a process. When Nehemiah got to Jerusalem, he discovered all kinds of schemes and plots against him, which proved totally ineffective. Once Nehemiah motivated the people to work, they couldn't be stopped. There were perfumers, goldsmiths, silversmiths, and many other professions doing the work. City-taking is not just for pastors of churches. Every kind of occupation is involved.

I believe, if we are going to take our cities and nation, then we must involve men and women of God who are placed by God in all kinds of places that we call "secular positions." Nehemiah himself was serving in a secular position. He was not a priest or pastor. When these two elements start working together, only then can the Kingdom come in its full power and glory. We are having much influence with many key people in the city of San Antonio who have a heart after God. They are all part of the army God is putting together to take this city. They are just as important and strategic as any pastor. They need to be strategically prayed for.

It says in Nehemiah 6 that when this army began to move together they completed the building of the wall in fifty-two days. They put a secure ring around the city, which prevented anyone from coming in. All corrupting influences, charlatans, and raiding mobs were kept out of the city because of that wall. The fight over building that wall was phenomenal. Nehemiah was a brilliant strategist, because he taught all the different leaders with local responsibilities to see the larger picture of their work. He brought them together, and all of them were warriors and builders together. They knew how to use tools for building, and they knew how to use a sword to fight (see Neh. 4:16–18).

There were a few in the list of leaders who were specialist swordsmen. The enemy had many different kinds of plots and plans to overthrow them, but Nehemiah's strategy preempted that and stopped the enemy's plans from ever getting off the ground. One of the things Nehemiah did was, when seeing a low part in the wall, he put a particularly strong person with a sword right in that cavity, saying, "If anyone comes through this hole, they will have this warrior to deal with!" I saw this as a strategy. In building leadership teams, we need to have more specifically directed intercessors. I believe men who are on the cutting edge of what God is doing need personal intercessors.

David had thirty-six mighty men altogether. However, three of them had the sole role of making sure that nothing ever got through to David. Their only purpose was to protect and guard David. They said, "You will have to go through us if you want to get to David." Another three men had responsibility to lead the other thirty, most likely in groups of ten. All of these things are written in the Bible for our instruction, especially for those on whom the end of the ages has come.

I work with a wonderful apostolic man in Austria, which is a tough place to see breakthrough. I have worked with this man for many years. He is an Italian married to an English woman. There are two Austrian men on his team, one married to a German woman and the other to an American. This is the core of the team that God is using. I have been a father apostolically to them for years. About eighteen months ago, we felt the time had come to plant a church strategically in Vienna. This city is incredibly tough. One of those six, if you like, was assigned to one of the low parts of the wall. I appointed certain intercessors to watch over that low part, because I thought there was a danger. If the devil is going to attack, he will attack there to try and break the whole thing up. We must understand that there is strategy to these things.

Section 7 – Ephesians Chapters 5 and 6

In the next passage of Ephesians, we are immediately introduced to the marriage relationship, then the parent-child relationship, and finally the master-servant, employer-employee, leader-follower relationship. This final category is someone who works for someone else for any reason. These are the three areas of great vulnerability, and Paul speaks to all this before he ever talks about going to war. Many people joyfully jump into Ephesians 6 without going through the process of Ephesians 1–5. As we have journeyed through this material, we have found many things that we must put in order before we come functionally to Ephesians 6:10 and following.

1. The Marriage Relationship

Why does Paul talk about marriage just before speaking about wrestling with principalities and powers? Paul knew the vulnerability of that relationship. If the marriage goes down, then that man is sunk as far as his potential to wage war against the enemy. If a woman's marriage collapses, then she will not be able to accomplish her full potential for the Kingdom. We must recognize these target areas: marriages, children, and covenant relationships.

So let's take this issue of submission in marriage. The husband is clearly instructed as to his role in the relationship. I have summarized this by saying that Christ and His church are the reality, while the husband and wife are the shadow. If a husband has any doubt as to how he is to behave, he simply needs to ask, "How does Christ treat the church?" If you treat your wife the way Jesus treats the church, then you will be doing well.

On the other hand, if a wife wants to know how she is to behave in response to her husband, then she must ask the question, "How does the church behave toward Christ?" This is the role she is acting out toward her husband. He loves her by giving himself for her. He nourishes and cherishes her. She honors, respects, and follows her husband as the church does Christ.

If I find a man functioning in some great ministry, but he has an absolutely starved wife, I know that something is deeply wrong. If I have any apostolic fathering responsibility, then I must get in there to address this issue, because I cannot leave it the way it is without serious consequences. As leaders and pastors, we must look at the state of the marriages in our leadership team. Of course, we must begin with ourselves. Ask yourself, "Am I like Christ as a husband? Am I nourishing her, feeding her what she needs?"

Tragically, the woman is often the head of her man in spirituality, even in many leadership situations. The man should be the source of enrichment for his wife and family. That is his responsibility. Be the source of nourishment for your wife. My wife and I have fantastic times in the word together. There are times when she gets things from God that are an absolute treasure to me. But I certainly flow back to her in equality. I feed her many things. We pray together and meditate together. We will brainstorm together, and I will try out some of my daring theological impressions. The way she handles them gives me a good idea of where I am going. This is our life. We spend a lot of time doing this, and it is enriching for both of us.

I also cherish my wife. The word *cherish* has the idea of value. It has the picture of handling a very precious possession like a very costly vase. It is love, but even more than that. You convey to her in tangible and intangible ways that she is the most precious and wonderful person God has given you. You are amazed and grateful that she would want to spend her life with you. She feels absolutely secure in your appreciation and care for her. You put a shield around her and protect her so that she does not have to carry the burden of things.

Financially, I make sure Eileen never has to carry the weight of our expenses or supply. Even if we are in a tough situation, it is still my burden.

Section 7 – Ephesians Chapters 5 and 6

We have certainly suffered a trial in our faith financially, but that has been the exception rather than the rule. She has always felt absolutely secure and cherished by me. Everywhere I go around the world, I can't stop talking about her. People say to her, "So you are the woman Alan is always talking about. You are this wonderful wife he is married to." This is the impression I ought to leave with people. This is not some politically polite move, either. It is the natural outflow of our life together. The relationship gets richer all the time. I believe this is the way God wants it.

This is true not because we are somehow fortunate. Instead, we let God shape our marriage in the way He wants it to be. I had to be a willing partner with God in order to change to become what Eileen needed in our relationship. We've had our moments, but it gets richer and better all the time. I know that our marriage is impregnable. There is no way the devil will ever get in between us, although he has tried. My job is to be Christ to her. Her job is to be the church back to me.

It goes on to say:

> So husbands ought to love their own wives as their own bodies; he who loves his wife loves himself. For no one ever hated his own flesh, but nourishes and cherishes it, just as the Lord does the church. For we are members of His body, of His flesh and of His bones. "For this reason a man shall leave his father and mother and be joined to his wife, and the two shall become one flesh." This is a great mystery, but I speak concerning Christ and the church. Nevertheless let each one of you in particular so love his own wife as himself, and let the wife see that she respects her husband (Ephesians 5:28–33).

2. The Parent-Child Relationship

The next relationship that must be impregnable to the devil is the parent-child relationship. Paul said:

> Children, obey your parents in the Lord, for this is right. "Honor your father and mother," which is the first commandment with promise: "that it may be well with you and you may live long on the earth" (Ephesians 6:1–3).

I want you to notice first that this passage is addressed to the children. This is what I call the black-and-white thinking of God. It simply says, "Children, obey your parents in the Lord because this is right!" This is not an issue for debate; just do it! That is the end of the argument. The children must be addressed in this way, and they must know from early on what is required of them. The parent leads and instructs. It is the child's responsibility to obey.

Then Paul addressed the fathers with very important instruction, "And you, fathers, do not provoke your children to wrath, but bring them up in the training and admonition of the Lord." Fathers must be careful in the way they handle their children. The responsibility of bringing up children and the way they turn out is placed firmly on the fathers and not upon the mothers. Obviously, I am not saying that mothers have no part to play in this. They have a very important role to play, but it is very clear where God lays the accountability. I am responsible, not my wife, for making sure my children grow up in the fear and admonition of the Lord.

One of the first things I want to teach my children is that they will honor their mother. They will also honor me. If you will do this kind of training, then you better start when they are two and three. That is the age where discipline and fathering must begin. Even before this stage, you should cuddle them and give them milk bottles. A father must bond with a child in a motherly way before he can move into his fatherly function. The bonding takes place by unconditional love and undemanding affection.

Section 7 – Ephesians Chapters 5 and 6

At about three years of age, you must get these principles so that you can begin to reason with the child. This is where the issues of Hebrews 12:5–11 become a natural as well as spiritual thing. I have to learn to father the way God fathers, because He is the perfect father. I learn from Him how to handle my children. I wish I had known God then the way I know Him now, because I would have fathered my children much differently and much better than I actually did. All I can do now is apologize to them, because I learned these things too late. Nevertheless, God has brought us through.

At least I knew how to pray for my children. If you put your children in the center of your prayers and carry faith for them, then there is nothing the devil can do. Every time my wife was pregnant, we would lay our hands on her tummy and commit that child to the Lord. We said, "We are claiming Your word that we will bring up righteous offspring. We are not having children for the devil to put his dirty hands on them. They will serve You from their earliest days. We will enforce this in Jesus' name!"

We must establish the principle of obedience firmly in the lives of our children. Notice that it does not say to the children, "Submit to your parents," but "Obey your parents." The word for children is *teknon*. This is the age where a parent says, "We are not going to debate these issues with you. Just do what we told you to do." You must establish the principle of obedience in their early years. However, when the child matures you release them to the principle of submission, which is a different dimension. As they come to maturity, you allow them to develop their own God-given conscience, letting the conscience rule in them rather than orders from dad. By the time they are grown up, if you have done it right, you have become their best friend.

I am my son's best friend. One of the most thrilling things in my life was when my son said that I am his hero. The same is true for the other children. However, I am so grieved over a deficiency in my relationship to my daughter. When she was young, I never gave her the cuddles and warmth she needed in those formative years. We worked all this through and prayed through everything together. Some years ago, when Rachel was thirty-five years of age, a mother of her own children and leading a ministry all her own, she said to me, "Dad, I have never sat on your lap to be cuddled by you." At this age in her life, she was asking me to give her what I failed to do when she was young. We had to live through this together the best we could. I was in my sixties. It was very precious and healing for both of us.

The real purpose of right fathering is to reveal the Father. It becomes very easy then for the children to transfer their obedient relationship from you as a natural father to a submissive and obedient relationship to their heavenly Father. The bond you build with them provides them with all the equipment they need to bond with God in a loving, affectionate relationship where they know God is for them. They have a God they can trust. They will obey and honor Him in even greater measure than they do you, because they have come to full maturity. This is a true father's greatest pleasure!

3. The Master-Servant, Employer-Employee, Leader-Follower Relationships

Paul then gave the following instruction to people in a subordinate relationship:

> Bondservants, be obedient to those who are your masters according to the flesh, with fear and trembling, in sincerity of heart, as to Christ; not with eyeservice, as men-pleasers, but as bondservants of Christ, doing the will of God from the heart, with goodwill doing service, as to the Lord, and not to men, knowing

Section 7 – Ephesians Chapters 5 and 6

> that whatever good anyone does, he will receive the same from the Lord, whether he is slave or free (Ephesians 6:5–8).

Once again, we learn how to behave in relationship to our master and Lord. We serve in any earthly relationship as a master or servant, leader or follower, employer or employee following the model of Christ who was the perfect servant and who is now the perfect master. This is essential for relationships in a leadership team in the local church or city-wide church. I have talked at length on this issue in another series on covenant relationships.

Paul's final instruction before finally moving into spiritual warfare is for masters, leaders, or employers,

> And you, masters, do the same things to them, giving up threatening, knowing that your own Master also is in heaven, and there is no partiality with Him (Ephesians 6:9).

I want to go back and look at a few things in review. We have explained this amazing dynamic of God being in us. Almighty God, who created heaven and earth, chose to work through our humanity in order to establish His Kingdom. He has limited Himself to work in this dispensation through humanity. Therefore, He must use the agency of humans. He could say, "I've had enough of humans. I will come into this deal Myself." The day God would do that would be the end of the day of salvation for humans. This would be divine judgment for us, bringing in the end of the age. There would be no place anymore for men and women to be saved. That day is coming, and I believe it is very close.

Until that day comes, God has limited Himself to work through humans because that is the nature of this dispensation. While He does this, He does not have to bring humanity to final judgment. The devil must work the same way. He must also work through human agencies.

Demons can have an influence on society, but they become even more effective when they have a human agency. That is why the human gates of hell need to be the focused targets of our prayers.

Let me remind you what happened when the demons who were working through the proud Pharisee Saul were kicked out. The humanity that was once used for the purposes of Satan to destroy the church became one of the most powerful agencies for God. Translate that to your towns and cities, into the political and religious scenes. Think of some of the leaders of great so-called Christian denominations or leaders of the most awful, deceptive religious systems in our nations. These are led and directed by men or women who are demonized. Imagine them turning around to become totally on-fire for Jesus!

This is already happening in Mormonism. Also, the whole Herbert W. Amstrong Children of God movement has repented of its error, and many of them are coming back into mainstream Christianity, on-fire for Jesus. None of these things are too hard for the Lord. Imagine what would happen if all the lights went on for the Jehovah's Witnesses. Imagine what would happen if all their zeal for door-to-door evangelism and passion to get people into their movement was suddenly used for the Kingdom of God. These things are not hard for God.

While the devil or any demon spirit has an agent in human form, they are able to act more effectively. That is why I want you to target known witches, influential religious leaders, and other antagonists of the Kingdom, not so they will rot in hell, but so that they might be delivered from their deception and become powerful advancers of the Kingdom of God. Once we start targeting these things with informed, strategic intercession, we will see incredible and wonderful breakthrough.

Section 7 – Ephesians Chapters 5 and 6

There is something else I have noticed. In all the leaders that pioneered the early church through to this tremendous breakthrough, including the apostles, known church leaders, and early church fathers, there is no record anywhere of any one of those leaders dying prematurely because he was attacked by a sickness. Not even one. Many of them were martyred, but the rest of them lived to a ripe old age.

When I saw this fact, it really triggered something in me. I cannot fully expound on this yet, because the power of it is still working in me. When you think about the assault on leaders in this land, then I conclude that we are sitting here letting the devil ravage our leadership through sickness and death. They are taken in premature death in the prime of their ministry. We must stop this in Jesus' mighty name. I feel a fury in my spirit against the attack of cancer in God's leaders. This is epidemic at the moment. I want you to join me in this crusade that none of the leaders that step out to pioneer the church of Jesus Christ will be taken out prematurely.

26

A WARRING CHURCH

Let's turn now to the second half of Ephesians 6. All I have said on this subject is an extension of God warring through our humanity. God is very much in the fight with us. We need to be very much in the fight with Him. We dare not think we can go against principalities and powers in our strength. But He must have us in order to wage effective warfare against the powers and principalities that rule our nation right now. This is true not just in the church, but also in the political sphere, educational sphere, judicial sphere, and so on. We will take all these spheres back from the devil.

There is something happening in America right now that is absolutely exciting. I just spoke with Eileen by phone, who is meeting with national intercessors giving reports about events in the White House and Congress. It is amazing how many public servants fear God and how many of them want God's way in our nation. Yet, at the same time, many of them do not vote the right way. It's probable that many of them do not have the courage to do so yet. We need to carry these things through in prayer.

Paul prayed for boldness. If the apostle of the church needed boldness, then how much more do our public servants need it? Paul said, "And [pray] for me, that utterance may be given to me, that I may open my mouth boldly to make known the mystery of the gospel" (Eph. 6:19). How many times did Paul pray that prayer? He was aware of the tremendous pressure to compromise, and that same pressure seeks to influence public officials to vote in a way that promotes the devil's program and nullifies God's. But this will not happen!

We Do Wrestle!

Come now to Ephesians 6:12,

> For we do not wrestle against flesh and blood, but against principalities, against powers, against rulers of the darkness of this age, against spiritual hosts of wickedness in the heavenly places.

The clear implication of this verse is that we do wrestle! We do wrestle against principalities, against powers, against rulers of the darkness of this age, and against spiritual hosts of wickedness in the heavenly places. Here are four things we wrestle against. We are also told what we do not wrestle against: flesh and blood. I will not waste my time fighting with the agents of demonic powers, but I am praying for their conversion. However, I am dealing with the principalities and powers that are behind them.

Caleb, in the battle against strong forces in his day, made this profound statement in Numbers 14:9, "...Their protection has departed from them...." As a conclusion Caleb said, essentially, "Therefore, we can eat them for breakfast!" So much of the power behind the forces working against God in our nation is demonic. When that power is taken from them, they suddenly become powerless and impotent.

Chapter 26 – A Warring Church

I saw this happen with communism very clearly. I used to go into Eastern Europe in the darkest, most fearful days of communism. We used to sneak in there, and you could feel the oppressive power that seemed to rule supreme over anything else. It seemed there was no way it would ever move. It would only get worse and worse until it filled the earth. That is what we were being told by certain schools of thought in those days. There came a day, I believe through the prayers of the saints, when that formidable foe began to crack. I sensed it for the first time in 1987. I went into some of the tougher communist nations, and it seemed that even the communist officials no longer believed in communism.

On one occasion, I sat in a café in Poland, which was an occupied country. Russian troops were everywhere. We sat next to a group of Russian soldiers. I sat with our Polish brothers, and they translated what these men were saying. They were telling a joke. It went like this, "There was a man in Red Square on May Day. He cried out to Khrushchev, 'You are a fool leading our nation to destruction.' This man was arrested and given ten years and ten days of imprisonment. One man asked, 'What are the ten days for?' They said, 'Ten days are for insulting the President of a Socialist Soviet Republic.' Then they asked, 'What are the ten years for?' They said, 'Ten years are for revealing State secrets!'" All the Russian soldiers laughed hysterically. This was the kind of mockery happening within the system. I realized that the demonic powers behind communism were destroyed. The system was like a machine that was running to a standstill. The power had gone out!

In the United States of America, the power behind secular humanism is being removed! The power behind Islam is being taken away! If you can see spiritually, then you realize that this is the most remarkable and unprecedented opportunity for the Church of Jesus Christ. We better not miss it. We cannot save America in our spare time!

Please hear me. If you do not have a passion for it, then you are no use to God in this purpose. Let's grab this opportunity with both hands. Let's get into the prayer closet like never before and get hold of our cities like never before. Be filled with overwhelming faith like never before. Let's pay whatever price is necessary to see this incredible breakthrough.

We do wrestle! As God directs me, I am going against every principality and power that rules over America. I know as God directs me He will also empower me. I am not scared by these demons. If they come against me altogether, then the God I serve is there with a flaming sword in His hand. He will not allow His servant to be destroyed when doing His will. I am absolutely without any fear. I am totally confident about my right to do what God tells me to do. I have no right to do what I think is a good idea. But if I am in the will of God, then I am unbeatable. If It Is God who is at work in me to do and will what is pleasing to Him, then I am invincible. It is not me, for I am nothing. But I qualify as a human being, which is exactly what God needs for His purposes. Talk to yourself; you too qualify.

I want you to put away any personal fears in your congregations. If you teach these principles correctly, then you can deal with the issues of fear. Should we go against principalities and powers? What happens if we do? Won't they begin to trouble us and attack us? When I saw this record among the early church apostles and church fathers, of no one dying of sickness, then I knew we are missing something. I expect us to get to the same place in Jesus' name.

Seven Pieces of Weaponry

There are seven pieces of weaponry described in Ephesians 6:14–17. I have included in each of these pieces the verb, which describes the intensity in which this dressing is done. For example, we are to gird our loins with the belt of truth. The verb *gird* means to bind something around our waist very tightly. You don't simply attach something loosely around your waist so that it falls off easily.

Then we are told to put on the breastplate of righteousness. The Greek verb for *put on* is *enduo*. We put this breastplate on in such a way that it does not slip. This righteousness is part of my life in every situation and circumstance.

Third, our feet are shod with the preparation of the gospel of peace. The Greek verb for *shod* is *hupodeo*. *Deo* was a word meaning imprison someone. So *hupodeo* means to extremely imprison something. You extremely imprison your feet with the gospel of peace. It is bound to you with a very tight binding.

Have you ever noticed in the passion of Jesus that He was pierced in His hands, side, and feet. In His resurrection, He still had pierced hands, because Thomas put his hands there. He still had an open side because Thomas put his hand there. It seems that throughout eternity Jesus will bear the marks of His passion. But when you come down to His feet, they have changed. In Revelation 1, John the apostle saw the glorified risen Christ. He said:

> His feet were like fine brass, as if refined in a furnace.... And when I saw Him, I fell at His feet as dead. But He laid His right hand on me, saying to me, "Do not be afraid; I am the First and the Last" (Revelation 1:15,17).

I want you to notice that the feet of Jesus have changed into flaming bronze feet. If you go through the scriptures, you will find that wherever Jesus is depicted in His glorified state, He is always pictured with these flaming bronze feet. They are always for one purpose, which is the treading down and crushing of His enemies. In His resurrection, the feet of Jesus have been changed into demon-crushing feet. In Deuteronomy 33, Moses, the man of God, blessed the children of Israel before his death. While I do recognize a special place for ethnic Israel, it is by faith that we become the Israel of God. I take these promises spiritually as a spiritual child of Israel, a son of God, an heir of Abraham.

Section 7 – Ephesians Chapters 5 and 6

In Deuteronomy 33:24 we find the blessing upon Asher. Hear what God says about Asher, "Asher is most blessed of sons; let him be favored by his brothers and let him dip his foot in oil. Your sandals shall be iron and bronze; as your days, so shall thy strength be."

I cried out very recently for the Asher blessing. God said to me, "Then dip your feet in oil." There is an anointing of the Holy Spirit which has come upon me that has given me the flaming bronze feet of my Lord Jesus Christ. These are devil-crushing feet! This is a reality. My wife and daughter Rachel have also received it. It is like a family trait. If you see demons around then watch Eileen's eyes. This delightful feminine lady suddenly becomes a roaring lion. She will get them every time. My daughter is the same. If there is anything demonic in the conference, it cannot stand her being there. It will manifest every time. She will simply kick it out. No demon can sit in a meeting when my daughter is preaching. She has flaming bronze feet.

We need this anointing. The gospel is the gospel of the Kingdom. An important dimension of this gospel is getting men and women saved, but even more important is bringing effective Kingdom advancement. I am here to establish the Kingdom of God. In the process of establishing the Kingdom, thousands of people will be brought out of independence and into submission to the King of kings. They will have their sins forgiven and their lives transformed as they recognize and submit to the King. It is the gospel of the Kingdom that has the power to save.

If I concentrate on establishing the Kingdom with a passion to get men and women into a submissive relationship to Jesus Christ, then I am bringing salvation to them in the most powerful and effective way possible. Frankly, it is the only way they can receive salvation. I have my feet shod with the preparation of the gospel when they become devil-crushing feet. I can cast demons out of people who are harassing and hindering them.

We've been through all the chapters of preparation in order to become these kinds of people. The whole purpose is that we become invincible in war. This is the clear argument and direction of the book of Ephesians. As a result, we become competent city-takers!

Then Paul went on to say in Ephesians 6:16, "Above all, taking the shield of faith with which, you will be able to quench all the fiery darts of the wicked one." The word *take* here means to strongly take hold of something. I cannot convey to you the intensity in which these actions are done. The only thing you don't do with intensity is taking the helmet of salvation, because the word *take* in Greek, *dechomai*, is a different word that has the idea of receiving something. In other words, it is something given to you as a free gift. You don't have to sweat for it. You don't have to get yourself saved. Instead, you must simply let God save you! You just receive it. There is nothing simpler than to allow God to save you.

All of these verbs emphasize tremendous truths for our spiritual warfare. Then we must take the sword of the Spirit, which is the word of God. With this formidable armor and these mighty offensive weapons, we are a terror to the devil. The sword of the Spirit and our gospel sandals are the offensive weapons. The other pieces are impregnable defensive armor.

Our responsibility is to then attack the strongman. In Luke 11, Jesus spoke about the same issue. Jesus outlined five levels of prayer, which finally led to a prayer level that gives you power to bind the strongman. You don't start there, but you must progress to this place. In Luke 11:21–22, it says:

> When a strong man, fully armed, guards his own palace, his goods are in peace. But when a stronger than he comes upon him and overcomes him, he takes from him all his armor in which he trusted and divides his spoils.

We need to rob the enemy of the armor on which he has relied. This must be part of our targeted prayer ministry. We must get hold of them in prayer and break them down one by one. I believe God will magnificently answer our prayers. We rob the enemy of the armor on which he has relied. Then it is very easy to invade territory he thought was his domain and plunder his property.

God will put into many judgmental Christians a new heart of compassion for the whole homosexual and lesbian culture. These broken yet precious people are in this position because many were broken and destroyed in their early lives by circumstances outside of their control. They have been deceived and perverted into this whole trap. Some have HIV, and they are facing death in a matter of years because there is no answer. This whole community will be invaded by the power of God. We will see many of them healed from AIDS as a sign of God's clear supernatural power. Many of them will turn to Jesus Christ, and they will become the main rescuers of that entire community. You will see a wonderful move of God in this area. However, as a church we must stop our holier-than-thou judgmental attitude. If we are saved, it is only because of grace. If we are anything, then we are what we are by the grace of God. If we can do anything, it is by His power, which mightily works within us. I can see very clearly these exciting days coming upon us.

Paul's Final Plea

Paul gave a final plea at the end of this passage, in Ephesians 6:18, "Praying always with all prayer and supplication in the Spirit, being watchful to this end with all perseverance and supplication for all the saints." We have a responsibility to protect one another. We are to be an army of intercessors who are there when someone is called to some public act. If a man or woman is raised to prominence in the will of God, then we need to put a shield around that person through intercession.

It does not matter whether the person is serving in the church or in public life. I believe we have miserably failed our politicians in the area who want to do the will of God.

I pray now with some Senators of the United States Congress. These are men of God filled with the Spirit. Each one I prayed with came to me in desperation. They said, "I went to Washington to champion the purposes of God, but I found the system so strong and the environment so unbearable that I must get out of it, because I cannot take it any longer." Instead of being able to overcome the darkness of Washington these men were being overcome by it. I believe, as a church, that we are very much responsible for these defeats. We have not protected them. We have not covered them. Instead of praying for our government, we complain about our government. Paul said this is the first thing we should do when we come together to worship as a body of people.

If you know any Senators who are on-fire for Jesus, then you need to be the power behind them that causes things to happen. Then you target your prayers toward your local town, including mayors, police chiefs, and other offices. We have a prayer shield around our police chief in San Antonio. He is alive in the Spirit and recently became a member of the Eagles Nest Fellowship. He's been on radio with Eileen, and he has shared his heart publicly, where he is with God. Since he has been surrounded with on-fire believing Christians, he has become more and more clear cut about his own direction and what he wants for his police force.

The chief circuit judge is a fine Christian woman. We are putting our prayers around her as well. We are forming a protective shield so that they may also speak as they ought to speak. We pray this for our pastors and leaders, but this also applies to every believer God has exalted to some place of influence in the public arena.

Section 7 – Ephesians Chapters 5 and 6

We must not assign these principles only to the church, but we must take them to every facet of society.

I want to get close to and empower some of our leading educators in order to rescue the public school system out of the devil's hands and bring it back to where it ought to be. We can do these things. This is our war. It is a praying war. Paul said in verses 19–20:

> And [pray] for me, that utterance may be given to me, that I may open my mouth boldly to make known the mystery of the gospel, for which I am an ambassador in chains; that in it I may speak boldly, as I ought to speak.

Paul was praying these things from prison. We believe that this letter was written from Rome. Paul was in the household of Rome, and he considered it an opportunity to influence the Roman household. Paul did not say, "Poor me! I am in prison!" No, he saw his circumstances as an opportunity. There are records of the early church fathers that suggest that one-third of the Roman household was converted through the witness of the apostle Paul. This is fantastic.

Then comes Paul's final greeting in Ephesians 6:21–24:

> But that you also may know my affairs and how I am doing, Tychicus, a beloved brother and faithful minister in the Lord, will make all things known to you; whom I have sent to you for this very purpose, that you may know our affairs, and that he may comfort your hearts. Peace to the brethren, and love with faith, from God the Father and the Lord Jesus Christ. Grace be with all those who love our Lord Jesus Christ in sincerity.

This is the book of Ephesians.

SECTION 8
Lessons from the Writings of John

27

JESUS' LETTER TO THE CHURCH IN EPHESUS

I want us to receive some lessons from the book of Revelation and John's other letters. I trust you understand that all of these letters were written for the church in Ephesus. Therefore, it holds particular significance for our study on this city and the purpose of the church to bring the Kingdom and defeat all other enemies.

This book was probably written about AD 90 and certainly no later than AD 95. The book of Revelation was written by the apostle John at the dictation of Jesus to the churches in Asia. Of course, Ephesus was the overseeing church in that region. All the letters were sent to the group in Asia, over which John had oversight from the regional center in Ephesus before His exile to Patmos about ten years earlier. All the churches had been through the fire, particularly during the fourteen-year persecution under Emperor Domitian, which was coming to its conclusion.

The letter to the Ephesians was written in approximately AD 64. Then in AD 68–69 there was the first furious persecution against the church under Emperor Nero. During that time, the apostle Paul and many others of the first group of apostles were martyred.

Section 8 – Lessons from the Writings of John

When the devil could not humble or break the church, he then broke out through political persecution. Up until Nero's command, the government had been quite neutral. The church experienced grave hostility and physical attacks from the Jews, but the Romans had remained indifferent one way or the other.

Now this ruling spirit disguised as Artemis, which had power over the Roman Empire, was now beginning to look for its gates in the political system. One of the most powerful gates it found was in a madman named Nero. Nero ruined the economy of the Roman Empire by his complete mismanagement. Then he even intentionally set Rome on fire because he wanted to rebuild certain places. His madness was to burn the whole place down in order to rebuild it. When it was suspected that he was the person responsible for the destruction, he turned all the blame onto the Christians. This resulted in terrible persecution in which many people lost their lives. The apostle John was in Ephesus, steadying the church during this difficult time. Timothy was also there, and the two of them were like two pillars in very difficult times. All they could do was simply hold on while all hell broke out against them.

The persecution under Nero ended in approximately AD 70. Then there was a ten-year period of slight relief, yet the situation was still uneasy. Then under the emperor Domitian, in AD 81, a more vicious attack came against the church. When the devil could not stop the church from within, he sought to ruin it from without. When he cannot stop the church any other way, he will seek to stop the church politically. He will use military might and any other means to stop it. We must not leave political strongholds in our country in the hands of the devil. First, it hinders us from advancing the Kingdom of God. If we leave the government the way it is, then the day will come when it will turn against us and be the main instrument the devil will use against us.

Chapter 27 – Jesus' Letter to the Church in Ephesus

I remember standing at a viewing place for the thirty-eighth parallel, which divides North and South Korea.. There was a very strong presence of American troops in South Korea. I was visiting David Yongi Cho's church at the time. As we stood near the thirty-eighth parallel, a Colonial of the American Army spat on the ground and said, "It ain't the might of America that is keeping South Korea free. It is the prayers of those Christians." He was absolutely right.

Every church that I went to in South Korea had an early morning prayer meeting every day. They all, without exception, had one all-night prayer meeting a week. There were also many places with permanent prayer functioning twenty-four hours a day. Whenever you went into these churches during a regular service, their first cry according to scripture was 1 Timothy 2:1–4. They cried out to God for all those who were in authority. They prayed that God might give peace. They prayed for righteousness in their government. All of this was meant to produce an environment where the gospel of Jesus Christ could be preached without hindrance. It was those prayers, and not political cleverness or military power, that kept South Korea open and protected.

I lived in India and have had contact with the country for about forty years. The real born-again believers have always been a small percentage. I've been in India during four different attempts by militant Hindus to change the constitution of India to make it an official Hindu nation. Therefore, all other religions would be oppressed. Also, proselytizing would be forbidden and punishable by law. The Indian constitution, written by the president in the 1940s, declares that India is a secular state with the right of every Indian to practice and propagate their own religion. The right of evangelism is written right into the constitution. On four occasions, political forces tried to change the constitution in order to stop Christians from evangelizing. Some of these attempts almost succeeded.

One occurred in 1976, when the President of India, Lal Bahador Sastri, along with the House of Representatives and Senate, presided over India. They prepared legislation to change the constitution, making it impossible to evangelize without strict penalties. The act was cynically called the Freedom of Religion Act. It said, "No one is allowed to coerce another to change their religion by promise of eternal reward or by threat of eternal punishment." How could you preach the gospel of Jesus Christ without violating the law? This law passed through several different levels of government, and all that was left before it passed into law was the president's signature. The Christians in India went to prayer with all their might. The president of India went to Russia on a state visit and had a sudden heart attack and died there. The government, which consisted of a coalition, blew up into a thousand pieces. The government fell, and as a result, that legislation never passed into law.

The praying minority has controlled the politics of India for forty years. We need to change our hearts in this regard. First, we must become militant in this area. It would open tremendous doors of opportunity to advance the Kingdom. If we do not commit to this, the government will turn against us and become the greatest persecutors of the church in America. The responsibility will fall upon our heads, because we failed to exercise our power to influence government through our prayers. I feel a great sense of solemnity and seriousness about this issue. This is my daily prayer. I hope you will get your church to be as faithful in praying for authorities as the Indian and South Korean churches have been.

Jesus Speaks to the Church in Ephesus

As we come to the end of this long and terrible persecution under Domitian, we find the churches still existing, but they are under tremendous fire. The first letter to the churches was to Ephesus, which was the key church in Asia. This was the mother church of all the other churches mentioned in Revelation. This was the regional church. From this church, the apostolic ministry of Paul, Timothy, and John touched the other churches in the region.

Chapter 27 – Jesus' Letter to the Church in Ephesus

The church in Ephesus was energetic, organized, and doctrinally correct, but they had lost their first love. This is what Jesus said to them:

> To the angel of the church in Ephesus write.... I know your works, your labor, your patience, and that you cannot bear those who are evil. And you have tested those who say they are apostles and are not, and have found them liars; and you have persevered and have patience, and have labored for My name's sake and have not become weary. Nevertheless, I have this against you, that you have left your first love. Remember therefore from where you have fallen; repent and do the first works, or else I will come to you quickly and remove your lampstand from its place. But this you have, that you hate the deeds of the Nicolaitans, which I also hate. He who has an ear, let him hear what the Spirit says to the churches. To him who overcomes I will give to eat from the tree of life, which is in the midst of the Paradise of God (Revelation 2:1–7).

Jesus said He knew their works. He knew their labor, and He knew their perseverance. Consider this in light of what Paul said in 1 Thessalonians 1:2–3:

> We give thanks to God always for you all, making mention of you in our prayers, remembering without ceasing your work of faith, labor of love, and patience of hope in our Lord Jesus Christ in the sight of our God and Father.

Compare this verse with Revelation 2:2 "I know your works, your labor, your patience." What is missing in the Revelation passage? In Thessalonica, their work was a work of faith. In Ephesus, their work was just work. In Thessalonica, their labor was a labor of love. In Ephesus, it was just labor. In Thessalonica, their perseverance was a perseverance of hope. In Ephesus, they simply endured. Can you see what has departed from the Ephesian church?

Section 8 – Lessons from the Writings of John

It seems to me that the faith, hope, and love of the church had died, and they were simply maintaining the status quo.

It is very easy to come to the point where you simply go to church. You run church meetings and have church organization. There are programs that are running, and all the energy of the church is used to maintain those programs. But the faith, hope, and love have departed. A church that has programs as a priority will end up like the church in Ephesus. The call of Jesus was: "Come back to your first love!"

I believe this is a three-fold love. First, it is an abandoned love for God. Second, it is love for one another. Third, it is love for the lost. When I really experienced the overwhelming love of God, it transformed my ability to love my brethren and filled me with a passion of love for the lost like I never had before. If you, or the church you represent, are like the Ephesian church here in Revelation, then you know what you have to do.

One of the difficulties I have in working in Eastern Europe today is that the old Pentecostal church, which stood during the difficult times of communist oppression, has become like this Ephesian church of Revelation. They went through the fire of persecution for several decades. Many of the wonderful older Pentecostal leaders went to jail. Others died for their faith. All of them paid a price. They stood in difficult times, determined to hold on and survive to bring the church through. However, for many of them it set them in a concrete mold of survival.

When you meet them today, it seems there is little love, faith, and joy in them. They are simply holding a position of truth. The tragedy is that when the Spirit of God tries to break through in these nations, they cannot move with Him. The younger generation is ready and willing. But during their fire of trial, they have been baked into a non-moveable position.

They will not give up one facet of the truth that they were prepared to die for. They are in a time-warp of Pentecostalism that is fifty years old. They will not change a thing. They are tragically the main obstacle to what God wants to do in those nations. This is the tragedy.

They spent years in prison for the faith, but now unwittingly they stand in the way of God. I meet with fantastic younger men, and the power of God is moving. There are glorious things happening. But our main problem is getting around the mountains of old traditions and habits in order to make way for the new things God wants to do in the nation. How can we honor them for the way they stood in terrible times of persecution and hardship, with great sacrifices, giving them what is really due their name? Yet, at the same time, how can we help them to move out of the way to let God do what He wants to do? This is one of the travails of my heart right now.

I see the situation in some nations in Eastern Europe as identical to this situation in Revelation. I have seen this same dynamic with men in Britain when they first began to see the Kingdom. They went out and began to speak boldly and were vilified by the denominations. This happened to the Pentecostals at the beginning of the last century in America, when they were also vilified by the denominational churches. They came out and formed Pentecostal churches. There was a mindset that is still detectable in some pockets of Pentecostal churches. I see the same mentality in these movements, "We can't change anything now, because we have the truth." Many of these churches end up getting in the way of God rather than being a help. This is the tragedy.

I don't want one particle of this to be in me or in those with whom I am associated and for whom I have responsibility. I want to be first and foremost a lover of God. Second, I want to be a lover of the brethren and a great lover of the lost.

Section 8 – Lessons from the Writings of John

I say, "Lord, if ever I begin to lose my first love, please ring bells in my heart so loud that I go crazy!" The thing I love about Reinhard Bonnke is that when someone gets saved he is as excited as if it was the first person he ever led to Christ. If someone gets healed, he is absolutely ecstatic like a little boy with a new toy. It is this boyish freshness that keeps him on the cutting edge of what God is doing today in the evangelistic field of Africa. God has used him to shake the very foundations of hell, putting faith into thousands and thousands of people. I pray that we will be that kind of person in our towns and cities.

28

THE GOSPEL OF JOHN

I want you to see how much of the New Testament is focused on the breakthrough in Ephesus. We have already seen that the context of Ephesus not only includes the book of Ephesians, but also the letters to Timothy. Finally, all the letters of John were written to the base church in Ephesus and to the churches in Asia. But first, I want to look at the gospel of John. We must see the purpose for which this gospel was written. The first three gospels (Matthew, Mark, and Luke) were written to evangelize a lost world. Matthew in particular speaks to the Jews. Mark speaks to the Roman world, and Luke speaks to the Greek world. These gospels were written somewhere between AD 52 and AD 65. Mark was almost certainly the first gospel written.

Then there was a thirty-year period of silence. However, from the time of his exile toward the last fourteen years of his life, the Spirit of God motivated John to write. The reason John was motivated to write was to prepare the ground for him to come out of prison and lead the church in the assault that finally cracked open the city of Ephesus. John wrote about three or four years before he was released from prison. When you read his second letter, for example, it is very clear that John knows he is on his way out.

Section 8 – Lessons from the Writings of John

These manuscripts were released and came to the church several years before John personally came to the city. They were preparatory for what God wanted to do in this city and region. You will notice that John's gospel does not contain much of the material that the other gospels contain. The reason is that the other gospels were already widely read and understood. John took new material and some common material and wove them together for a specific purpose. John wanted to stir and quicken a church that had become stale and hesitant because of persecution.

By the time John wrote his gospel, there were already third generation Christians. I have watched this dynamic in other settings when third generation Christians come to maturity. For example, I have been involved in the country of Nepal since the earliest days of anything happening there. I can now go to Nepal to see the condition of those first Christians who paid such an enormous price to stay alive. Every elder in every church has been to jail for at least one year. In fact, almost every church member is a jail bird. Little old ladies went to jail for one year, including their dogs.

Now they are out of jail and far more on fire for Jesus than when they went in. There was a passion and fire within them. God emancipated them in every way, mentally and economically. They began to see the prosperity of the Kingdom materially manifested in their lives. Their children grew up in the blessing that they paid a tremendous price to obtain. The children have nice clothes, and they enjoy nice schools. They enjoy the fatness of the Christian life, but because they did not pay the same price for it, dullness exists in them that does not exist in their parents. Finally, when it comes to the grandchildren it can become simply a culture rather than a passion. They were born into the Christian culture, and therefore, they do Christian things. But the question is: How do we keep the fire going from one generation to the next? I can see that John the apostle is dealing with the same problem here.

John was writing to the third generation of Christians. In their case, there was a continual price of persecution to pay, which in some sense helped them to see the exclusivity of living in the Kingdom or living in the world. Nevertheless, the church managed to settle down into a church life that had lost the power. With that kind of church, you cannot take a city. John wrote his gospel with a clear target in mind. He wrote to his readers that they might believe and that believing they might have life in His name (see John 20:31). You will find that the theme of John's gospel and his first letter is *life*. John did not tolerate religious ceremony or outward form, but he spoke about the eternal life that was with the Father and was manifested in the Son.

John's gospel is built around eight miracles. John called them signs or wonders, attesting miracles to the life that was in Jesus. Each miracle was not only a great miracle, but allegorically they were parables with profound spiritual truth. Around the miracle you will find teaching that compliments the profound meaning of the miracle. This is the way to read John's gospel. This is the thrust of John's gospel. The purpose was to bring these Christians to real life. The key was believing.

The first miracle was the turning of water into wine. This miracle brings out the distinction between the deadness of religion and the power of life. John 2 records the miracle, and John 3 deals with being born again. In John 4, we find the miracle of the healing of the nobleman's son. This nobleman has a son that was dying. He asked Jesus, "Please come and heal my son." This man was under the impression that he must get Jesus to come physically to lay his hands upon his son before anything would help. Even then, it seemed to be a desperate plea. Jesus said to the nobleman, "Unless you people see signs and wonders, you will by no means believe" (John 4:48).

Section 8 – Lessons from the Writings of John

This is the kind of faith that can only believe when the atmosphere is conducive for faith. This is part of the context we looked at earlier. The woman at the well brought her town first of all to proxy faith or leaning faith. In other words, they believed in Jesus because of what she said. Finally, they came to the place where they themselves believed because they heard Him. It is essential that we help our teenage children not to simply absorb the culture of our Christian life. They need the very fire of God birthed in them by their own mighty encounters with God.

I believe in many of the healing crusades, as with Benny Hinn and Reinhard Bonnke, people are healed as they come to faith in the atmosphere of that event. However, after leaving the crusade, many of them loose their healing. The reason is because the miracle was a fruit of faith. A person must continue in faith following the event in order to maintain the healing. Many people lay hold of things in meetings because of the environment of the meeting. You lay hold of things in a conference because the atmosphere is conducive for believing. However, when you go home and return to your dead situation, things begin to leak out, and you cannot hold on to what you received, because the atmosphere is now hostile instead of favorable. It is essential to make the transition from being dependent on environmental circumstances to being a person who changes the environment because of what you are carrying.

This nobleman in John 4 was given an option. In English, Jesus spoke six words to him, "Go your way; your son lives" (John 4:50). This man had the word of God and the physical presence of Jesus. He could either continue pulling on the sleeve of Jesus, begging Him to come and lay His hand on his son, or he could turn away from the physical Jesus and go home with the word of God that was given to him. He chose the second option. The word of God had come into him, and it was like a seed that would bring forth its harvest if he walked in it.

Chapter 28 – The Gospel of John

He walked away from the physical presence of Jesus with only six words to go on. As he started to walk away from Him, he did not feel any different. It did not seem like anything had changed. He may have been thinking, "I am the biggest idiot in the world to walk away from Jesus. All I have now are these six words. What can these six words do?" However, this man was passing an invisible barrier that many of us must pass. This man had the chance to pass from faith that can only work in the right environment to the kind of faith that can work anywhere.

Once you come to this kind of faith, instead of being a beneficiary of what other people's faith has produced, you begin to be the initiator of faith for other people to enjoy. There will always be a larger crowd of those who come and enjoy the blessings of faith than there are of those who make the blessing available. I want you to transition from being someone who comes to enjoy the blessing to becoming the kind of warring pioneers who can make the blessing happen for others to enjoy. This kind of faith is essential for substantial breakthroughs!

As this nobleman was on his way home, the seed began to germinate and sprout. On this long journey home, I can almost see his attitude changing. By the time he reached home, he had begun to believe this stuff. He had actually begun to dance. His depression had turned to joy. He was no longer in despair, but said, "When I get home, my son will be alive and well!" A group came out to meet the nobleman before he reached home. They said to him, almost in disbelief, "Your son lives!" I believe this was the harvest of everything that was working in him all the way home. When I saw this, I said, "God, I want to be this kind of believer!" *It is one thing to go into environments where things happen, but it is another thing to be part of the group that creates the environment for things to happen.*

Section 8 – Lessons from the Writings of John

We will make revival happen in Texas. Obviously, we are workers together with God. He will make it happen, but we are the instruments by which He makes it happen. Thousands and thousands will be beneficiaries, but they are not the people God used to make the blessing available. People will come in and receive the kind of faith that will believe, because miracles are taking place. When I saw this, I cried out to God, "I want to have the kind of faith that makes things happen."

Then, in John 5, Jesus came to a lame man who had sat by the pool of Bethesda for thirty-eight years looking for a miracle. There was a certain day when an angel came to stir up the waters, and the first person to jump in would receive healing. This man was living on the tentative possibility of being healed. But after coming for thirty-eight years, hoping for something that had not happened, even though he maintained the routine, expectation had actually died in him long ago. He was simply going through a religious exercise. Thousands and thousands come to healing meetings and our churches with the same attitude. You might ask, "Do you believe in healing?" They will say, "Yes, I believe in healing." But the faith in them is as dead as the faith in that lame man by the pool of Bethesda.

Jesus came to him and asked him a surprising question, "Do you want to be made well?" (John 5:6). Why was he coming there for thirty-eight years if he didn't want to be made well? Jesus knew this man's heart. Many people come to churches and come forward to be prayed for, but inside they are no more expectant for something to happen than this man. Imagine thirty-eight years times 365 days. Imagine how many attempts that man had taken toward healing. Men carried him to the pool, and it was the same old routine. People go to church, they go to conferences, meeting after meeting, and their unspoken expectation is, "I will be the same when I get home as I was when I came here."

You could work through this study in the same condition. By now I trust you have realized that this could be a crisis moment for you, for your church, and for your city. It is that faith that will make all the difference. Jesus asked him, "Do you want to be made well?" The man immediately began to make excuses. He said, "Well, there is no man to help me into the water…" (see John 5:7). In other words, I am looking for the right person to come with the right anointing so that I can be the beneficiary of his anointing and faith working through him.

The man's second statement was, "When the waters are stirred…." I want you to know that there are moments when God moves. Charles Finney said in his writings, "Lectures on Revival," "You can make a revival happen anytime anywhere providing you fulfill the conditions." We are often imprisoned by a false understanding of God's sovereignty, "I can't do anything. I am helpless. We are helpless until God decides, 'The time has come to move.'" We hear of wonderful meetings that took place in a church somewhere, and we think because we didn't go that we missed something. This is the second excuse, where someone waits for their moment. Until that moment occurs in the sovereignty of God, I am a helpless spectator until God decides to move.

The third excuse was, "Someone gets down into the water before me." In other words, God limits His blessings to a few fortunate people. My Bible says that God is rich toward all who call upon Him. My Bible says that with God there are no favorites. Everyone who calls upon the Lord will not be disappointed. That is what my Bible says. God does not have grace for the first twelve people, and then He suddenly runs out. The blood of Jesus Christ, according to 1 John, is sufficient not only for our sins, but also for the sins of the whole world. That is how powerful His blood is. If the whole world cried out to God, "Save us!" there would be adequate resources in the cross to do it for everyone. "Lord, heal us!" Every sickness would disappear.

"Lord, cast out these demons!" Every demon would flee. That's how big and powerful our God really is.

Jesus said, "If you believe in Me as the scriptures have said..." (see John 7:38). In other words, if the Jesus you believe in is as big as the Bible says He is, then out of your innermost being will flow rivers of living water. How big is your Jesus? Is He just big enough for you, or is He big enough for the whole world?

Jesus turned to this man and said, "Rise, take up your bed, and walk" (John 5:8). In the Greek, this statement is in the present imperative tense, which means it is like a military command, and the point in time is now. Imagine an army sergeant coming into the army barracks and the soldiers are asleep when they should be in formation outside. He comes in and says, "Excuse me. I am sorry to disturb you, but the captain is outside waiting for you on parade. Could you please put on your uniforms and as quickly as possible come out on parade? It would be very nice if you could do this now." Can you imagine a sergeant saying something like this? No, instead, the sergeant would walk into the barracks and say, "Get up!" This is precisely what the Greek says. Jesus did not say in a nice soft tone, "Arise." He said with military force, "Get up!" There was the fierceness of a military command behind what He said. The time for him to get up was immediately. We need to get up!

Then Jesus said to the man, "Take up your bed!" That mat was like a bed of excuses. I remember talking with Reinhard Bonnke about this in Africa. He said, "Alan, everywhere I go people say, 'This place is so hard. The devil is so strong around here.'" This was Reinhard's own testimony. He was a missionary in one African city pastoring a church with three hundred people. He said, "Oh, the devil was so strong. For ten years we believed in how strong the devil was in our city. Then one day we had a visit from a Zulu evangelist.

He came to our church and did not seem to know that the devil was so strong around our place. Alan, this man came and charged the devil like a lion! I realized that I had been deceived for ten years into believing too much that the devil is strong around here. That encounter with this Zulu evangelist changed my life."

I pray this will have the same effect upon you. Charge the devil like a lion. Say, "He is not strong around here!" Whatever excuses you have, roll them up! You say, "I'm not very skilled or gifted." Roll it up! "I don't sing. I don't have a great worship team." Roll it up! The Jesus I am coming to know is bigger and more glorious and mightier than I have ever comprehended. He is sufficient. I will roll up my bed. I will not say, "This is a hard place. This is a tough place. We have all these witches and darkness, New Age, and so on." Roll up that bed in Jesus' name!

The third command Jesus gave to this man was, "Walk!" This word is in the present continuous tense, which means this is something you do and go on continually doing. This man was powerfully and wonderfully healed.

We don't have the time to go through the rest of John, but can you see how powerful this gospel is? Every page is filled with purpose in order to bring people to the warring militancy of faith, into this passion for the very eternal life of God to be lived through us. By the time John's readers read through this book a few times, something was happening in the church. God was preparing them for John to physically come out of prison.

29

THE LETTERS OF JOHN

I want you to see how carefully the Spirit of God was preparing this moment of breakthrough. He laid the foundation of the word two or three years before the actual event of breakthrough. The word had time to soak in them, work in them, until they were a different people than they were before. In 1 John 1:1–3 this eternal life is described:

> That which was from the beginning, which we have heard, which we have seen with our eyes, which we have looked upon, and our hands have handled, concerning the Word of life–the life was manifested, and we have seen, and bear witness, and declare to you that eternal life which was with the Father and was manifested to us–that which we have seen and heard we declare to you, that you also may have fellowship with us; and truly our fellowship is with the Father and with His Son Jesus Christ.

John tells us that in the person of Jesus Christ the full magnificence of eternal life was presented to him, so that he could touch it, hear it, handle it, and look intently upon it. It totally impacted him. The first effect of that eternal life was like a magnet that drew him with an irresistible power.

Section 8 – Lessons from the Writings of John

The second effect of that life was to make him desperately hungry for that life. The thing about Jesus is that the nearer and nearer you come to Him, the more you look, there is no disappointment. Instead, it is far more magnificent than anything you might have dreamed possible.

One of the tragedies in getting close to some Christian leaders is discovering that they are great on the platform, but when you meet them in their hotel room you seem to be meeting another person. That can be very disappointing. This is not the case with Jesus. All the way through He was the same glorious eternal life. Just to be near Him was one of the most captivating experiences. As you draw closer and closer to that life and see the ever-increasing glory of that life, your own life becomes so shabby by comparison. This life, in the best sense of the word, has a condemning effect, "I wish I could live like Him and not like me." This is a very necessary step.

You can see John now in a desperate state. This is the same person who laid his head on the breast of Jesus. It looks like he is trying to climb inside of Him. He said, "I can't have enough of that life." Then John came to the place of seeing the great gap between the best of what he could be and all that Jesus naturally is. The gap is so wipe. John longed for that gap to somehow be bridged or removed, but on this side of Calvary it could not happen. Jesus went to the cross. The Spirit who was promised was sent. At some time that the Bible does not reveal, an actual transaction of life occurred. John, who could not stand Peter or James because of the competition between them, suddenly changed. These men suddenly became one new man in Christ. This one new man in Christ gloriously proclaimed the same eternal life.

The word *manifest* means to show something in a way that is tangible to the natural senses. That life was manifested to us.

Chapter 29 – The Letters of John

But then John said something that is absolutely staggering, "That which we have seen and heard we declare to you, that you also may have fellowship with us; and truly our fellowship is with the Father and with His Son Jesus Christ" (1 John 1:3). John was saying, "You want to know what eternal life is like? For years I ran after it, but now I have it. If you want to know what eternal life is like, then come and spend a weekend with me, and I will show you. I can proclaim it. I can show it forth to you." This is the miracle.

That is the miracle the early church had lost by the third generation of believers. They had Christian religion. They had Christian doctrine. They had Christian programs. They had Christian activity, but something had happened to the life. This is what Jesus was calling the Ephesian church back to in the book of Revelation. It was the relationship with Him in love, which produces this life. John was saying, "I can proclaim this to you. You can see what the eternal life of God is like by spending a weekend with me. I will show it to you." This eternal life had a John color to it, but it was the same eternal life. When Jesus walked the earth, this eternal life had a unique Jesus color to it. This will never be reproduced, but the eternal life can have an Alan Vincent color to it. It can have the color and personality of anyone reading this, but it is the same eternal life.

John wrote these things with a purpose in mind, "…that you also may have fellowship with us." Please remember what this word *fellowship* really means. It means to be joined together in a common life and to be joined together in a common purpose. John went on to say something even more staggering, "And truly our fellowship is with the Father and with His Son Jesus Christ." John was brought into a common life, having been brought into the eternal life of the Godhead. This does not mean he had been deified. It does mean that the eternal life of God was now flowing through John's humanity the way it was flowing through the Lord Jesus Christ.

Section 8 – Lessons from the Writings of John

It is the same eternal life that was in Adam before he fell. It brings the same ability to rule over all that God has created.

One of the first things said about that life is its power to have dominion. It is the eternal life that brings the Kingdom of God, because it is the eternal life that has the dominion. Without the eternal life, you have no hope of ruling. Only that life has the power to rule. The moment Adam was cut off from that life, he lost all power to rule over God's creation and all power to rule over himself. Eternal life is the key to ruling functionally. Jesus was able to functionally rule as a man because He lived by that life. Adam functionally ruled in the same way until he stepped out into independence.

John said, "Truly our fellowship is with the Father and with His Son Jesus Christ." In other words, we share a common life together, and we share a common purpose together. My common purpose, along with God the Spirit, God the Father, and God the Son, is to bring in the Kingdom of God with all power and all glory so that Jesus is the undisputed ruler and king of that Kingdom. I am as committed to this as the Godhead is! What about you?

At the end of this letter, John wrote:

> This is He who came by water and blood–Jesus Christ, not only by water, but by water and blood. And it is the Spirit who bears witness, because the Spirit is truth. For there are three that bear witness in heaven: the Father, the Word, and the Holy Spirit; and these three are one. And there are three that bear witness on earth: the Spirit, the water, and the blood; and these three agree as one. If we receive the witness of men, the witness of God is greater; for this is the witness of God which He has testified of His Son. He who believes in the Son of God has the witness in himself; he who does not believe God has made Him a liar, because he has not believed the testimony that God has given of His Son (1 John 5:6–10).

If God says, "You have the same eternal life that powerfully flowed through Jesus; this is what I gave you when you were born again," and you say, "I don't think that is true," then God says, "Don't make Me a liar!" If we deny this truth, then we hinder the practical reality of these things. If we have a church or group of people who believe this as much as the apostle John believed it, then no city can resist the power of that eternal life. This was the power and source of John's life.

Don't make God a liar. If God has given you this eternal life, don't say, "It can't be the same life Jesus had. It might be a dilution of what He had, but it cannot be the same life." There is no such thing in the Kingdom. John said further in 1 John 5:11–13:

> And this is the testimony: that God has given us eternal life, and this life is in His Son. He who has the Son has life; he who does not have the Son of God does not have life. These things I have written to you who believe in the name of the Son of God, that you may know that you have eternal life....

Nothing could be simpler than this. Either you have the Son of God and have the life, or you do not have the Son, and you do not have the life. There are no varieties and varying degrees of strength in that life. It is either the full eternal life of God, or it is nothing. Which do you have? If you have the Son, then you have the eternal life. That eternal life in you is as capable of doing the works of God as the eternal life in our Lord Jesus Christ. I fully believe this. I am totally and utterly consumed by this.

John said, "I am writing these things to you so that you will get this message." A church that believes this is inevitably a city-taking church. The only way we can know Him and have fellowship with Him is to walk in the light, confessing every sin and allowing the mighty blood of Jesus to do its work. This is a continual process. There is a point where we get it, but we also continue in it.

Section 8 – Lessons from the Writings of John

Looking back to 1 John 1:7, we see that the same idea applies to sin:

> But if we walk in the light as He is in the light, we have fellowship with one another, and the blood of Jesus Christ His Son cleanses us from all sin. If we say that we have no sin, we deceive ourselves, and the truth is not in us. If we confess our sins, He is faithful and just to forgive us our sins and to cleanse us from all unrighteousness. If we say that we have not sinned, we make Him a liar, and His word is not in us (1 John 1:7–10).

If we say the same thing as God about our sin, then He will deal with any and every vestige of sin in our lives. What I am as a creative handiwork of God is absolutely fantastic. I say that about all humility. However, the aberration of sin has hindered the full glory of that life being shown through my particular and unique personality. When the sin is dealt with, there is nothing else there to stop that life from coming forth. There is fundamentally nothing wrong with me in terms of how God made me. He did not make a mistake. All I must do is let the power of God's blood and the power of God's light deal with sin so that what is leftover is completely capable of radiating the fullness of God's eternal life. However, I must be honest about it. I must walk in the light as He is in the light.

The Greek word, in 1 John 1:9, for *confess* is *homologeo*. Confession is not saying, "Oh, God! I am a terrible sinner!" Instead, *homologeo* means that I come into agreement with God about my sin. Literally, the Greek says to say the same thing. We come into agreement with God about our sin, and God will deal effectively with it by forgiving us and turning us away from our sin. If we pretend it is not there, or refuse to admit that it is there, then there is a problem.

The honesty of our walk is a priority. This is what it means to walk in the light. It is the honesty. I must be real with God. I must be real with my brothers. I must be honest in my marriage. Anything that is hidden is darkness.

Darkness is sin's dwelling ground. If I live a hidden life, not allowing myself to come out into the open for fear of rejection or what people will think, then I will remain a prisoner. The power of this eternal life will be restricted due to my dishonesty.

Living in the reality of Father's love relaxes you to be able to cope with all other relationships. Although I enjoy fellowship with others, I do not absolutely need it. I am right with God, and He and I get along really well. As I walk in the light, confessing my sins, God is faithful and just to cleanse it all away. There is nothing the devil can nail me on, because I have an advocate with the Father, Jesus Christ, the righteous. He is not only the propitiation for my sins, but also for the sins of the whole world.

In 1 John 2:6, it says, "He who says he abides in Him ought himself also to walk just as He walked." How did Jesus walk? He walked in absolute fellowship with the Father. As we move through this incredible letter, we discover some of the marks of this eternal life. These marks are your birth right, since you are born again. Here are the marks of a person who has eternal life:

- Walks in the light
- Knows Him who was from the beginning
- Keeps His commandments
- Loves the brethren
- Does not sin (This is not an automatic, inevitable thing. Instead, not sinning is a possibility available through the power of that life from moment to moment. I don't have time to explain how powerful the blood and cross are to bring us to the place where sin is not a necessity. Sin is not a necessity, although it is always a possibility. The ability not to sin is a possibility, but the impossibility of not sinning does not exist. This is the balance of Christian perfection in a few words.)

- Walks as He walked
- Overcomes the world
- Overcomes the evil one

The Second Letter of John

This is a small letter written by John, written to the elect lady and her children. This makes me wonder whether she was a female pastor of a church. It certainly makes you wonder. He says:

> The elder, To the elect lady and her children, whom I love in truth–and not only I, but also all those who have known the truth–because of the truth which abides in us and will be with us forever: Grace, mercy, and peace will be with you from God the Father and from the Lord Jesus Christ, the Son of the Father, in truth and love. I rejoiced greatly that I have found some of your children walking in truth, as we received commandment from the Father. And now I plead with you, lady, not as though I wrote a new commandment to you, but that which we have had from the beginning: that we love one another. This is love, that we walk according to His commandments. This is the commandment, that as you have heard from the beginning, you should walk in it (2 John 1–6).

Can you see the tremendous emphasis on truth? It was said of the Lord Jesus by the apostle John in John 1:14, "…We beheld His glory, the glory as of the only begotten of the Father, full of grace *and truth.*" We need to see why these two things were in such glorious balance in the Lord Jesus. Jesus said, "I am the way, *the truth,* and the life…" In His high priestly prayer, He said, "Father, I have kept them in *your truth.* Your word is truth." This is a major doctrine in the New Testament, and many have lost it. I don't remember hearing many messages in the church on truth.

At the end of 2 John, John said the following:

> Having many things to write to you, I did not wish to do so with paper and ink; but I hope to come to you and speak face to face, that our joy may be full (2 John 12).

John already had the sense that he was coming to the end of his imprisonment. These letters went before him in order to prepare the ground so that when he got there he would have a people who were in eternal life; who were in the truth; a warring company who were soaked in the new revelations God was speaking through this apostle. Can you see how the preparatory word of God was an essential part of the preparation? God always prepares a man, but he also prepares a people. John did not go as a John Wayne individual hero to take on Artemis. Although he was the spokesperson, we must see the army of warring believers that were the power behind what he said. The preparation of the people was as important as the preparation of the man.

The Third Letter of John

In the third letter of John we find the same emphasis being repeated:

> Beloved, I pray that you may prosper in all things and be in health, just as your soul prospers. For I rejoiced greatly when brethren came and testified of *the truth* that is in you, just as you walk *in the truth*. I have no greater joy than to hear that my children *walk in truth* (3 John 2–4).

Then, in verse 8, he added, "We therefore ought to receive such, that we may become fellow workers *for the truth.*" Can you see how important this thrust is to the apostle John? Again and again John talked about the importance of the truth. I believe the apostle Paul had the same thing in mind when he said, "Pray for me that I may speak as I ought to speak." It is possible to lie by not speaking the truth.

Section 8 – Lessons from the Writings of John

Just saying the truth might cause problems so you keep silent. That is nothing more than lying, although you have said nothing. You leave an untruthful situation unconfronted because to speak the truth would be too costly for you.

In John's letter, he was often very sharp when discerning between truth and error. He was definitely the apostle of love. That love is particularly expressed in his love for the truth. Because of love, John would not tolerate one fiber of lying. He confronted it head-on because he knew it meant the difference between life and death, between victory and defeat. It is often not politically advantageous to speak the truth, but very costly. I want us to pray for many of our politicians who love Jesus Christ. I am praying that they may be emboldened like the apostles Paul and John to speak the truth whatever the situation and whatever their circumstances. The truth must be more important to them than political expediency. This would have a powerful affect upon our government.

These are the things the Spirit of God caused the apostle John to write to a people He was preparing for the final assault on Artemis (Diana) in Ephesus. That demon would be driven out of town, and the entire machinery of that demon's false kingdom would collapse in ruin. The advance of the Kingdom of God would march across Europe with many battles and conflicts to be fought, but now it would be an invincible advance. These were the issues that were raised. I asked God, "Why is this such an important thrust? Why did You cause your precious servant John to make this trumpet call to the church before they stepped out to take the city for God?"

Please notice in 3 John that we meet a person called Gaius, who is called "the faithful." We also meet Diotrephes, who is the unfaithful. He is described as someone who "loves to be first" (3 John 9). He is very sectarian and malicious in his talk. He even stops people from entering the church.

Chapter 29 – The Letters of John

There is also a commendation of Demetrius, who is spoken well of by all the brethren and even by the truth itself. That is an interesting phrase. John was expecting to see these people very soon.

After fourteen years on the Isle of Patmos during the persecution under Domitian, John's release finally came in AD 95. (It is interesting to note that Domitian died the same year.) This grand old man who had allowed years of prison to work such a great work in him now returned to Ephesus glowing with power and a new anointing of great authority. If we are in the Kingdom, then this same dynamic will work for us. If we are shut in by some physical prison or restricting circumstances, it can all work for good in our life. John came out of prison with a new anointing and greater authority.

The final showdown was now at hand to overthrow the great principality in the temple of Diana or Artemis. The temple of Diana was one of the Seven Wonders of the World. It was extensively developed by Alexander the Great. It was then improved upon by the Romans. People came from all over the Roman Empire to this temple to receive favor from this deity. There was a church in Mumbai that was known throughout India for healings that took place, provided you went to church for nine consecutive Wednesdays. Of course, you had to pay the appropriate price each time. Things did happen there that made the deception so convincing. Whatever the devil did, even if it was healing, always involved a hook.

This temple of Diana was the center of the dark demonic power that ruled empires from the time of Darius. This demon ruled and controlled the Roman Empire, the Greek Empire, the Egyptian Empire, the Persian-Median Empire, and finally the Babylonian Empire.

387

Section 8 – Lessons from the Writings of John

This was not a small, inexperienced demon. This was a mighty principality. According to Ramsay MacMullen, who is quoting Eusebius, John entered the very temple of Artemis (or Diana) and standing before the high altar commanded this great principality to flee in the mighty name of Jesus. I quote, "In the very temple of Artemis himself, he prayed, 'O God...at whose name every idol takes flight and every demon that is here take flight at thy name...' And while John was saying this, of a sudden the altar of Artemis split in many pieces....and half the Temple fell down. Then the assembled Ephesians cried out, '(There is but) one God, (the God) of John!....'"[1]

Up until this point, the cry of Ephesus had been, "Great is Diana the god of the Ephesians." Even though there was a living and powerful church in Ephesus, the cry of the city had not changed. Diana was still being hailed as the great goddess of the Ephesians. We need to listen to the cries of our city. Do any of them cry, "Jesus is Lord!" I know many Christians in certain cities who cry this cry, but does the city itself make this cry? What do people in the streets cry out?

If you go into the Bronx of New York city, who cries out "Jesus is Lord"? Instead, the cry you hear in the Bronx is: "Watch out for the mafia. Don't park your car there. That is a mafia parking place." What is the cry of New York? It could be: "Money is Lord"; "Mafia is Lord"; "Drugs are Lord"; or "Pleasure is Lord." It could be any of these cries. What is the cry of Boston? It might be: "Intellect is Lord." Some of the greatest educational institutions of the world are located there. But we want a new cry to come out of Boston. Imagine all the university professors at Harvard falling on their knees, saying, "Jesus is Lord."

---

[1] Ramsay MacMullen, Christianizing the Roman Empire AD 100–400 (New Haven, CT: Yale University Press, 1984), 26.

A new cry came out of Ephesus, "There is but one God, the God of John!" They said:

> "We are converted, now that we have seen thy marvelous works! Have mercy upon us, O God, according to they will and save us from our great error...." And some of them lay on their faces and made supplication, others bent their knees and prayed; some tore their clothes and wept and others tried to take flight.[2]

No one was unaffected by this mighty assault!

We want to see this in Houston and San Antonio. He can do it in New York and Boston and Washington D.C. Let all the Senators and entire Congress cry out, "We have sinned greatly. Have mercy upon us, O God! We tried this ridiculous separation of church and state, not allowing You to have Your say. Forgive us for our foolishness. Our founding fathers never intended this separation, and we have lied through our teeth to manipulate things to our advantage. God, forgive us our sin!" Can these days happen in America? I believe they can!

There was an immediate amazing effect in the city of Ephesus and the continent of Europe through the overthrow of the principality in the Temple of Diana, or Artemis, that is revealed through extrabiblical material. We can read the early church fathers for more information on this breakthrough and overthrow. Two good books, which give excellent summaries and bibliographies on the subject, are:

- *Christianizing the Roman Empire AD 100–400* by Ramsay MacMullen
- *How God Saved Civilization* by James L. Garlow

---

2   Ramsay MacMullen, Christianizing the Roman Empire AD 100–400 (New Haven, CT: Yale University Press, 1984), 26.

Section 8 – Lessons from the Writings of John

Ramsay MacMullen is a Yale University professor. The thesis of his book is very relevant for us. He believed that the Christians' ability to Christianize (Kingdomize) Europe came through the church's newfound ability to confront major demonic strongholds and cast them down. That was his thesis. He used Artemis and the city of Ephesus as the first of several examples in a series of confrontations that eventually broke open the whole of Europe for the gospel of Jesus Christ. All other forms of religion and gods were left in the dust as completely powerless and irrelevant.

BRING THE **KINGDOM** TO YOUR CITY

AFTERWORD

Diana's Comeback

However, these defeats did not mean that these demonic powers were eradicated. They were dethroned, but they needed to stay dethroned through a mighty warring church that continued to walk in eternal life and the truth. Unfortunately, this did not happen.

Diana began to lose her credibility all over the Roman Empire. Within fifty years this deity was no longer worshipped. This is a fact. The influence of Artemis, or Diana, dwindled to almost nothing, and many Ephesians turned to the Lord. Within fifty years of this event, the worship of Isis/Artemis/Diana had virtually ceased all over the Roman Empire. Ephesus then became the main center for advancing the Kingdom of God into Europe for the next two hundred years. Ephesus gradually became the power center for the forceful advance of the Kingdom throughout the Roman Empire. There were further persecutions and many more battles, but now nothing could stop the advance. The gospel of the Kingdom and the worship of Jesus as King now began to permeate all of society.

In AD 313, under Emperor Constantine, Christianity became the official state religion of the Roman Empire, but Constantine never renounced his former devotion to the pagan gods. Constantine and his pagan priests merged many of the pagan festivals and rituals of Isis, Artemis, and Diana with Christianity to make an easier transition. In this way, Diana/Artemis/Isis made a comeback as the Mother of Jesus within the church. This same spirit that disguised as Diana, Artemis, or Isis was not finished. The tombs of both Mary the mother of Jesus and John are traditionally in Ephesus. Mary went with John following her son's death, because Jesus said to John, while hanging on the cross, "John, behold your mother." John took Mary into his household and cared for her. When John went to Ephesus, she went with him. Mary died in Ephesus, which is where her tomb lies. John died a natural death in Ephesus at about the age of one hundred. John was not martyred. He was gloriously healthy until his last breath.

This spirit that had lost all power and authority was angry and conniving. The principality changed its clothes and its name and, masquerading as Mary the mother of Jesus, deceived many. Wearing its new disguise as Mary, this spirit gradually took over the church from within and was soon exercising strong control over it. This is where the error of Mary comes from. I mentioned before about recent discoveries in the ancient port of Alexandria of idols with Isis holding baby Horace in black marble, which are identical to the Black Madonnas scattered over Central and South America. It is very clear to these secular archaeologists that one came from the other.

It seems that the spirit who had in the past been known as Baal, Isis, Artemis and Diana always worked to get to the center of political, economic, and military power so as to get control of the world. It took off the clothes and imagery of Diana and put on the clothes and imagery of Mary the Mother of Jesus and began to corrupt the Church from within.

Other deceptions such as Freemasonry and Islam can be traced back to the same source. This is what we are up against in Europe and many other places around the world.

If God could bring the beleaguered church in Ephesus and the apostle John to the place of power and authority to throw it down, then He can do the same for us! I believe God is arming the church for war. After centuries of surges of power with years of neglect in between, I believe the Spirit of God is now arming the church of Jesus Christ for the final showdown. I believe we are privileged to be part of this generation!

OTHER BOOKS AND RESOURCES BY ALAN AND EILEEN VINCENT

BOOKS ON AMAZON

Biography by Eileen Vincent:
- Kingdom Works The Life and Legacy of an Apostolic Father

Alan Vincent as Author:
- Fight the Good Fight of Faith, following the example of Jesus
- Heaven on Earth Releasing the Power of the Kingdom through you
- The Kingdom at War Using Intercessory Prayer to Dispel the Darkness
- The Power of the Cross

Alan Vincent as Contributor:
- Invading Babylon, The 7 Mountain Mandate.

Eileen Vincent as Author
- No Sacrifice too Great, The story of C.T. Studd and Priscilla Pioneer Missionaries.
- Faith Works, The true story of Radical Obedience.

Other titles are available but no longer in print.

MORE FROM ALAN VINCENT

Teachings are available on multiple platforms including:
- Free at *alanvincentteachings.com*
- Spotify
- YouTube

Printed in Great Britain
by Amazon